'A valuable exploration of co-nourishing aspects of Zen Buddhism and psychoanalysis, amplifying and adding to this growing field. It at once gives valuable critiques of work already done and opens further possibilities of being and experience. Seiso Cooper mediates and helps expand dimensions of growth that further open life.'

Michael Eigen, *author of* Contact with the Depths, The Sensitive Self, *and* The Challenge of Being Human

'*Psychoanalysis and Zen Buddhism* is in a class by itself within the ever-expanding literature comparing Zen Buddhism and psychoanalytic thought. Cooper succinctly clarifies points of departure. He is consummately equipped to take the reader on a profound yet exciting journey into the depths. The reader comes away with an appreciation of the realizational perspective, while obtaining a nuanced understanding of Bion's and Dogen's inherent theoretical differences.'

Melvin E. Miller, *coeditor of* Self and No-self: Continuing the Dialogue Between Buddhism and Psychotherapy, *psychoanalyst in private practice, Montpelier, Vermont, USA*

'Seiso Paul Cooper uses an experiential voice to illuminate how sitting in silence common to both Zen Buddhism and psychoanalysis engenders clarity in the present. He addresses with erudite skill the misunderstanding and misuse of what Zen practice has come to mean in western thought. By returning to the sources of zazen, misconceptions of both theory and practice are reset and contextualized. Here lies the way of "unknowing," an essential state of mind to both awakening and emotional change.'

Robby Stein, *Bion videographer, Tavistock-trained child psychotherapist*

Psychoanalysis and Zen Buddhism

In this book, Cooper brings together psychoanalysis and Zen Buddhism by offering a comprehensive and integrated model, described as "The Realizational Model," that is consistent with the core concepts of Soto Zen Buddhism and psychoanalytic practice.

Focusing primarily on Soto Zen Buddhism as presented in the original writings of the Japanese scholar monk Eihei Dōgen (1200–1253), and supported and elaborated by relevant contemporary scholarship in relation to the writings of the British psychoanalyst Wilfred Bion (1897–1979), this book addresses the issue of how can one understand, assimilate, and integrate conceptions of the human mind that originate in the 13th and 20th centuries, as they are visited and inflected by the unconscious preconceptions of a 21st-century perspective. Expressing authentic Buddhist tradition within the frame of psychoanalytic thinking, and supported by online guided audio meditations that accompany the text, this work offers a uniquely interdisciplinary perspective of invaluable clinical significance.

Case material garnered from 35 years of psychoanalytic practice as well as examples from daily life support the abstract concepts discussed in the text, rendering it equally relevant for psychoanalysts and psychotherapists, as well as students of Zen wishing to explore its practical applications.

Seiso Paul Cooper is a licensed and nationally certified psychoanalyst, ordained Soto Zen priest, and transmitted teacher in the Soto Zen lineage of Shunryu Suzuki and Dainin Katagiri. He is a member of the Soto Zen Buddhist Association and the American Zen Teacher's Association. He is the cofounder and guiding teacher: Two Rivers Zen Community; founder: Realizational Practice Studies Group; former Dean of Training, National Psychological Association for Psychoanalysis; faculty, training analyst, and supervisor: Institute for Expressive Analysis, Metropolitan Institute; a member of the editorial board: *Psychoanalytic Review*; and award-winning author: *Zen Insight, Psychoanalytic Action: Two Arrows Meeting* (2019) and *The Zen Impulse and the Psychoanalytic Encounter* (2010). He maintains a private psychoanalytic psychotherapy and supervision practice in Montpelier, Vermont. He has presented his work on Buddhism and Psychoanalysis internationally. He currently organizes, facilitates, and leads silent retreats in the formal Soto Zen style, especially tailored for mental health professionals both at retreat centers and online.

Psychoanalysis and Zen Buddhism

A Realizational Perspective

Seiso Paul Cooper

LONDON AND NEW YORK

Designed cover image: "Enchantment" Seiso Paul Cooper, 2022

First published 2023
by Routledge
4 Park Square, Milton Park, Abingdon, Oxon OX14 4RN

and by Routledge
605 Third Avenue, New York, NY 10158

Routledge is an imprint of the Taylor & Francis Group, an informa business

© 2023 Seiso Paul Cooper

The right of Seiso Paul Cooper to be identified as author of this work has been asserted in accordance with sections 77 and 78 of the Copyright, Designs and Patents Act 1988.

All rights reserved. No part of this book may be reprinted or reproduced or utilised in any form or by any electronic, mechanical, or other means, now known or hereafter invented, including photocopying and recording, or in any information storage or retrieval system, without permission in writing from the publishers.

Trademark notice: Product or corporate names may be trademarks or registered trademarks, and are used only for identification and explanation without intent to infringe.

British Library Cataloguing-in-Publication Data
A catalogue record for this book is available from the British Library

Library of Congress Cataloging-in-Publication Data
Names: Cooper, Seiso Paul, author.
Title: Psychoanalysis and Zen Buddhism : a realizational perspective / Seiso Paul Cooper.
Description: 1 Edition. | New York, NY : Routledge, 2023. | Includes bibliographical references and index.
Identifiers: LCCN 2022041221 (print) | LCCN 2022041222 (ebook) | ISBN 9781032267630 (hardback) | ISBN 9781032267654 (paperback) | ISBN 9781003289821 (ebook)
Subjects: LCSH: Psychoanalysis and religion. | Zen Buddhism—Psychology.
Classification: LCC BF175.4.R44 C656 2023 (print) | LCC BF175.4.R44 (ebook) | DDC 150.19/5—dc23/eng/20221212
LC record available at https://lccn.loc.gov/2022041221
LC ebook record available at https://lccn.loc.gov/2022041222

ISBN: 978-1-032-26763-0 (hbk)
ISBN: 978-1-032-26765-4 (pbk)
ISBN: 978-1-003-28982-1 (ebk)

DOI: 10.4324/9781003289821

Typeset in Garamond
by codeMantra

For the benefit of all suffering beings:
　　　　May peace prevail on earth

Contents

Acknowledgments   xi
Foreword by Robby Stein   xiii

PART ONE
Introduction   1

1   "No Fixed Point": An Introduction   3

2   The Primacy of Experience   14

3   *Mokusho*: Silent Illumination Open to Whole Being   21

PART TWO
Review   31

4   Literature Review: Precursors   33

5   D.T. Suzuki and Dōgen   51

6   A Zen Wave: Review   69

PART THREE
The Definite and the Infinite   87

7   Emptiness and Dependent Co-Arising   89

8   Dōgen's Expression of Suchness   96

9   Bion's Use of "O" and "K"   102

PART FOUR
Realizational Perspectives   113

10 Assimilation and Accommodation   115

11 Bion and Dōgen: Realizational Practice, Emotional Truth   129

PART FIVE
Practice   143

12 Thinking's Bad Rap   145

13 Ada: A Clinical Study   154

14 Shikantaza: "Basic Fact of Sitting" Practice Session   160

Index   167

Acknowledgments

This offering has emerged with the kind and generous inspiration, encouragement, creative suggestions, and support from many individuals, including my students who never fail to inspire and motivate me. My Zen and psychoanalytic teachers have provided generously with their teachings and ongoing encouragement, support, and feedback. I am deeply grateful for the opportunity to engage in deep practice and study into the writings and teachings of Eihei Dōgen on numerous retreats with Shohaku Okumura, Roshi who provided an integration and balance between scholarship and authentic practice. I am especially appreciative of my psychoanalytic mentors, Alan Roland and Michael Eigen, who encouraged and guided me through my initial forays into both areas of self-investigation and expression into these two highly subjective disciplines. My gratitude extends to my colleague and friend Mel Miller for his thoughtful reading and editing suggestions as well as engaging in countless and fruitful hours of constructive conversation and for our collaborations on a number of panels and conferences which contributed to the development of this offering. My appreciation extends to James Grotstein for his enthusiastic, valuable, and encouraging response to my writing. I am indebted to Eric Rhode for his original intellectual peregrinations, his creative insights, and his encouragement in terms of integrating these two areas of practice and study. Stimulating conversations and collaborations with Mark Finn, along with shared practice time on retreats, continue to be a rich source of inspiration and clarity of vision. Many thanks to Robby Stein for his response and creative associations that enhanced and contributed to fine-tuning the writing. My deep appreciation extends to Kate Hawes and Georgina Clutterbuck at Routledge for their enthusiastic response and continued support throughout the entire production process. Last, but not least, I am deeply grateful to my wife and best friend Karen Morris for her love, support, sensitive and deep reading of various chapter drafts, her helpful questions and suggestions, and unflinching, consistent encouragement through this entire process.

I gratefully acknowledge the permission kindly provided to reprint the following materials:

Chapter Eleven, "Bion and Dōgen: Realizational Practice, Emotional Truth," which is a revised and expanded version of my article originally published as Cooper, P. (2020). Realizational perspectives: Bion's psychoanalysis & Dōgen's Zen. *American Journal of Psychoanalysis*, 2020 (80): 37–52.

An extract from Byrne, C. (2019). Verses of silent illumination: Hongzhi Zhengjue's poetic vision of Caodong Zen. *International Journal of Buddhist Thought & Culture,* Vol. 29(2): 171–205; more specifically, the author's translation of verses from "mozhao ming" written by Hongzhi Zhengjue.

Foreword by Robby Stein

Bion's reflection "hasn't anyone seen a psychoanalyst turn into a psychoanalyst" in his autobiography *A Memoir of The Future* (1991) speaks to the core issue of what happens within the consulting room. This transition from "as if" to being "the thing itself" is what all therapists must face. From the Zen perspective, this place is close to the term "suchness" and occupies a ground shared by both Psychoanalysts and Zen practitioners alike. Seiso Paul Cooper uses an experiential voice to unwind and illuminate how sitting in silence common to both practices brings us clarity in present time. Through a realizational perspective, Seiso explores how both *zazen* and psychoanalytic practices intersect. As a supervising analyst, Zen practitioner, and teacher, he addresses with erudite skill the misunderstanding and misuse of what Zen practice has come to mean in western thought. By returning to the sources of *zazen*, misconceptions of both theory and practice are reset and further contextualized alongside Bion's suggestion that within each session the analyst must be free from memory and desire. Bion's writings on the limits of language and the transformation of experience provide an invaluable link to the setting that we all experience within our practices. A Realizational Perspective traverses both the theoretical underpinnings and practical methods available to all therapists who wish to unlock the emotional truth inherent between patient and practitioner. Here lies the way of "unknowing," an essential state of mind to both awakening and emotional change.

Robby Stein, PsyD, MPsych Psych, Bion Videographer,
Tavistock Trained Child Psychotherapist

Part One

Introduction

Chapter 1

"No Fixed Point"
An Introduction

Zen Buddhism, it seems, is everywhere. There is no question about it. We hear about "Zen moments," "Zen lifestyle," "Zen Palate," "Zen living," "Zen fashions!" There is a holiday pop-up store in New York City called "Zen Garage" that sells handbags made from antique mid-eastern fabrics, a recent book *The Zen of Psychotherapy* that has absolutely nothing to do with Zen Buddhism, and even a tile matching computer game called "Zen Match." What these various expressions have to do with Zen Buddhism beyond being commercially trendy is of concern. Many of these commercialized misuses of the term Zen have been generated often for clearly self-promotional purposes.

Eihei Dōgen, the 13th-century founder of the Sōtō Zen tradition in Japan and one of the main characters in this ensuing narrative, asserts and insistently concerns himself with what he refers to as "Authentic Zen," or what the Zen scholar Steven Heine asks for in the subtitle of his book *Will the Real Zen Buddhism Please Stand Up?* (2008).

Mark Finn, a Buddhist practitioner and a psychoanalyst, summarizes this unfortunate situation cogently, and convincingly in his review of my book *The Zen Impulse and the Psychoanalytic Encounter* (2010), he writes, "Some authors in the Buddhist psychoanalytic dialogue write as though they alone had come to observe the intersection of the two psychologies" (2011, p. 420). Finn's terse and poignant observation finds elaboration with Raul Moncayo, a transmitted Zen Buddhist teacher and ordained Sōtō Zen priest as well as a psychoanalyst and psychoanalytic educator in the Lacanian school, who comments on this unfortunate situation in terms of the apparent lack of acknowledgment, engagement with, or critiques of other works on the subject in terms of finding a place for their work in the incremental development of the subject. In the introduction to his book on Zen Buddhism and Lacanian psychoanalysis, *The Signifier Pointing at the Moon*, he writes: "This book differs from books that are written 'as if' this was the first book on the subject" (2012, p. xiii). He continues by commenting that:

> Unfortunately, books are often marketed in this way. Whether in psychoanalysis or Buddhism, many books ignore or don't mention other authors who have written books on the same topic. [He attributes this to] ... an

aspect of power and capitalism (master's discourse) that creeps into the ideology of the social sciences and spiritual literature. Without critical theory or a metalevel analysis that can take various social, cultural, and ideological factors into account, market forces and the ego will continue to rule the production and diffusion of knowledge even in the universities.

(p. xiii)

Specific cultural and ideological factors will be considered in Chapter Seven, "Emptiness and Dependent Co-arising," and in Chapter Ten, "Assimilation and Accommodation," in terms of the reception of Zen Buddhism within the psychoanalytic community in relation to the transmission of Zen Buddhism in the west by Buddhist teachers.

Consistent with and mirroring this trend toward the popularization of Zen in the wider culture, increasingly, psychotherapists and psychoanalysts of various persuasions have read about, practiced, or explored Zen Buddhism either casually, incidentally, or with deep and committed immersion. Some, like myself, are ordained priests and formally transmitted teachers as well as trained and experienced psychoanalysts and psychoanalytic educators who are leaving a notable mark in this expanding psychoanalytic niche, as is evidenced by their publications (Bobrow, 2010; Kennedy, 1984; Moncayo, 2012).

Since Erich Fromm, D.T. Suzuki, and Robert DeMartino's groundbreaking publication *Zen Buddhism and Psychoanalysis* (1960), which has been reprinted multiple times as well as currently enjoying publication in both audio and electronic versions since its initial publication in 1960, the literature on Zen and psychoanalysis has expanded into a virtual subdiscipline with its own specialized literature. References to Zen Buddhism, as well as other Buddhist traditions—primarily Southeast Asian Theravada Buddhism and various Tibetan Buddhist schools—can be found increasingly in the psychoanalytic literature, which will be reviewed and explored in Chapter Six, "A Zen Wave: Review."

It is no accident that one of the landing places for the western iteration of Zen Buddhism is within the highly subjective and experiential domain of psychoanalysis, a shared emphasis that will be addressed in Chapter Two, "The Primacy of Experience." With this shared experiential emphasis in mind, Chapter Three, "*Mokusho*: Silent Illumination: Open to Whole Being," will provide a description of the Chinese Chan practice of *mokusho* or silent illumination, along with detailed practice instructions.

Chapters Four, Five, and Six provide a review of the literature. This review is followed by a series of chapters that provide definitions of basic terms that are central to Mahayana Buddhism, which is one of the two major traditions of Buddhism that includes Chan in China, Zen in Japan, and Son in Korea. Chapter Seven discusses the two core Mahayana Buddhist principles of emptiness and dependent co-arising, followed by Dōgen's usage of the related term *Immo* (suchness) in Chapter Eight. This experiential emphasis and the resulting orientation that I describe as a "realizational perspective" will be elaborated in Chapter Eleven, "Bion and Dōgen: Realizational Practice, Emotional Truth."

Based on the Buddhist principles of emptiness and dependent co-arising, defined and discussed in Chapter Seven, "Emptiness & Dependent Co-arising," I view the two disciplines as mutually interacting and exerting an impact both on the current forms and directions that psychoanalysis and Zen take. I will explore the causes and conditions for this observation in terms of tradition and contemporary expression in Chapter Ten, "Assimilation and Accommodation." Despite the many diverse contemporary expressions and developments, as Heine notes in his discussion regarding the transmission of Zen from China to Japan and that holds contemporary relevance, there is: "Yet the durable heritage of the century of transition that began in the early 1200s continues to affect deeply multiple current appropriations and adaptations of the venerable religious movement" (2018, p. 13).

This "durable heritage" finds expression in the later writings of the British psychoanalyst Wilfred Bion, the other main character in this offering, in his concept of "invariance" (1965) that Michael Eigen in his discussion of Bion's "Faith in O," which will be discussed in Chapter Nine, "Bion's Use of 'O' and 'K'" that Eigen notes, "As Bion repeatedly reminds us, we may expect to find invariant structures in any subject. One way or another a constant thread runs through Bion's journey toward the beginning" (1985, p. 321). Speaking of beginnings, in terms of both Zen's "durable heritage" and Bion's "invariance," I'd like to begin with this Zen dialog between the Chinese Chan (Zen) master Nangaku (677–744) and his teacher, the sixth ancestor of Zen in China, Hui-neng (638–713).

"WHERE HAVE YOU COME FROM?" A ZEN DIALOG:

Nangaku Ejo became a disciple of the Sixth Patriarch, Master Daikan Eno

The Sixth Patriarch asked:	Where have you come from?
Nangaku said:	I have come from Master Ankoku on Mount Su.
The Sixth Patriarch said:	Something ineffable has come like this.
(Nangaku could not reply.) {After eight years} He came to understand the words and said:	When I first came here, Master, you accepted me with the words, "Something ineffable has come like this."
The Patriarch said:	How do you understand the words?
Nangaku said:	If I try to represent it in some way, the explanation does not hit the mark.
The Patriarch said:	Do you rely on practice and realization or not?
Nangaku said:	It would not be true if I insisted that there is no practice and realization, However, it is impossible to taint the situation by distinguishing practice and realization.
The Patriarch said:	This "not to taint" is just what the many Buddhas wanted to preserve. You are the same as that. I am the same as that, and many patriarchs in India are also like that.

(Excerpted from Book Two, Case One of Dogen's *Shinji Shobogenzo*. In: G. Nishijima, 2003, p. 137).

We can understand the phrase "not to taint" as to not separate or to treat practice/realization dualistically. Dōgen frequently uses the term *shusho ichinyo*, "practice realization oneness," to emphasize this radically nondualistic orientation. This is a crucial point for Dōgen. He mentions it elsewhere. For instance, in the *Hensan* (Thorough Exploration) chapter of his *Shobogenzo* (True Dharma Eye), he repeats: "To describe a thing does not hit the target" (1243a, p. 208). Dualistic tendencies such as conceptualization, logical linear thought, internalized habit formations, and by extension Wilfred Bion's psychoanalysis, in which he argues that the encounter should not be tainted by memory, desire, understanding, preconceptions, or internal representations, strikes a similar chord.

Nangaku's comment dovetails with Bion's opening statement in the Introduction to *Attention and Interpretation* (1970), where he comments that language can only approximate reality, because language is based on sensuous experience and the data of psychoanalysis is nonsensuous, an issue that will be further explored and clarified in Chapter Twelve, "Thinking's Bad Rap."

In his commentary to this dialog between Nangaku Ejo and Daikan Eno, the Sōtō Zen teacher and Dōgen translator Gudo Nishijima notes, "Master Nangaku said that it was difficult or impossible for any explanation to capture reality" (2003, p. 137). This is precisely Bion's point. He articulates a highly subjective and experience-based formulation of psychoanalytic practice. This experience-based orientation form of *zazen* that I plan to emphasize, as I mentioned, is *shikantaza* or "just sitting," a practice that as a didactic and experiential conclusion to this offering will be elaborated in Chapter Fourteen, "*Shikantaza*: Basic Fact of Sitting: Practice Session." Along with Chapter Three, mentioned above, both chapters provide instructions for actual Zen meditation practices that are supplemented with links to online audio files with systematically guided instructions.

Despite differences between both Dōgen's and Bion's basic assumptions, this highly subjective and experience-based attention to the present moment along with the related themes that include: a radical openness to unknowing; a shared orientation to the relation between intuition and cognition; a shift from attention to static mind states and objects to an emphasis on fluid functions and actional relationships. Together, these points of attention contribute to the formulation that I describe as a "realizational" approach to psychoanalytic practice, which is centered on practice and experience, regardless of theoretical or doctrinal assumptions, and functions as a unifying and integrating theme for what follows.

With these points in mind, I would argue that Nangaku's "not to taint" can also refer in contemporary times to the trap of "medicalizing," secularizing," or "psychologizing" Zen Buddhism through the process of taking specific practices piecemeal out of the larger fabric of the Buddhist religious system to add to one's psychotherapeutic "bag of tricks." Such seems to be the fate, for example, of the secularization of the Theravada Buddhist practice of *vipassana* by western psychologists and that has come to be referred to as "secular mindfulness." This religious practice has become accommodated to and assimilated by the medical profession in North America, for example, by behavioral-cognitive therapists (see, for instance, Masuda & O'Donohue, 2017).

My view and therefore my own personal bias that, to use Nangaku's words, might "taint" this offering, centers on my experience of study and practice that places Zen Buddhism firmly and squarely at the center of a religious tradition, which has more to do with soteriological or realizational intentions and endeavors and less to do with medicinal or healing intentions, except incidentally. On this point, Peter Hershock (2014) observes that the primary unifying factor in all spiritual and mystical traditions is this emphasis. This tension operates between medical/scientific/objective and religious/mystical/subjective models and how they shape the shared dialog.

Zen Buddhism, from my perspective and experience, functions as a religion. Zen articulates a soteriological intent and explicates structured, systematic teachings and practices developed to support the realization of that intent, which can be described as "freedom from suffering" as summarized in the Buddhist articulation of the "Four Noble Truths," the acknowledgment of suffering and its causes and the activation of freedom and its causes. The causes of freedom are elaborated systematically as the "Eightfold Noble Path" that includes Right View, Right Thought, Right Speech, Right Conduct, Right Livelihood, Right Effort, Right Mindfulness, and Right Concentration. A point of significance regarding religious belief systems is the Mahayana premise—originally articulated by the Indian Buddhist philosopher and the 14th patriarch of Zen Nagarjuna (150–250 C.E.)—that all belief systems should be refuted, including the Buddhist belief system. Perhaps we need to also question this Buddhist "no belief" belief system as well, or as in Zen parlance is described as maintaining "no fixed point."

However, in the absolute sense, with the rise of Mahayana Buddhism and the Emptiness tradition, all positions are viewed as fundamentally empty, including the view that all views are empty. On this point, Dōgen writes in *Bendowa* ("A Talk About Pursuing the Truth," 1231) in response to a questioner:

> Be well assured that for a Buddhist the issue is not to debate the superiority or inferiority of one teaching or another, or to establish their respective depths. All he needs to know is whether the practice is authentic or not.
>
> (Waddell & Abe, 2002, p. 16)

From this perspective the relative polarization between traditionalist and modernist or between religious and secular views is not the point. An alternative conceptualization that might be stated as the modernist view identifies and names the actual lived and expressed practice exerted in each moment since Zen's inception. Simultaneously, traditionalist intentions function to identify and articulate, as Bion would describe as the "invariance" (1965, p. 6) within one's consistent conception of this practice as it is presently structured.

This reality of Zen as a functioning and highly structured religious system has become problematic for many westerners who have found their way into Zen initially hoping to free themselves up from their original Judeo-Christian indoctrination that, as many of my students and patients, among converts to Zen, say they have found to be repressive, meaningless, brittle, and hollow and which led them, albeit often misguidedly, to alternatives such as Zen in the first place. Often, such individuals felt motivated in this direction through the misguided offer of a promise that Zen is "not a religion, philosophy, or theory," rather it is a "way of life," that is, it functions as a universal mysticism, a view promulgated by D.T. Suzuki and popularized by Alan Watts (1957), which will be explored in Chapter Four, "Literature Review: Precursors." Further, fueled by Japanese nationalism, this view purports that Japanese Zen functions as a "universal mysticism" that transcends and is superior to all other forms of mysticism, spirituality, or religion. In contrast to their early religious experiences, the depiction of Zen as an iconoclastic, antinomian, anti-intellectual free-for-all, at first glance, presented as a welcome, appealing, and refreshing alternative to their disappointment with the religious systems of their birth. True, these tendencies do exist in the Zen tradition. However, there is more to it than that, such as the expected tight adherence to monastic rules, precise performance of various rituals, and following tight schedules. Pulling on this one thread out of the larger fabric of Zen Buddhism as a comprehensive religious structure is, in my view, shortsighted, and in many cases, unless addressed and worked through by the practitioner, has been a source of disillusionment, disappointment, discouragement as well as acting out and reinforcing rather than working through character pathology. There has been plenty written on this subject (e.g., see Heine, 2008; van der Braak, 2020). It is within the context of this issue that the Zen scholar and critic of the medicalization and secularization of Buddhism in the west Andre van der Braak sums up this erroneous or at least incomplete perception of Zen regarding function and structure in terms of practice and ritual space as follows: "Part of what distinguishes zazen from a meditation technique is first of all the religious framework within which it takes place. A zendo is a locus of reverence and ritual, not the spiritual equivalent of a gym or health club" (2020, p. 153).

Suffice it to say that I have no interest in a Zen denuded of ritual, study, or practice. Nor am I interested, at the risk of appearing naïve, in secularizing or medicalizing Zen for the sake of accommodating to and being assimilated into an ofttimes seemingly rigid and dogmatic psychoanalytic landscape. Nor am I interested in arbitrarily imposing Zen scriptures, structures, or rituals upon my psychotherapy patients. The influence of my lifetime immersion into Zen Buddhism functions primarily on an experiential, spontaneous, and unconscious level, as practice and studies over the years have influenced my mode of being in the world. However, upon a request initiated by the patient, I will offer instructions and/or resources for study and practice.

My emphasis and insistence on describing Zen as a religious system and endeavor seems to go a long way toward explaining my interest in a small yet expanding group of psychoanalysts, whom we might describe as part of the Bionic development and who view psychoanalysis from a realizational perspective. This orientation threads its way through the work of writers who have creatively dovetailed off the Bionic perspective (Eaton, 2019; Eigen, 1998; Grotstein, 2007; Lopez-Corvo, 2005, 2006; Ogden, 1997a, 1997b; Reiner, 2012, 2019; Rhode, 1998; Symington & Symington, 1996; Vermote, 2017, 2019).

In another sense, what we may describe as a "secular-religious" dichotomy is no more than a conceptual bubble, or a shadow engendered by dualistic thinking and possibly an attachment to a particular "territory," if you will. In either case, the crucial question, as I see it, becomes, "What is our *relationship* to any tradition and its related practices: scholarly, medical, scientific, mystical, philosophical, spiritual, or religious?" Asserted a bit differently:

> What ways do the teachings available through Zen study and practice and/or through psychoanalytic study and training interact with each other and impact our mode of being in the world and how we approach and relate with those individuals who seek our expertise?

Returning to the core Mahayana Buddhist teachings of emptiness and dependent co-arising that I refer to above and from which Zen Buddhism emerged that all phenomena are empty of inherent, permanent, or "own" existence, then it is an easy step to understand that there is, by the same token, no reified, concrete, traditional Zen Buddhism; only the living Zen that we practice in the here and now. How then do we reconcile this fluid relativist view with the seemingly fixed eternalist view that "authentic practice" in Dōgen's view is the practice rooted in Zen ancestry, for instance, when he speaks of our practice being identical with the Buddha's practice or Bodhidharma, the first ancestor of Zen in China's practice, a point that he repeats throughout his extensive writings. For instance, in *Bendowa* (1231), he writes:

> [Someone] asks, "Why do you see it [Zazen] as the only authentic gate?"
> I say: Great Master Śākyamuni exactly transmitted, as the authentic tradition, this subtle method of grasping the state of truth, and the tathāgatas of the three times all attained the truth through zazen. Thus the fact that [Zazen] is the authentic gate has been transmitted and received. Furthermore, the patriarchs of the Western Heavens and the Eastern Lands all attained the truth through zazen. Therefore I am now preaching [Zazen] to human beings and gods as the authentic gate.
> (Nishijima & Cross, 1994, p. 7).

The Zen scholar Dale Wright, for example, addresses this point in terms of the many intentions an individual may bring to reading a religious text. He writes, regarding the realization of "the Great Matter," which he describes as enlightened being: "… when we examine our reading practice, the activity in motion right now, in what way and to what extent is it motivated by whatever we take to be the 'great matter?'" (1998, p. 34). Further, he writes, "What is the character and quality of our aim in reading? Can this practice be deepened and improved so that it may truly matter whether we have done it or not?" (p. 34). He continues by noting what, in my view, is the point in terms of the impact of what some may describe and relate to as "secular," while others, like myself, will characterize as "religious":

> It will matter, however, if, in reading the Huang Po texts, (The subject of Wright's discussion), we deepen our own sense of the matters about which the text speaks since these matters may be manifest in our lives as well.
>
> (p. 35)

No Fixed Point

In Zen parlance, we can address this question and how one might fruitfully approach this offering through the notion of "no fixed point." That is, not allowing our preconceptions, wishes, desires, or memories to saturate the mental space needed for clear perception of the currently manifesting reality: *Genjokoan* in Dōgen's terms. However, keeping an open and clear mind to the evolving experience of the moment doesn't necessarily require that we "purify" or rid ourselves of preconceptions or fixed views. The important point centers on whether or not one is aware of preconceptions and how one relates to them.

In the reality of the moment, our preconceptions are equally part of and influence the field. The relational interaction, which is both Dōgen's and Bion's emphasis, includes our preconceptions that are the result of the causes and conditions of our lives. Both analyst and analysand are interacting within a dependently co-arising context with the influence of both conscious and unconscious factors. From the vantage provided by no fixed point, accurately intuiting or "reading" the needs of the situation will determine one's response. Bion addresses this issue by making a distinction between forced memories and spontaneously arising memories that he refers to as "evolutions," a term he uses to clarify the distinction between these two different types of memory and which he describes as follows:

> There is something that has often been called 'remembering' and that is essential to psychoanalytic work; this must be sharply distinguished from what I have been calling memory. I want to make a distinction between (1) remembering a dream or having a memory of a dream and (2) the experience of the dream which seems to cohere as if it were a whole, at one moment absent, at the next present. This experience, which I consider to be essential to evolution of the emotional reality of the session, is often called a memory, but it is to be distinguished from the experience of remembering.
>
> (1970, p. 107)

This orientation raises the following relevant questions. What is plausible within the Zen Buddhist agenda for a psychoanalyst whose theories and associated preconceptions, whether conscious or unconscious, are organized and dominated around notions such as ego development, independent selfhood, and separation/individuation? How does the psychoanalyst respond to and take seriously core Buddhist notions such as no inherently and separately existing self, oneness, an ultimate, all-inclusive interconnectedness, and in the case of Dōgen's Zen, the paradoxical and radical nondualism that includes dualism? These same questions are equally relevant for the Western student who is new to Zen and who, for the most part, has spent a lifetime internalizing values and belief systems that are seemingly contradictory in relation to Zen views and that from a Western point of view seem to defy reason.

A major difficulty in negotiating these waters, to elaborate this point a bit further, stems from an often expressed faulty or incomplete understanding of basic Zen Buddhist concepts and the context from which they emerged. For instance, to assert one example, the Buddhist notion of "no-self" when viewed from the negatively tinged lens of a modern western nihilist perspective generates a profound misunderstanding that can create serious reality consequences. The incidence of inappropriate behaviors such as the sexual exploitation of students by some Buddhist teachers serves as an all too often, well-documented, and disturbing prime example.[1] Such problems might be remedied by a more explicit and deeper experiential understanding of the concepts involved. For example, I find it instructive to understand "no self" as a shorthand for no permanent, inherently existing self that exists independently of causes and conditions. The self-sense or "I-sense" (Cooper, 1999a) rises contextually subject to causes and conditions, but doesn't exist in an absolute, transcendent, separate, hidden, or permanent way. This point of distinction will be further elaborated in Chapter Seven, "Emptiness and Dependent Co-arising."

I am one person, my preconceptions are determined by my immersion in both psychoanalysis and Zen, as well as my personal history, which led me to these two disciplines in the first place. The question becomes: can I take a backward step and respond to the present situation based on my intuition and understanding of the moment beyond what might be viewed as an exclusively "secular" or "religious" lens? So, for example, my response to a patient will hopefully evoke an informative and performative response that engenders lived self-awareness and psychic change. Such a response may take the form of a traditional psychoanalytic interpretation, a notation, a suggestion, or a moment of silence, as will be elaborated in Chapter Thirteen, "Ada: A Clinical Study." In contrast, but not necessarily so, my response to a Zen student will be directed toward enhancing deepened practice with the intention that the student experiences self-engendered realization and insight into the true nature of reality and may take the form of a question or a declaration. I become, to use another Zen metaphor, "the finger pointing at the moon" for the student. However, it is up to the student to look past my finger. Can we take the backward step from our own preconceptions, memories, wishes, desires, and seemingly fixed identities in order to loosen our own fixed positions? Can we resolve the koan, "How did this polarization originate in the first place?" "What is my investment in any view?" "What purpose does it serve?" True to the Middle Way can we make room for a balanced and nuanced discussion? Can we create and acknowledge the space to hold differing points of view in an equally shared dialogical space from which something new might evolve? This point of view is clearly where I situate myself both psychoanalytically and religiously and has influenced the direction of the following offering.

Given the above points, I'd like to conclude with a few words about the causes and conditions of my own study and practice.

Beginnings

My interest in Buddhist practices in relation to psychoanalytic psychotherapy is primarily focused on how practices such as *zazen*, Zen Buddhist sitting meditation, and related core principles fundamentally impact the practicing therapist. An alternative view centers on specific Buddhist practices such as various forms of meditation as supplemental therapeutic techniques to introduce to the patient, although, as I see it, these two approaches are not necessarily mutually exclusive or contradictory and, in many cases, may be complementary.

Shikantaza is the practice of the Zen teachers who have directly influenced me, and most importantly, I feel that it is the most compatible with the highly subjective, experience-based internal listening/intuiting process that is unique to psychoanalytic therapy when conducted from a realizational perspective.

When I first started practicing psychoanalysis and psychotherapy, I maintained rather strong, which in retrospect one might describe as rigid, boundaries between the two disciplines. However, this early position has softened over the years through the support and encouragement of my colleagues and teachers and especially with the recent easy access to my publications on the subject through the expansion of the Internet over the years. I frequently find myself in the position of asking during an initial consultation whether the individual requesting my assistance is seeking me out as a psychotherapist or as a Zen Buddhist teacher. Of course, I am both, and both will be present during sessions because I am, of course, one person who has been deeply influenced by both practices that have become internalized into my mode of being in the world. However, my emphasis and responses will shift, depending on the needs, concerns, and interests of both students and patients. With these points, the next chapter, Chapter Two, "The Primacy of Experience," will serve as an entry into this offering.

Note

1 For example, see Mark Oppenheimer's article "The Zen Predator of the Upper East Side" 2014.

References

Abe, M. (1985). *Zen and Western Thought*. Honolulu: University of Hawaii Press.
Bion, W. (1965). *Transformations*. London: Karnac.
Bion, W. (1967). Notes on memory and desire. In: J. Aguayo & B. Malin (Eds.), *Wilfred Bion: Los Angeles Seminars and Supervision* (pp. 133–149). London: Karnac, 2017. [Originally published in: Bion, W. (1967). Notes on memory and desire. The *Psychoanalytic Forum*, 2:272–3, 279–80.]
Bion, W. (1970). *Attention and Interpretation*. London: Karnac.
Bion, W. (1991). *A Memoir of the Future*. London: Karnac.
Bleandonu, G. (1994). *Wilfred Bion: His Life and Works*. 1897–1979. London: Free Association Books.
Cooper, P. (2010). *The Zen Impulse and the Psychoanalytic Encounter*. London: Routledge.
Cooper, P. (2019). *Zen Insight, Psychoanalytic Action: Two Arrows Meeting*. New York & London: Routledge.
Coupey, P. (2020). *In the Belly of the Dragon: A Zen Master's Commentary on the Shinjinmei by Master Sosan (D. 606)*. Chino Valley, AZ: Hohm Press.
Dōgen, E. (1227). Fukanzazengi. In: N. Waddell & M. Abe (Trans.), *The Heart of Dōgen's Shobogenzo* (pp. 1–6). Albany: State University of New York Press, 2002.
Dōgen, E. (1231). In: Nishijima & C. Cross (Trans.), *Master Dogen's Shobogenzo, Book 1* (pp. 2–23). London: Windbell Publications, 1994.
Dōgen, E. (1231). Bendowa. In: N. Waddell & M. Abe (Trans.), *The Heart of Dōgen's Shobogenzo* (pp. 7–30). Albany: State University of New York Press, 2002.
Dōgen, E. (1243a). Hensan. In: Nishijima & C. Cross (Trans.), *Master Dogen's Shobogenzo, Book 3* (pp. 207–214). London: Windbell Publications, 1997.
Dōgen, E. (1243b). Zazenshin. In: Nishijima & C. Cross (Trans.), *Master Dogen's Shobogenzo Book 2* (pp. 91–106). London: Windbell Publications, 1996.
Dōgen, E. (1243c). Zazengi. In: N. Waddell & M. Abe (Trans.), *The Heart of Dōgen's Shobogenzo* (pp. 109–110). Albany: State University of New York Press, 2002.
Dōgen, E. (1244). Zanmai o zanmai. In: Nishijima & C. Cross (Trans.), *Master Dogen's Shobogenzo Book 3* (pp. 281–284). London: Windbell Publications, 1997.
Epstein, M. (1984). On the neglect of evenly suspended attention. *Journal of Transpersonal Psychology*, 16(2):193–205.
Epstein, M. (1988). Attention and psychoanalysis. *Psychoanalysis and Contemporary Thought*, 11:171–189.
Maezumi, T. (2002). *Appreciate Your Life: The Essence of Zen Practice*. Boston: Shambhala Publications.
Milton, J. (1667). *Paradise Lost*. London: Samuel Simmons Printer.
Pelled, E. (2007). Learning from experience: Bion's concept of reverie and Buddhist meditation: a comparative study. *International Journal of Psycho-Analysis*, 88(6):1507–1526.
Roberts, S. (2018). *Being-Time: A Practitioner's Guide to Dōgen's Shōbōgenzo Uji*. Somerville: Wisdom Publications.
Rubin, J. (1985). Meditation and psychoanalytic listening. *Psychoanalytic Review*, 72:599–614.
Speeth, K. (1982). On psychotherapeutic attention. *Journal of Transpersonal Psychology*, 14:141–160.

Chapter 2

The Primacy of Experience

The underlying basis of what follows is the principle that Zen Buddhism and psychoanalysis are two of the most highly subjective and experience-based disciplines. I believe that both Dōgen (1200–1253) and Bion (1897–1979) have taken this orientation as the epitome of their respective approaches. In fact, it is their subjective and experience-based foundations that energize both Zen and psychoanalysis as unique and impactful processes in both performative and informative ways. This subjective and experiential orientation reflects a cultural shift that finds expression within psychoanalysis as it initially emerged through Freud's endeavor to seek legitimacy in the scientific community for his nascent psychoanalysis as an objective science, but over time it has evolved increasingly in a subjective and experiential direction.

Consider this dramatic example of experiential learning in the moment from the Zen perspective: A samurai came to visit a Zen master to ask him a question that had been tormenting him for a long time. Naturally, this samurai didn't practice *zazen*, but the way of the sword. His question seemed completely sincere:

> "What is hell?" he asked the Zen master.
> The Zen master told him he didn't feel like answering that question right now.
> "Why not?" asked the samurai.
> "Because you're too stupid."
> "What do you mean, too stupid?"
> "You're too stupid, you wouldn't understand."

The samurai was offended. He was probably imagining what his lord, the shogun, would think if he saw him just then. So, he tried to ask the question again, but the master cut him off:

"What could you possibly understand? You're a cardboard samurai! A loser!"

At that point, the samurai really got mad:

"And you! What are you? A good-for-nothing parish priest! A boot-licking Buddha-lover!"

> "You're just a coward!" laughed the Zen master.
> "That's it, said the samurai. I'm cutting off your head!"

> He began to draw his sword. The master completely unfazed, laughed even harder.

> "With what—with that rubber sword?":

> Trembling with rage, his face dripping sweat, the samurai raised his weapon over his head. Just as he was about to strike, the master pointed at him and said:

> "There. That's hell!"
>
> (Coupey, 2020, pp. 104–105)

Similarly, Bion emphasizes the experiential and subjective orientation to psychoanalysis in his opening to his book *Attention and Interpretation* (1970). He begins by noting:

> I doubt if anyone but a practising psycho-analyst can understand this book although I have done my best to make it simple. Any psycho-analyst who is *practising* can grasp my meaning because he, unlike those who only read or hear about psycho-analysis, has the opportunity to experience for himself what I in this book can only represent by words and verbal formulations designed for a different task.
>
> (p. 1)

Note that Bion emphasizes the word *practising*, and he is setting up his observation that language is based in and designed to communicate sensuous experience, which is not in the intuited and experiential realm of the psychoanalytic process and not the subject of psychoanalysis. In fact, language, according to Bion, holds the potential to obscure the intuited awareness of psychoanalytic experience and at best can only approximate reality, except when the intuited awareness of the illusive "O," or the emotional truth of the session, evolves into "K," Bion's symbol for knowledge.[1]

He maintains this position consistently throughout his writing. For example, in *Memoir of the Future*, published in 1991, he asserts:

> Non-artistic methods of communication are less accurate than those used by artists... I can say this with conviction of the psycho-analytical experience also. I cannot describe this experience in any convincing way to someone who does not share it, any more than the moving picture of men landing on the moon tells me what it feels like. It is delusory to suppose that contemporaneity makes it communicable.
>
> (p. 110)

In the same piece he further explicates a distinction between knowing *about* psychoanalysis, but who have not experienced it firsthand for themselves and individuals who have directly engaged in the experience of psychoanalysis. He compares the former to "trained animals" and writes, "They can learn to pretend they are familiar with the psychoanalytic experience as a clever animal learns tricks: the human animal can learn how to play tricks which might convince the ignorant" (p. 111).

However, despite this emphasis on lived experience, which he argues that language can only approximate, he doesn't refute or discard language, since ineffable experience, which he describes simply as O, can only be intuited experientially, and becomes "known" through evolution into K, which can then be communicated through language in the form of an interpretation or notation and, at best, as I noted, approximates experience, both of the analysand and the analyst's intuition of the analysand's experience. That is to say, to draw from Bion's notion of "transformations" (1965), there is an ongoing and paradoxical consensus of the intuited (or perceived) reality of the moment, as well and as equally significant, uniqueness of each individual's perceptual experience and resulting expression of that experience. For instance, to take a concrete example, two individuals will agree that a particular object of perception is a teacup. However, the actual perception and experience of the teacup is multi-determined by many internal and external factors such as past experiences, light, shadows, and vantage point.

Using painting as an example, in *Transformations*, Bion argues that each individual's experience and perception of any particular scene will be expressed differently in the resulting artistic production. He notes that through what he describes as an "invariant," the transformation between objects of perception, a pond, in his example, the artist's process and the final rendition of the pond on the canvas will be recognizable to the viewer. This point can be developed further from the Zen perspective by considering the notion of *karma*, simply translated as "action" or "activity," and *samskaras* habit (karmic) formations, which can be thought of as an underlying, often unconscious preconceptions that contribute to repetitive and reified organizing principles. From this point of view, the activities, perceptions, and interactions with the environment that influence each individual's experience result in a unique perception of reality as well as unique, patterned, and repetitious ways of being in the world.

Over time, these influences develop into unique, consistent, habitual, and often automatic and unconsciously motivated ways of perceiving and interacting with the world both internally and in terms of interpersonal relations. The repetitive quality of *samskaras* finds visual representation in the Buddhist *Bhavachakra* (Wheel of Life and Death) as a potter at the wheel who enacts the pattern of continuously making the same pot repeatedly.

By emphasizing experience, Bion opens the gate to entering a realizational approach to psychoanalysis. He quotes this passage from John Milton's *Paradise Lost* (1667), "The rising world of waters dark and deep (are) won from the void and formless infinite" (in: W. Bion, 1965, p. 151). Bion argues that opening into this formless void, this intuited reality requires moment-to-moment presence by the action of relinquishing sensory input, memory, a wish for a result, and understanding. In other words, previous learning must be set aside, including what the analyst has previously learned about the analysand. In Zen parlance, this has been described as "the face before your parents were born." Bion's approach is both radical and all-inclusive. For example, he writes: "The psychoanalyst should aim at achieving a state of mind so that at every session he feels he has not seen the patient before. If he feels he has, he is treating the wrong patient" (1967, p. 138) and "What we are concerned with is not only what we know and understand, but what we do not know and do not understand" (1991, p. 264). This sense of nondirected and all-inclusive openness that Bion advocates finds expression throughout the Zen Buddhist literature. For example, the contemporary Sōtō Zen priest and teacher Shinshu Roberts, in her recent discussion of Dōgen's notion of *Uji*, or "being time," writes:

> If our worldview ... entertains all possibilities, this enables us to let go of our attachment to any particular ideas about our situation and thereby actualize the totality of the moment." She goes on to write that "I" includes the other, and "when this inclusivity is actualized, we are fully present with whatever is happening in its totality, and we respond. This response is unobstructed. It alleviates suffering.
>
> (2018, p. 49)

In this manner, Dōgen advocates the unimpeded and full expression of our moment-to-moment being, unrestricted, as Bion would emphasize, without the interference of memory, desire, or understanding (1967, 1970). This experiential emphasis conveys a sense of acceptance and optimism, which Taizan Maezumi, Roshi, the founder of the Los Angeles Zen Center, advises the student to: "Trust yourself as you truly are; you are already the Buddha Way itself. Be intimate with it. Do not make yourself separate with your opinions, your judgments, your ideas, with whatever you think your life is" (2002, p. 66).

I would add, also without the restrictions and limitations of judgment. An interesting parallel can be found in Dōgen's use of water as a metaphor for the suchness of ultimate or absolute reality as a fluid, ever-evolving infinite becoming that characterizes what Buddhists describe as *sunyata*, translated as "emptiness," "voidness," or more recently as "boundlessness." Briefly stated, by emptiness Buddhists note that nothing exists permanently, inherently, separately, or free from causes and conditions. All existence arises and fades dependent on causes and conditions that engender an interdependent network that we are all part of. We will return to a detailed analysis of emptiness and the complementary concept, dependent co-arising, in Chapter Seven, "Emptiness and Dependent Co-arising."

The radical nondualism and nonexclusive orientation that drives the realizational perspective, by definition, includes the logical, sequential linearity of the definite, defined by Bion as the "medical view" (1970, p. 83) and the circularity and rhythmicity of the infinite, which he defines as the "religious vertex" (p. 75).

It would be fruitful to make a comparison of this fundamental Zen Buddhist view of "One reality, two views," expressed in the notions of the relative (empirical) and the absolute (ultimate) perceptions of reality with the medical and religious vertices.

Similarly, yet in contrast to the microcosm—the dyad—examined by psychoanalytic thinkers, Dōgen elaborates a macrocosmic view and he makes it clear that realization must include an awareness of both the relative and the absolute. Suffering, based on his macrocosmic or cosmological view (Abe, 1985), has its source in a failure to see beyond the personal and limited view of the relative and to confuse it for an ultimate view of the "True Reality of All Beings." In their unique ways and with diverging interests in mind, both Dōgen and Bion advocate a "binocular vision" that takes account of both the absolute and the relative.

Meeting Bion

Bion's opus is vast, varied, and deep. During my early explorations into his ideas as a psychoanalytic candidate, I was advised "to pull on threads that appeal to me and to see what evolves" (personal communication with Michael Eigen). I found myself in the midst of what Bion's biographer Gerard Bleandonu (1994) describes as his "epistemological period." As a long-term Zen Buddhist practitioner, early in my psychoanalytic training, I was exploring articles that discussed the interrelationships between Buddhist meditation and psychoanalytic therapy. Wilfred Bion's mandate to relinquish memory, desire, and understanding (1967, 1970) is often quoted or referenced in this body of literature, usually in comparison to the relation between psychoanalytic listening and Theravada Buddhist-based mindfulness meditation practices (Epstein, 1984, 1988; Rubin, 1985; Speeth, 1982; more recently, Pelled, 2007). My interest intensified and I began to delve into Bion's brief, yet highly condensed, but pivotal article "Notes on Memory and Desire" (1967).

Similarly, as the result of the profound impact of my experience of a retreat at Hokyoji, an 800-year-old monastery in Ono, Japan, and my encounter with the abbot and with the monks in residence, my study and practice of Buddhism led me to the Japanese Sōtō Zen School and to the equally vast and complex writings of the school's founder Eihei Dōgen and to its core practice, derived from the Chinese Ch'an practice of *mokusho* (silent illumination).[2] Dogen's iteration of *mokusho* developed as *shikantaza* (just sitting).[3]

The similarly highly condensed and brief epistle *Fukanzazengi*, "Universal Promotion of the Principles of Zazen" (1227), drew my attention as it describes in clear, cogent, and convincing details the specific procedure for *shikantaza* practice from the Sōtō Zen Buddhist perspective while simultaneously explicating the core beliefs that drive this practice. Dōgen advocates this form of Zen sitting practice as the authentic practice of the ancestors. While references to *shikantaza* find expression throughout Dōgen's writings, he explicated, developed, and expanded this practical emphasis either directly or indirectly in several other pieces, including *Bendowa* (1231), *Zazenshin* (1243b), *Zazengi* (1243c), and *Zanmai O Zanmai* (1244).

Similarly, centuries later, Bion elaborated his brief discussion offered in his 1967 article "Notes on Memory and Desire," which he elaborated further in his book *Attention and Interpretation* (1970). Despite their radically cultural and historical differing sources, *Fukanzazengi* and *Notes* share the common feature of presenting brief, terse, direct, clear, and straightforward, albeit highly condensed, foundations for practice based on direct experience and the core underlying assumptions in their respective disciplines: Sōtō Zen Buddhism that evolved as a major school in the East Asian Mahayana tradition and a revisioned psychoanalysis that developed and branched out from Freudian and Kleinian perspectives. These shared experiential viewpoints find consolidation and integration in what I describe as the "Realizational Perspective." These early influences and the experiences that they engendered and that they continue to exert have formed the basis for my continuing development as a practicing psychoanalyst and psychoanalytic educator and for my development and continuing refinement as a Zen practitioner and teacher.

Notes

1 O and K will be elaborated in Chapter Nine, "Bion's Use of O and K."
2 For elaboration, see Chapter Three, "*Mokusho*: Silent Illumination: Open to Whole Being."
3 For details and instructions, see Chapter Fourteen, "*Shikantaza*: Basic Fact of Sitting Practice Session."

References

Abe, M. (1985). *Zen and Western Thought*. Honolulu: University of Hawaii Press.
Bion, W. (1965). *Transformations*. London: Karnac.
Bion, W. (1967). Notes on memory and desire. In: J. Aguayo & B. Malin (Eds.), *Wilfred Bion: Los Angeles Seminars and Supervision* (pp. 133–149). London: Karnac, 2017. [Originally published in: Bion, W. (1967). Notes on memory and desire. The *Psychoanalytic Forum*, 2:272–273, 279–280.]
Bion, W. (1970). *Attention and Interpretation*. London: Karnac.
Bion, W. (1991). *A Memoir of the Future*. London: Karnac.
Bleandonu, G. (1994). *Wilfred Bion: His Life and Works. 1897–1979*. London: Free Association Books.
Coupey, P. (2020). *In the Belly of the Dragon: A Zen Master's Commentary on the Shinjinmei by Master Sosan (D. 606)*. Chino Valley, AZ: Hohm Press.
Dōgen, E. (1227). *Fukanzazengi*. In: N. Waddell & M. Abe (Trans.), *The Heart of Dōgen's Shobogenzo* (pp. 1–6). Albany: State University of New York Press, 2002.
Dōgen, E. (1231). *Bendowa*. In: N. Waddell & M. Abe (Trans.), *The Heart of Dōgen's Shobogenzo* (pp. 7–30). Albany: State University of New York Press, 2002.

Dōgen, E. (1243b). *Zazenshin*. In: Nishijima & C. Cross (Trans.), *Master Dogen's Shobogenzo Book 2* (pp. 91–106). London: Windbell Publications, 1996.

Dōgen, E. (1243c). Zazengi. In: N. Waddell & M. Abe (Trans.), *The Heart of Dōgen's Shobogenzo* (pp. 109–110). Albany: State University of New York Press, 2002.

Dōgen, E. (1244). *Zanmai O Zanmai*. In: Nishijima & C. Cross (Trans.), *Master Dogen's Shobogenzo Book 3* (pp. 281–284). London: Windbell Publications, 1997.

Epstein, M. (1984). On the neglect of evenly suspended attention. *Journal of Transpersonal Psychology*, 16(2):193–205.

Epstein, M. (1988). Attention and psychoanalysis. *Psychoanalysis and Contemporary Thought*, 11:171–189.

Maezumi, T. (2002). *Appreciate Your Life: The Essence of Zen Practice*. Boston, MA: Shambhala Publications.

Milton, J. (1667). *Paradise Lost*. London: Samuel Simmons Printer.

Pelled, E. (2007). Learning from experience: Bion's concept of reverie and Buddhist meditation: a comparative study. *International Journal of Psycho-Analysis*, 88(6):1507–1526.

Roberts, S. (2018). *Being-Time: A Practitioner's Guide to Dōgen's Shōbōgenzo Uji*. Somerville: Wisdom Publications.

Rubin, J. (1985). Meditation and psychoanalytic listening. *Psychoanalytic Review*, 72:599–614.

Speeth, K. (1982). On psychotherapeutic attention. *Journal of Transpersonal Psychology*, 14:141–160.

Chapter 3

Mokusho
Silent Illumination Open to Whole Being[1]

I have been emphasizing the importance of experience throughout this text. This chapter will be part didactic in terms of definition, background, and instructions and part experiential in terms of entering a silent practice session by describing and offering a meditation practice based on the practice of *mokusho* (Chinese: *mozhao*), "silent illumination," which developed in China beginning in the 7th century and eventually evolved into *shikantaza* or "just sitting" in the Japanese Sōtō Zen tradition during the 13th century through the Eihei Dōgen's teachings. *Shikantaza* practice will be explored in Chapter Fourteen, "*Shikantaza*, Basic Fact of Sitting Practice Session," as a conclusion to this offering. A brief discussion regarding *mokusho*'s origins provides an entry into this practice. The description of this form of meditation and the actual practice will make experientially clear a sound rationale for recommending it to psychoanalytic practitioners. This orientation will be followed by guided instructions and a few minutes of silent practice time. Three rings of a bell will signal the beginning of the silent session of meditation practice. The silent period will conclude with one ring of the bell.

As mentioned previously, Zen practices reflect and function as expressions of the core assumptions of the tradition. *Mokusho* is no exception. The term silent illumination can be viewed as a representation of the identity of the one and many or as a complete expression of absolute and relative being as inseparable. That is the "silent" aspect of the practice refers to and expresses oneness and "illumination" points to the "reflection" of the clear and cogent mind. Together, they represent the interrelationship between the one and the two, which is a fundamental doctrinal concept. This understanding explains, as will be described below, why "silence" and "illumination" operate together. The interacting dynamic between the two aspects of *mokusho* that is clearly described in the literature also explains why the misconception of silent illumination as an exclusively quietist practice makes no sense.

Origins

Mokusho developed over an extended period of time beginning with Bodhidharma (5th century), an Indian monk who became the first ancestor of Zen in China and practiced what came to be described as "wall gazing." The practice continued to develop with various iterations until it became singled out as a distinct practice associated with the Caodong (Sōtō) school of Zen during the 11th century through the teachings of Hongzhi Zhengjue (1091–1157), although other variations are described in the literature. *Mokusho* integrates the earlier Indian Buddhist practices of *shamata* (calm abiding) and *vipashyana* (insight practice) into a single practice. The full teaching of *mokusho* and the relationship between calming and insight is asserted tersely and completely in Hongzhi's poem *Mozhao Ming* "Inscription on Silent Illumination" (1131), which the Chan scholar Christopher Byrne describes "as a poetic and philosophical text, which offers a bold and authoritative statement on the superiority of Caodong doctrine and practice" (2019, p. 174).

Here are the relevant verses culled from the 72 verses of the poem:

> Only silence is the supreme speech,
> Only illumination is the universal response—
> Responding without attainment,
> Speaking without being heard.
>
> Calling and answering with clear authentication,
> perfectly responding to one another.
> When there is no silence within illumination,
> anger and aggression arise.
>
> With clear authentication, calling and answering,
> responding to one another perfectly.
> When there is no illumination within silence,
> confusion leads one astray.
>
> (Byrne, 2019, pp. 177–178).

Hongzhi's verses make it clear that both aspects of calming and insight are necessary and work together in the one practice. Regarding the interacting relationship between silence and illumination, the Chan teacher Sheng Yen writes:

> In silence there is illumination; in illumination there is silence—the two cannot be separated. ... This is because within silence there is free-flowing wisdom—dynamic and alive. So, in Silent Illumination, one does not enter samadhi, at least not in the sense of utter stillness.
>
> (2008, p. 63)

Understanding the inclusion of both silence and illumination and the interaction between the two is crucial for a clear understanding of the practice, which, as noted above, has historically been criticized as an exclusively quietist form of meditation, as has been misunderstood by some writers.[2] Yen notes further that *mokusho* is a very simple practice:

> Silent illumination is a simple method—so simple, in fact, that this simplicity becomes its difficulty. Ultimately, it is the method of no-method, in

which the practitioner leaves behind all seeking, all attachment, all expectations, and just lives Chan directly.

(2001, p. 144)

This simplicity consists of gently settling the agitated mind and deluded thinking by engendering revaluated or authentic thinking by creating the space for it, which allows the stillness and clarity of the realized mind to arise naturally.

Huineng (638–713), the sixth patriarch of Zen, advises the student that "If you give rise to thoughts from your true self-nature, then, although you see, hear, perceive, and know, you are not stained by the manifold environments and are always free" (in: P. Yampolsky, 2012, Kindle location 4077).

Huineng uses the image of a lamp and a flame to emphasize this point:

> Students of the way do not say that there is a difference between samadhi coming first and then producing prajna, and prajna coming first and then producing samadhi [And] They are like a lamp and its light. If there is a lamp, there is light; without a lamp, there is darkness. The lamp is the body of the light, the light is the function of the lamp. The name may be two, but in essence they are basically one and the same.
>
> (T. Cleary, 1998, p. 31)

The Chinese Chan teacher Yongjia Xuanjue (665–713) describes the process:

> For this reason, Chan practice involves "purifying and wiping away the various deluded conditioning and illusory habits." Thoughts and emotions are only temporary functions of the mind. We can't get caught up with them. We need to expose, embrace, work with, and let go of them. In this process, we regain the most natural state of being: empty yet wakeful; still and aware.
>
> (G. Gu, Trans. 2021, p. 18)

Simplicity

Is it really that simple? Yes! Then what reason is there to make meditation such a complicated and elusive affair? There is no reason. However, I'd like to address this question in two ways. First, ego would like to take credit for figuring out something complicated and difficult, not something so simple and easy. Ego would like credit for creating some complex procedure. Ego likes to reinvent the wheel. Second, ego is also a devious and very clever trickster and can attempt to hold on to its threatened territory with all sorts of inventions and complications that can be reduced to resistance to authentic practice. Investigating further, resistance stems from the threat of existential anxiety. This becomes verifiable experientially through sitting practice. That is, we do not exist in the solid, separate, or independent way that we imagine ourselves to exist. We are faced with the paradoxical reality that we exist in a relative sense subject to causes and conditions, but, as will be discussed in Chapter Seven, "Emptiness and Dependent Co-arising," we do not exist permanently, inherently, or separately from causes and conditions. This belief can create complications that can serve as a very powerful resistance to authentic practice and the lived realization of what Zen often describes as the true reality of all beings or framed as what Buddhists describe as the Three Marks of Existence. They include the emptiness of all phenomena, the reality of *anatta* or the illusion of an inherently or permanently existing self, and finally, of the suffering that derives out of impermanence. In this regard, *mokusho* is simple and practical.

In *mokusho*, we just sit and notice what is rising and falling without attachment, aversion, or judgment. The practitioner develops an awareness of the whole body just sitting. The technique after a period of guided relaxation consists of a continuous awareness of the whole body as a unity. When you notice that you are caught in some preoccupation, simply check your posture and continue being aware of the whole body simply sitting.

Intention

This process of simple awareness is guided by the "intention to raise *Bodhicitta*," the mind of true awareness to the arising and passing of all experience without grasping or pushing away. We just notice and we continue to focus on just sitting. We just stay present, simply being with the truth of the reality of the moment, whatever that may be. This entails a relaxed and open awareness. In this manner, as Sheng Yen notes, we practice "by quietly settling the churning mind of deluded thinking, it seeks to allow the perfect quiescence and luminosity of the enlightened mind to naturally emerge" (2001, p. 140). This luminosity is simply the awareness of what is.

He adds, "Unless *mokusho* is practiced properly, it is no more useful than soaking stones in cold water to brew a cup of tea" and "Misusing it can also amount to escaping into the demon cave to weave dreams of unconcern" (2006, p. 162).

The short of it is that *mokusho*, silent illumination, is not the same as doing nothing. We notice the mind's tendency to become attached to objects of consciousness, such as sounds, physical sensations, and thoughts, including feelings, memories, and future concerns. Whatever we experience in this practice of choiceless, objectless, goalless awareness, we simply notice and return to the present moment and to the basic fact of sitting. To repeat, in this practice, your attention is focused on sitting just as you are. You are not trying to gain anything, reach any place. You are also not trying to get rid of anything. You simply sit and return your attention to a sense of the whole body just sitting in the present. The present is your target. This is *mokusho*, plain and simple.

The mandate here, as I like to describe it to my students, is to "Just keep sitting, no matter what!" or, when you get lost in thought trains to just remind yourself: "just being as it is, just sitting." Remember, letting go of thoughts is not the same as trying to eliminate thinking altogether. "Just being" is just a simple reminder to take a backward step and to simply continue to notice exactly what is happening in the present moment.

But what is this simple basic fact of sitting? To cite an old koan, "What is sitting with the face before your parents were born?" This face is the face before concepts, ideas, or feelings, memories, wishes, and desires became activated. This is the "True Dharma Eye," the seeing before and beyond concepts. What is this sitting before concepts form? What is this sitting when concepts form, after concepts form? What is this sitting in the moment before the bell sounds; inside the sound of the bell; outside the sound of the bell; after the sound of the bell? What is this sitting when the bird flies away in the endless sky and you are simply being here, just sitting still, just noticing? What is sitting upright? What is the basic fact of sitting, the sitting of the left hand nestled gently in the right palm, thumb tips lightly touching? What is the mind of sitting in silence? What is the mind of sitting in the truck sound; after the truck sound; in the wind sound; after the wind sound? Dōgen Zenji says that we must thoroughly investigate all of these mind moments. By thorough investigation, he means to just keep sitting, no matter what! We investigate by sitting without pushing away or grasping or chasing after anything. In other words, "avoid picking and choosing." Avoid avoiding! In other words, exercise nonattachment to the rising and passing of all experience.

Simply abide in the dharma position of your uniqueness as you are; abide in the common ground of whole being; in separateness; in deep connectedness, what is this "basic fact of sitting?" Abide in the sitting of this question. Abide in the sitting of the present moment, in the dharma position of who you are right now, just sitting. The past is gone; it is no more than a memory puff. The future has not yet arrived; it is no more than a fantasy, or a wish, and a desire. The present moment is gone as soon as it arises, again and again, moment after moment. The only reality is just this present moment of silent illumination. But please be careful. Don't grasp at the present either. Grasping is one of the Three Poisonous Minds: ignorance, attachment, and aversion. We tend to pick and choose, to grasp and to push away, because ignorance splits mind into a grasper and a grasped and creates the likes and the dislikes that engender picking and choosing. This is only natural because we are human beings. This is not a problem if you simply sit and notice. Ignorance creates desirer and desired. Ignorance creates attachment and aversion, grasping, pushing away. But the mind that sees and the mind that is seen is the same mind—the one mind. The mind that hears and the mind that is heard is one and the same mind. The mind that speaks and the mind that is spoken to is one and the same mind. Dōgen writes in *Soku-Shin-Ze-Butsu*, "Mind Here and Now is Buddha" (1239a):

> "We realize in practice that "mind here and now is buddha," we realize in practice that "the mind which is buddha is this," ... we realize in practice

that "mind-and-buddha here and now is right," and we realize in practice that "this buddha-mind is here and now."

And:

"The mind that has been authentically transmitted" means one mind as all dharmas, and all dharmas as one mind.

(Nishijima & Cross, 1994, p. 53)

So, be careful not to turn the one mind into a something. There is really nowhere to stand, no solid ground, just sitting as it is. *Mokusho* is its own ground. Don't grasp the nowhere either. Grasping the nowhere is also one of the three poisonous minds. Whatever one grasps at: a memory, a concern, a creative flash, enlightenment, samsara, nirvana, the present, they can all function as anchors and resistances. If you raise the anchor and just keep sitting, what will happen? What is left? Just this: the silence of illumination and the illumination of silence; the silence of just noticing and the illumination of simple awareness.

The renowned Zen teacher Kodo Sawaki Roshi, also known as "Homeless Kodo," was reputed to say: "Zazen is good for nothing!" (in: K. Uchiyama & S. Okumura, 2014, p. 138). Well, what is this nothing that *zazen* is good for? Bodhidharma, the First Ancestor of Zen in China, said to Huike, his successor, "Realization is a process of self-scrutiny." Bodhidharma could not accomplish this for Huike who had to do this for himself. Therefore, Bodhidharma directed him to look within by instructing him to "Show me the mind that needs to be pacified." Incidentally, Dōgen reiterates the relationship between self-experience and realization in *Hossho*, "The Dharma Nature" (1243d). He writes:

When we learn in practice, sometimes following the sutras and sometimes following good counselors, we realize the truth independently, without a master. Independent realization without a master is the working of the Dharma-nature.

(Nishijima & Cross, 1997, pp. 127–129)

Following Bodhidharma's directive (my paraphrase), Huike looked and looked but continuously came up empty-handed. He returned to Bodhidharma and said: "I have found nothing." Bodhidharma responded: "Your mind is now pacified." The present mind is manifesting right here, right now; no need for grasping, no need for searching here, there, or everywhere. Just keep sitting, no matter what! Yes, just keep sitting, no matter what! And, to just keep sitting is the matter that is ineffable, unnamable, and unsayable what!

Settling into Practice

With these points in mind, begin to prepare for practice. Keep in mind that the preparation is an equally important part of practice. First, make very sure that you are very comfortable. If you are using a chair, sit closer to the front edge. This will help keep the spine erect in a good posture. Whether you are sitting on a zafu or a cushion, a chair, or on a bench, it is very important to make yourself comfortable.

If you don't, you will become preoccupied with the discomfort. The discomfort will become a source of attention or an object of your meditation. In silent illumination practice, we don't fix our attention on anything, except what we might call "the basic ground of our being." We remain open to all experience both internally and externally as the present moment continuously evolves and changes. Next, gently rock your body slightly back and forth and from side to side. Find your balance point and then simply be still. This rocking also helps to ground you in the present moment.

In *zazen*, we sit with our eyes open. Notice that your eyes are open about halfway, with a soft gaze set at about a 45-degree angle to the floor. Open eyes help to prevent sleep or daydreaming. Also, open eyes represent being open to all reality. In this way, as you practice, you let all reality flow without trying to block out anything without judgment or preferences. Remember, you are just sitting. If you are new to sitting with your eyes open, you might have some difficulty at first. Your eyes might close. If they do, that's O.K. Simply notice that you are "sitting with eyes closed." When you are ready, gently open them again and continue. No judgment, no pressure or forcefulness, just sitting. Keep in mind that you are centered in the middle: relaxed, not lazy, firm, not rigid or forced.

First, check in with the body and the mind. Begin with the body. Check your posture, sit firmly upright and erect, but not stiff. Relax your shoulders. Rest your left hand in your right palm, thumb tips lightly touching as if you were holding a very thin piece of paper. Rock gently back and forth and from side to side, just a bit to find your own balance point. Avoid leaning back in your chair. Feel the breath coming and going as if from the abdomen. Let go of any control. When there is a short breath, just notice that the breath is short. When there is a long breath, notice that the breath is long. That's all; nothing more, nothing less. No need for counting, following, or controlling the breath. This practice is a choiceless awareness, nothing excluded, nothing prioritized. So, it is the same with thoughts, memories, future expectations, sounds, scents, and body sensations. Just notice, very simple. That's all you need to do.

Simply scan the body slowly and gently without lingering on any spot for more than a moment or two. Begin by bringing your attention to the crown of the head. Following your breath, feel your attention spreading out along your scalp down into the forehead, eyelids, and eyes, cheeks, jaw, throat, back of the neck, shoulders, chest, upper back, solar plexus and rib cage, middle back, lower back, belly, buttocks, thighs, kneecaps, and back of the knees, calves and shins, feet; if you are sitting in a chair, feel the soles of the feet resting gently and fully on the ground. See that you are comfortable and relaxed. Gently adjust your posture and feel a sense of bodily ease and that you have settled into your seat. Check the mind. Is there any sense of anticipation or expectation for something special to happen, any wish to change something? Is there any sense or feeling of grasping for something or of wanting to get rid of anything? If you see something, simply watch it as if from a distance. Recognize that there is no need to change anything. Just noticing is enough. This sense of neutral nonjudgmental and nonreactive observation allows your intuitive wisdom to work without any need for action on your part. Our tendency to do something, to exert an effort, to change something comes from old habit formations that can operate in a very subtle, almost unnoticeable way. By just sitting with no gaining mind, we are creating the space to just observe. So simply watch whatever arises, maybe lingers, and eventually dissolves into the silence that they rose from and into the present awareness of just sitting. This neutral quality of just sitting with no gaining mind and simply watching can bring into awareness a sense of ease and stillness. This sense of ease and stillness is ever-present and has always been with you beyond any effort on your part. This is the natural intuited wisdom of not-doing that brings these feelings into awareness without any effort. Be aware that this sense of ease is already inherent to your being before you sat down, before you made an attempt to exert any effort, and simply rest in this space—BELL.

Concluding Comments

You can also integrate these principles into your approach to sitting with your psychotherapy patients. In the same way that we just practiced sitting now, you just sit, when you are with your patients, be aware of the totality of your whole being sitting and listening. Throw your whole being into what you are doing in the therapeutic encounter. So, we train ourselves to engage our whole being in what we are doing. Whether sitting in meditation, eating, washing dishes, or doing psychotherapy, you are not engaged in discursive, wandering, or deluded thoughts. All of you—environment, body, and mind—is right there. Whatever you do, whatever the task at hand, your whole life is there at that moment. This is what Bion means by relinquishing memory, desire, and understanding. Now you may think that throwing your whole being into the practice or into the task at hand creates unnecessary tension. However, by totally exerting your whole being into whatever you are doing, you are also being relieved from doing anything else at that moment. Therefore, when you are doing that one thing, that is all you need to care about. So, you can approach your patient in a very relaxed manner and with an attitude of openness and wonder.

Please keep practicing, even if only for a few minutes a day. It is very important, not only for you but also for the people who we come into contact within your clinical practice and in your daily life.

Notes

1 *Mokusho* "Opening to Whole Being" guided audio practice instruction link: https://soundcloud.com/paul-cooper-290569931/mokusho-opening-to-whole-beingmp3
2 For example, see Chapter Five, "Suzuki and Dōgen."

References

Byrne, C. (2019). Verses of silent illumination: Hongzhi Zhengjue's poetic vision of Caodong Zen. *International Journal of Buddhist Thought & Culture*, 29(2):171–205.

Cleary, T. (1998). *The Sutra of Hui-Neng Grand Master of Zen*. Boston, MA: Shambhala.

Dōgen, E. (1239a). *Soku-Shin-Ze-Butsu*. In: G. Nishijima & C. Cross (Trans.), *Master Dogen's Shobogenzo, Book 1* (pp. 49–55). London: Windbell Publications, 1994.

Dōgen, E. (1243d). *Hossho*. In: Nishijima & C. Cross (Trans.), *Master Dogen's Shobogenzo, Book 3* (pp. 125–129). London: Windbell Publications, 1997.

Gu, G. (2021). *Silent Illumination: A Chan Buddhist Path to Natural Awakening*. Boulder, CO: Shambhala Publications.

Uchiyama, K. & Okumura, S. (2014). *The Zen Teaching of Homeless Kodo*. Boston, MA: Wisdom Publications.

Yampolsky, P. (2012). *The Platform Sutra of the Sixth Patriarch: The Text of the Tun-Huang Manuscript*. New York: Columbia University Press (Kindle Edition).

Yen, S. (2001). *Hoofprints of the Ox*. Oxford. Oxford University Press.

Yen, S. (2006). *Attaining the Way: A Guide to the Practice of Chan Buddhism*. Boston, MA & London: Shambhala.

Yen, S. (2008). *The Method of No Method: The Chan Practice of Silent Illumination*. Boston, MA & London: Shambhala.

Part Two

Review

Chapter 4

Literature Review

Precursors

Zen first appeared on the American scene during the 1920s primarily through the extensive writings of D.T. Suzuki (1870–1966).[1] Due to his command of English in contrast to other Zen teachers of the time, he served as the primary source of information regarding Zen Buddhism in the west. In a study of Asian religion and western culture, Iwamura notes, "For a generation of Western spiritual seekers in the 1950s and 1960s, he seemed the essence of the Oriental teacher of ancient wisdom" (2010, pp. 27–28). Suzuki's presentation engendered fascination, wonder, and the promise of spiritual realization and freedom. I am no exception to his influence, having encountered his writings during the mid-1960s when I was young, impressionable, and like many in my generation, looking for answers that western religious traditions failed to answer for me.

His explication of a hybrid Zen influenced by his deep emersion and assimilation of western science, philosophy, and religion resulted in a modernist version to be presented to and assimilated by the western audience. This point requires elaboration regarding the impact that Suzuki's Zen had on his western audience with particular relevance to his relationship with the western psychoanalytic community. Harrington summarizes Suzuki's background clearly and succinctly:

> The real Suzuki was also a man who, alongside his deep study of Japanese and Chinese texts and traditions, had spent decades—especially in the first half of his life—becoming deeply conversant with the latest Western psychological theories. Those years of self-study were critically important to his development of a way of talking about Zen that would ultimately draw the attention of some of the leading psychoanalytically oriented therapists of the day. It was almost surely not Suzuki's original intent, however, specifically to catalyse a dialogue between Western psychotherapy and Eastern Zen. What role then did his long-standing engagement with Western psychology play in his own thinking? The short answer is: psychology was the language of universality and modernity; and if Zen was to survive, Suzuki believed, it needed to learn to speak that language.
>
> (2016, pp. 6–7)

The significance of these influences played a major role in the dependently co-arising dynamic that interacts between Suzuki and his audience in terms of what material becomes assimilated and what internal accommodations the receiver of the new material makes. These issues will be elaborated and explored in Chapter Ten, "Assimilation and Accommodation."

Suzuki's influence coupled with his accommodations, the result of his assimilation of western ideas, combined with his sectarian exclusively Rinzai Zen vision, however, engendered a skewed and incomplete version of Zen, which can effectively be described as "hybrid." Suzuki's Zen, due to these factors and associated biases, was characterized and frequently received by his western audience as exclusively intuitive, iconoclastic, sectarian, and nationalistic.

Suzuki emphasized personal individual experience through self-inquiry or what Dōgen from a very different perspective describes as *Hensan* or "Thorough Investigation" (1243a). His approach created a sharp contrast to blind faith in dogma and blindly following unexplained empty and therefore meaningless rituals that I encountered in the religion of my childhood. His writing exerted a strong impact on me in my personal pursuit for self-understanding during the troubling time of the Viet Nam era. In his eulogy to Suzuki, Thomas Merton, the Trappist monk mystic and poet, captures the feeling of the time poignantly:

> The impact of Zen on the west, striking with its fullest force right after World War II, in the midst of the existentialist upheaval, at the beginning of the atomic and cybernetic age, with western religion and philosophy in a state of crisis and with the consciousness of man threatened by the deepest alienation, the work and personal influence of Dr. Suzuki proved to be both timely and fruitful: much more fruitful than we have perhaps begun to realize.
>
> (1967a, p. 3)

While over time, through practice, study with various teachers, and the increasing availability of writings on Zen Buddhism, I developed a rather critical view of Suzuki's presentation. However, during that period in my life, his writings exerted a deep influence in my understanding and practice of both Zen and psychoanalysis. Regarding this latter point, the purpose of this discussion of Suzuki's version of Zen is intended to demonstrate his influence on the early generation of psychoanalysts and to clarify, albeit often misguided, the view and initial response to Zen Buddhism.

Understanding Suzuki's place in the incrementally evolving, expanding, and continuously developing dialog between Zen and psychoanalysis demands what van der Braak in a discussion of traditionalist and modernist views of Zen Buddhism as a "reimagining of Zen" writes:

> In order to come to a reimagining of Zen we have to locate the inappropriate projections inherent in earlier imaginings of Zen, so that they can be revised or replaced with more appropriate ones (in a rather pragmatic sense).
>
> (2020, p. 11)

In terms of the larger picture of Zen Buddhist sects with their many overlapping identities and notable differences, this discussion is intended to clarify and highlight the point that Suzuki's explication of Zen Buddhism does not represent the whole tradition as one might have initially imagined. His specifically Rinzai orientation is limited by a sectarian and an apologist view as well as by the historical and cultural contexts that his work emerged from and was presented to the North American reader. For example, his nationalist leanings find expression in his comment that "pure Zen can only be found in Japan not in China where it originated" (1949, p. 96).

His experiential, truth-seeking approach to Zen highlights an anti-ritual, anti-intellectual, and radically iconoclastic view that derives partly from his sectarian bias that came to be misunderstood as an antinomian agenda that negated the need for a moral code or religious practices. Viewed through a lens colored by these preconceptions, the spiritual freedom that Suzuki points toward has been confused as a license to disregard or ignore morality. His portrayal of historical Zen teachers as iconoclasts resulted in a critical view of religious structures, ritual performance, thinking, and a devaluation and misperception of the practice of Zen meditation. Critical examination clearly demonstrates that his rendition of Zen was basically one-sided and limited by his own sectarian biases. He emphasizes the Rinzai Zen tradition, which he characterized as grounded in naturalism and an intuitionist stance that tends to devalue study, language, and soteriological practices such as meditation. This orientation created the false impression that this version of Zen encompassed all of Zen. In a sense, one slice, albeit an important slice, was confused for the whole pie. For example, his exclusion of the Sōtō Zen, tradition, and his ambivalent response to Dōgen, which will be explored in the next chapter, was compromised by his exclusive emphasis on the Rinzai Zen tradition. His revisioning of Zen for the west was structured around his accommodation to his perception of the prevailing western framework. In this regard, van der Braak describes Suzuki as a "romantic interpreter of Zen" who "attempted to go beyond the mind" and aimed at directly beholding the "spirit," "possibly through a faculty of mystical intuition or other extra-rational means" (2020, p. 103).

We can't lay this problem exclusively at Suzuki's feet. As will be addressed in Chapter Ten, "Assimilation and Accommodation." The dependently co-arising context in which assimilation and accommodation take place includes a western reader, for example, the psychoanalyst, whose internalized preconceptions saturate the psychic space with psychoanalytic theories, ideas, and beliefs. Hence, interpretations of Zen are biased and filtered through a lens that often prioritizes individualist and nihilist biases,[2] thus turning a blind eye toward Zen's extreme conformity to communal structures and behavioral restrictions. For instance, Wright summarizes the filters operating and influencing assimilation and accommodation in terms of the priority placed on western individualism:

> Being "not different," however, is not the image of greatness projected by modern western Zen whose practitioners would turn to Zen in the wake of

> European romanticism precisely in an effort to differentiate themselves. This twentieth-century tradition could not help but absorb the values of modern individualism and to read Zen from the only perspective available to it.
>
> (1998, p. 126)

For the Zen monastic, for instance, individual freedom finds expression within the background of religious structures that conform to generations of orthodoxy rooted in a highly defined history. Dōgen, for example, was in many ways an innovator, as exemplified in his novel, in his often radical approach to understanding traditional koan interpretations and his commentaries on traditional *mondo* (master and disciple conversations).[3] At the same time, he seeks legitimacy and articulates an orthodoxy rooted in tradition, tied to the lineage of ancestors, for example, by comparing the student's enlightened mind to Buddha, Bodhidharma, and the lineage of Zen patriarchs.

Wright describes two potential ways of understanding this seeming paradoxical situation:

> Two models of this process are attractive. One places identity and difference in sequence. The monk first appropriates the tradition by gaining its identity and then enters into a dialectical process of differing from himself. The past is transmitted as paradigm and challenge. ... The second model has the two processes occurring simultaneously. Because acts of identification occur in new contexts, critique and differentiation take place all along.
>
> (1998, p. 126, f. 25)

As noted above, the role of ritual has been played down by Suzuki through his emphasis on the iconoclastic behaviors of Zen teachers, which has given a false impression of Zen as a wild, undisciplined, anything goes affair. This misconception that eschews orthodoxy, conformity, or commitment to a religious structure as well as the developmental process of identity and differentiation described by Wright. This incomplete perception of Zen that excludes or devalues these religious structural elements has added to a false depiction of the larger framework of Zen Buddhism. The role of ritual in Zen, for example, in terms of practice, can better be understood in terms of the structure that Zen ritual functions, such as a stage on which practitioners as actors ritually play out their so-called spontaneously emerging iconoclastic self-states. In my own experience of participation in various Zen communities, an all-encompassing and pervasive conformity that extends to all areas of ritual and ritualized behavior consistently appears to be the "name of the game." For example, the contemporary American Zen teacher Reb Anderson, speaking of ritual, offers this opinion on the significance of ritual structures:

> By giving up our habitual personal styles of deportment and bringing our body, speech, and thought into accord with traditional forms and ceremonies, we merge in realization with buddha.

And:

> When correctly understood and practiced appropriately, the traditional rules and procedures of Zen training provide a context within which student and teacher together can realize selflessness and practice wholeheartedly, wholesomely, and in harmony with all beings.
>
> (1999, p. 53)

The skewed and overidealized western reception of Suzuki's articulation of Zen has been examined and criticized through contemporary scholarship. For example, Heine (2008) advocates a more balanced and nuanced approach to understanding Zen, which he notes has been traditionally negatively biased against a religious orientation along with its associated practices and structures. He writes:

> Each of these approaches, when given consideration in and of itself, may be seen as worthwhile or even brilliantly insightful in offering a significant contribution to comparative cultural history. The problem is that respective outlooks, when weighed against one another, tend to come across as reactive and partial, or biased and one-sided.
>
> (2008, p. 5)

In this regard, Suzuki exemplifies this bias. Heine advocates an approach "... tempered by a self-reflective, self-critical methodology, [that] is open-ended and balanced in relation to the other" (p. 5).

The body as ritual expression, as a visible container is essential, as Dōgen notes in *Shoji*, "Life and Death" (year not recorded). He writes, "Those who reject the body reject the Buddha." (Buddha in this context functions as metaphor and descriptor of awakened mind.) *Zazen* in this context is depicted as a highly structured "ritual enactment" (Leighton, 2008, p. 167). Practice becomes a direct expression of the realized Buddha mind. The body in the practice of still seated meditation functions as a ritual container, and in its stillness, a realizational expression contains all states of mind and associated sensory input, engendering a perceptual transformation that has been described as no different than the Buddha's mind, no different than the ancestor's mind, no different than whole being. This passage from Dōgen's *Hensan*, "Thorough Exploration" (1243a), exemplifies this point:

> Old Master Shakyamuni and Old Man Gensha are experiencing the same state. Old Master Shakyamuni and Old man Gensha are investigating to the limit the experience of satisfaction and the experience of dissatisfaction: this is the principle of thorough exploration. Because Old Master Sakyamuni experiences the same state as Old Man Gensha he is the eternal buddha. Because Old Man Gensha is in the same state as Old Master Sakyamuni, he is a descendant.... Old Master Sakyamuni and Old Man

Gensha simultaneously experience the same state... Old Man Gensha and Old Master Sakyamuni are experiencing the same state and thoroughly exploring it.

Dōgen continues with his imperative that practice is essential:

> Unless the truth of thorough exploration is actually manifest in the present, experience of the self is impossible and experience of the self is unsatisfactory; experience of others is impossible and experience of others is unsatisfactory; experience of "a person" is impossible, experience of "I" is impossible.
>
> (Nishijima & Cross, 1997, p. 211)

In my own experience, there has been a vast difference between the iconoclastic presentation of Zen and the actual practice of *shikantaza* (just sitting). Both my Asian and American teachers encourage students to actively engage in textual study, various rituals, practice, hierarchical structures, and subscribe to fundamental Buddhist doctrines such as karma, emptiness, and dependent co-arising, all of which influence how I think about, experience, and interact with patients and students. I find the notion of active engagement to also be internal and attitudinal, for instance, in my view that the core ritual expression of realized being is enacted the moment the practitioner sits for *zazen*. In this regard, I may be viewed as a naive traditionalist. However, I maintain what might be called a "modernist" view that finds expression in my metaphorical, symbolic, psychological, demythologizing response to Buddhist cosmology. For example, I view the Six Realms depicted on the *Bhavachakra*, "Wheel of Life and Death," as momentary oscillating psychological states that we all experience rather than actual discrete realms of existence. In this regard, a clear-cut distinction between traditionalist and modernist views of Zen seem moot.[4]

Influences on Psychoanalysis

D.T. Suzuki was a prolific writer. He exerted a profound influence on the western reception of Zen Buddhism in many fields, including psychoanalysis (Fromm, 1960; Horney, 1945; Kelman, 1960), religion (Merton, 1967b, 1968), philosophy (Alan Watts, 1932, 1948, 1957), and in the literary arts in the writings of Aldous Huxley, Jack Kerouac, and others. For example, influenced by Suzuki's Zen orientation, the psychoanalyst Karen Horney provides a poignant example that she refers to as "wholeheartedness of spirit" to describe the psychoanalytic stance of total openness to the patient's ongoing currently manifesting experience. Horney (1945) quotes Suzuki's narration of a Zen encounter dialog to explicate this orientation. She prefaces the story by commenting: "It is interesting to note in this connection that in Zen Buddhist writings sincerity is connected with wholeheartedness, pointing to the very conclusion we reach on the basis of clinical observation—namely, that nobody divided within himself can be wholly sincere" (1945, pp. 162–163). She then quotes the following Zen dialog:

Monk: I understand that when a lion seizes upon his opponent, whether it is a hare or an elephant, he makes an exhaustive use of his power; pray tell me what is this power?
Master: The spirit of sincerity (literally, the power of non-deceiving).

Horney then offers a quote from D.T. Suzuki in way of explanation:

> Sincerity, that is, not-deceiving, means "putting forth one's whole being," technically known as "the whole being in action" ... in which nothing is kept in reserve, nothing is expressed under disguise, nothing goes to waste. When a person lives like this, he is said to be a golden-haired lion; he is the symbol of virility, sincerity, wholeheartedness; he is divinely human.
> (p. 163)

For many years, there was a tendency among psychoanalysts interested in Zen to idealize Suzuki and to swallow his limited version of Zen Buddhism whole without critical examination. The available criticism emerged from outside of the profession and therefore did not tackle theoretic or technical issues.[5] For example, in an extensive review of Koestler's critique of Suzuki and eastern religions, Fader asserts: "Although hardly a scholar of Asian religions, Koestler, the Hungarian popular journalist and outspoken anti-fascist, published a scathing critique of Hinduism and Zen" (1980, p. 46). He describes Zen as amoral, ambiguous, godless, cruel, and lacking coherence. Regarding Suzuki, he asserts:

> It is time for the Professor to shut up and for Western intelligentsia to recognize contemporary Zen as one of the 'sick' jokes, slightly gangrened, which are always fashionable in ages of anxiety.
> (1960, p. 58)

Suzuki responded to Koestler's misinformed critique. Interestingly, he based his critique on Koestler's misinterpretation of Zen rooted in cultural differences. He notes in part that Koestler "unfortunately, seems not to be cognizant of 'the stink' radiating from his own 'Zen'" (1961, p. 17).

Not unlike Koestler's critique, the available general critiques of Zen were also misguided, since they were based on Suzuki's hybrid, sectarian-biased, and incomplete presentation.[6]

On the other hand, the psychological community expressed deep admiration for the man and for his work. For example, Jung contributes introductions to several translations of eastern wisdom tradition texts, including *The Tibetan Book of the Dead* (Evans-Wentz, 1927), *The Tibetan Book of the Great Liberation* (Evans-Wentz, 1954), *The Secret of the Golden Flower* (Wilhelm, 1931), and with specific relevance to this discussion, *Introduction to Zen Buddhism* (Suzuki, D.T., 1949).

Jung raises general questions regarding the value of Asian religious systems and their practices for the western psyche. However, he does not consider the value, accuracy, or completeness of Suzuki's limited version of Zen, which, as I mentioned above, is replete with a sectarian and biased depiction of Zen Buddhism. Rather, Jung clearly idealizes and accepts Suzuki without question. For example, he writes: "Daisetz Teitaro Suzuki's works on Zen Buddhism are among the best contributions to the knowledge of living Buddhism that recent decades have produced" and "We cannot be sufficiently grateful to the author, first for the fact of his having brought Zen closer to Western understanding, and secondly for the manner in which he has achieved this task. (1949, p. 9).

This response to Suzuki's writings is understandable, as his work was basically "the only game in town" at the time in terms of their accessibility for the western reader. Bernard Faure, a scholar of East Asian religions, attributes this tendency toward a wholesale positive reception of his work to Suzuki's charm and presence. He notes:

> Suzuki's success had also a lot to do with his undeniable personal charisma. … It is therefore hard to dissociate the image of the man, with his genuine simplicity, warmth, and his status of enlightened layman, from the assertions concerning the Chan/Zen tradition.
>
> (1993, p. 54)

For example, in his eulogy to Suzuki, Fromm wrote, "You spoke to a man, and nothing but a man. It is because of this that he will be present always; a friend and a guide whose physical presence was secondary to the light which radiates from him" (1967, p. 89). It is clear from Fromm's comments how deeply he admired Suzuki as a person.

Steven Heine describes Suzuki as an "international sensation" (2008, p. 17). I would imagine that a sense of enthusiasm, wonder, and curiosity regarding this previously unknown and seemingly exotic East Asian discipline with the promising possibility of rendering psychoanalysis more effective added to this largely uncritical reception.

Suzuki's biases, such as in this example, are coupled with a lack of serious and comprehensive scholarship and explication of East Asian Zen Buddhism, particularly in terms of his writings targeted for the western audience.

Nevertheless, Suzuki's influence exerted an unquestioned impact into the nascent interest in Zen Buddhist thought among the psychoanalysts who were drawn to his teachings.

Harrington, for example, in a review of the relationship between Zen and psychoanalysis, concludes:

> It was Suzuki who, more than anyone else, first encouraged American psychotherapists to think of Zen as psychotherapy by other means, and the

Asian religious traditions as a resource, not just for spiritual insights, but also for clinical projects.

(2016, p. 23)

Suzuki's hybrid and one-sided presentation of Zen influenced the popular writer, Alan Watts. His resulting (mis)understanding of Zen serves as an example of D. T. Suzuki's spreading influence on the popular culture of the time.

Alan Watts

Following on the heels of D.T. Suzuki's teachings, Alan Watts, the British philosopher and popularizer of Zen Buddhism in America, further perpetuated the biases in Suzuki's work, which resulted in an erroneous and widespread reception of Zen Buddhism in the west. However, ultimately Suzuki eventually criticized Watts for his misunderstandings with respect to confusing freedom with license and conflating religious realization and libertarianism. Watts wrote: "What Zen most emphasizes in its disciplinary practice is to attain a spiritual freedom and not revolting against conventionalism" (1957, pp. 7–8). He describes this freedom in a very direct, concrete, and lived manner: "The freedom may consist sometimes in eating when hungry and resting when tired" (p. 8). Further, he emphasizes this point by concluding, "Zen may find its great followers more among conformists than rebellious and boisterous non-conformists" (p. 8).

Suzuki eventually leveled a sharp and more broad-based critique regarding his view of the status of the western misperception and ensuing misrepresentation of Zen to the public in an untitled article dated 1960 that was published posthumously in the Eastern Buddhist (Suzuki, 1970). His comments clearly reflect on the dependently co-arising interaction between west and east:

> Since Zen began to be more or less popularized among a certain group of young Americans whose immature minds, I am afraid, are liable to go off the track immoderately, Zen has been grossly misrepresented. Even among sober-minded professional people this danger seems to be growing. It is true that Zen holds in it something tending to invite a certain kind of misinterpretation; this is inevitably attached to every new approach to reality. Further:
>
> There is another kind of danger coming from quite a different source which is not on the side of the Western writers or students. Zen is not an easy subject to write about, and it is not meant for anybody to do so. [Suzuki then emphasizes the importance of the dual influence of study and experience.]
>
> First of all, a certain personal experience is needed, to attain which requires a number of years. Secondly, experience alone is not enough. One must be acquainted with the whole range of Zen literature… The masters, it is true, had no intention to leave any such things for posterity. It was their disciples who collected them and compiled them into "Sayings," which

consist generally of their sermons and *mondo* ("questions and answers") they had with their pupils. Historically and doctrinally, they are very informing and abound in deep reflections. Those who desire to elucidate Zen literally as far as this treatment is possible must study all these sermons and *mondo*, at least the most important ones.

(1970, pp. 1–2)

Of note, this article was reprinted in an edited collection (Franck, 1982) with this critical opening paragraph removed, which invites serious future speculation.

Despite his admiration of Suzuki's teachings, Watts also commented on his limitations. In the Preface to his popular book *The Way of Zen* he writes:

But as yet no one—not even Professor Suzuki—has given us a comprehensive account of the subject which includes its historical background and its relation to Chinese and Indian ways of thought. The three volumes of Suzuki's *Essays in Zen Buddhism* are an unsystematic collection of scholarly papers on various aspects of the subject, enormously useful for the advanced student but quite baffling to the general reader without an understanding of the general principles. His delightful Introduction to Zen Buddhism is rather narrow and specialized.

(1957, pp. 7–8)

Resistance

As a case in point Watts exemplifies the resistance that interferes with assimilation and accommodation processes that when left unquestioned, create a false understanding of Zen. Based on his writing on Buddhism, such as in his book *The Way of Zen*, it is quite clear that he assimilated an impressive amount of new information. His knowledge of basic Buddhist principles, as evidenced in this book, is almost encyclopedic. However, for the most part, he fails to accommodate this body of information into his preexisting psychic structures, which remained unaltered. As a result, he presented a radically distorted expression of Zen that, as I noted above, reinforces and conflates libertarianism and an antinomian attitude with spiritual freedom. He fails to question or alter his false views and related dysfunctional self-destructive behaviors.

In terms of his naturalist leanings coupled with his critique of meditation and his almost exclusive emphasis on spontaneity with respect to what he describes as "spiritual freedom," Suzuki clearly exerted an influence on Watts. For example, Suzuki writes:

Zen in its essence is the art of seeing into the nature of one's own being, and it points the way from bondage to freedom. By making us drink from the fountain of life, it liberates us from all the yokes under which we finite beings are usually suffering in this world.

(1949, p. 13)

However, in his reading, Watts poses Suzuki's comments against institutional religious structures and language, which, based on Suzuki's comments, clearly underlines how Watts misread Suzuki. Serious practitioners were also quite critical of Watts' Zen. For example, in *Zen Dust*, Ruth Fuller Sasaki comments on "... misinformation being spread about ... by those professed exponents of Zen in the West who had not actually undergone Zen training" (in: R. McDaniel, 2015, p. 95).

Over time, as the seeds of authentic Zen that had been planted and cultivated, blossomed as the teachings spread by teachers who were deeply immersed in formal Japanese monastic training. These teachers included Taizan Maezumi, who founded the Los Angelis Zen Center; Shunryu Suzuki who wrote the influential and popular *Zen Mind, Beginner's Mind* (1970) and who founded the San Francisco Zen Center, Green Gulch Zen Farm, and Tassajara Mountain Zen Center; Dainin Katagiri, who founded the Minnesota Zen Meditation Center in Minneapolis; and the American teacher Phillip Kapleau, who wrote the popular *Three Pillars of Zen* (1965). In this writing, Kapleau leveled a sharp critique of Watts' distorted views on Zen.

Over time, Watts began to lose credibility and influence. Nonetheless, he exerted a strong impact. While Watts explored the great texts of many Asian religious systems, his primary source of interest was clearly in Suzuki's writings. This influence culminated in his book *The Spirit of Zen*. McDaniel describes this book as a "reader's guide to Suzuki" (p. 98). In the preface to his popular *The Way of Zen*, Watts expresses Suzuki's influence on his own thinking. He writes, "My own Spirit of Zen is a popularization of Suzuki's earlier works, and besides being very unscholarly it is in many respects out of date and misleading, whatever merits it may have in the way of lucidity and simplicity" (1957, p. 8).

Not unlike Suzuki, for instance, Watts' naturalist stance finds expression in his critique of meditation practices. He argued that realization cannot authentically evolve through *zazen* because for him *zazen* practice was simply a replacement of one set of conventions with another. While I agree that this possibility exists depending on what intentions the practitioner brings to the meditation seat and the relationship that is formed with a teacher, study, and practice, Watts does not explore the variations in intention or the individual's relationship to any practice, which, based on the well-documented relationship between teacher and student, is a key point in Zen tradition.

There is an underlying dualism in Watts that also finds expression in Bion's ideas, which will also be explored. However, it is not clear whether this is a shared parallel development or a one-sided influence. I find it unlikely that Watts had a major influence on Bion because Bion drew from a wide range of sources. In his book *Attention and Interpretation* (1970), he references Plato, Keats, Meister Eckhart, John Milton, and the Jewish mystic Isaac Luria. However, there are no references to Buddhism. Gerard Bleandonu (1994), his biographer, references Bion's interest in the American counterculture movement of the 1960s. He notes that Bion appreciated the younger generation's budding interest in eastern religions, especially Hinduism, which was reminiscent of his early childhood in India.

In any case, this dualist tendency shared by Watts, Bion, and western philosophy runs counter to the radical nondualism of Dōgen's teachings. Overlooking this dualism has led to some misguided approaches, such as the spurious comparison between Bion's "O" and Buddhist emptiness. Another example, of Suzuki's influence to briefly mention, is Fromm's (1960) misguided devaluation of language and idealization of silence articulated in his peregrinations on Zen and psychoanalysis.

Lopez-Corvo (2005, 2006) also draws from the charismatic and controversial Alan Watts, who, while highly influential and extremely popular in the west, was clearly not a Zen teacher. Philip Kapleau (1912–2004) was a teacher of Zen Buddhism in the Sanbo Kyodan tradition, founded by Hakuun Yasutani in 1954, and which evolved as a blending of Japanese Soto and Rinzai schools. In 1966, Kapleau became the first American to found and teach at a Zen training center (the Rochester Zen Center). In his popular *Three Pillars of Zen* (1965), he criticizes Watts as "obviously unpracticed in Zen" (p. 23). Further, he clearly demonstrates how Watts distorted Zen teachings to rationalize his own lack of discipline and failure to actually practice *zazen*. For instance, Kapleau writes: "Alan Watts even tries to prove, by citing portions of a well-known dialogue, that Zen masters themselves have impugned sitting" (p. 23). For instance, a well-known Zen saying attributed to "Homeless Kodo," "Zazen is good for nothing" (Uchiyama & Okumura, 2014, p. 138), might on the surface be misconstrued as an overall dismissal of sitting practice. As an aside, it might be more fruitful from a practice perspective to ask, "what is this 'nothing' that Kodo speaks of?" In the Sōtō context, Kodo is addressing and critiquing facilitative or instrumental goal-oriented practices but not expressive practices. Additionally, he simultaneously expresses the primary core central Sōtō notion of *shusho ichinyo*, "the oneness of practice and realization," an orientation attributed to Dōgen. More emphatically, practice is good in and of itself as an expression of our enlightened nature.

Erich Fromm

During this early period in the continuing evolution of the relationship between Zen and psychoanalysis an increasing number of psychoanalysts demonstrated an interest in the developing dialog. However, it was Erich Fromm who became prominent through his friendship with Suzuki and with the publication of *Escape from Freedom* (1941), which thrust him into the public eye.

In an article appearing in the *Eastern Buddhist*, Fromm describes how he met Suzuki and his impact:

> My wife and I first became acquainted with Zen through his books, and later by attending his seminars at Columbia University in New York; after that, by many conversations here in Mexico. Sometimes we thought we had understood—only to find later that we had not. Yet eventually we believed that the worst misunderstandings had been overcome and that we had understood as much as one can with only the limited experience which is our lot. But undoubtedly whatever understanding of Zen we acquired was greatly helped not only by what Dr. Suzuki said or wrote, but by his being.
> (1967, p. 87)

Among Fromm's various interests, he focused on his endeavor to understand the human tendency to be drawn to authoritarianism. He viewed Zen, at least in Suzuki's exposition, as an alternative worldview that might hold the potential for freedom. Fromm speculates on Zen's potential to address his concerns:

> Zen-Buddhism, a later sect within Buddhism, is expressive of [a]...radical anti-authoritarian attitude. Zen proposes that no knowledge is of any value unless it grows out of ourselves; no authority, no teacher can really teach us anything except to arouse doubts in us; words and thought systems are dangerous because they easily turn into authorities whom we worship. Life itself must be grasped and experienced as it flows, and in this lies virtue.
> (Fromm, 1950, p. 40)

Fromm's 1960 essay on Zen and psychoanalysis is frequently quoted in integrated studies. Fromm points toward a realizational perspective by emphasizing experience. He writes:

> He must avoid the error of feeding the patient with interpretations and explanations which only prevent the patient from making the jump from thinking into experiencing ... This process produces a good deal of anxiety, and sometimes the anxiety would prevent a breakthrough, were it not for the reassuring presence of the analyst. But this reassurance is one of "being there," not one of words which tend to inhibit the patient from experiencing what only he can experience.
> (1960, p. 126)

He views the primacy of experience as a crucial aspect of psychoanalytic healing. On this point, he takes issue with Freud:

> Freud never expressed himself with full clarity on the difference between intellection and the affective, total experience which occurs in genuine

"working through." Yet, it is precisely this experiential and not-intellectual insight which constitutes the aim of psychoanalysis.

And:

It is characteristic of all true insight in psychoanalysis that it cannot be formulated in thought, while it is characteristic of all bad analysis that "insight" is formulated in complicated theories which have nothing to do with immediate experience.

(p. 132)

This early interest in Zen among Fromm and other psychoanalysts was primarily intellectual, speculative, and basically not practice-oriented. However, this orientation changed over the years due to the arrival of Zen teachers from Japan who emphasized and promoted practice, attracted western followers, and over time, produced a new generation of highly experienced practitioners, often formally ordained priests and transmitted teachers who became deeply immersed in and trained as psychoanalysts. This group of practitioners represents a wide range of psychoanalytic orientations, including Object Relations (Bobrow, 2010), Multimodal (Cooper, 2010, 2019), Self-Psychology and Intersubjectivity (Magid, 2002; Suler, 1993, 1995), and Lacanian (Moncayo, 1998, 2012).

Basic Misunderstandings

The typical early reception of Zen in the West has been incomplete and riddled with misunderstandings. Two basic misunderstandings that are fundamental created a skewed image that negated Zen as a comprehensive religious system. They include a dualist approach that separates noumena and phenomena and a prevailing yet often subtle nihilist orientation that separates and devalues language and thinking and idealizes silence and not thinking. For example, commenting on this matter, the Zen scholar Dale Wright notes that:

A major misunderstanding of Zen experience centers on the devaluation of language, and by implication, thinking. This misunderstanding extends to the nature of enlightenment experiences, which are characterized as beyond words, and which from this point of view, such experiences become severely limited by language. [As Wright notes] this uniquely western position that Zen experience transcends language, a position either developed or assumed, so far as I can see, in all English language works on Zen that attempt to articulate what "enlightenment" is.

(1992, p. 113)

Critiques of Fromm's impressions of Suzuki's Zen do exist. However, they tend to be general and do not specifically address the influence of Zen on psychoanalytic technique or theory. For instance, in a review that appeared in *Philosophy East and West*, the academic philosopher and Zen practitioner Paul Wienpahl comments, "Fromm gives an excellent account of psychoanalysis and then tries, unsuccessfully, to relate it to Zen Buddhism" (1965, p. 81).

Language and Thinking

Based on Suzuki's influence, Fromm developed a dualistic misunderstanding of Zen teachings by his devaluation of language, which he views as an interference with a clear perception of reality.

Historically, the Zen critique of language was not directed at language itself. Rather, it was a reaction to the scholarly overattachment to the scriptures at the expense of intuitive knowing and experiential learning. After all, Zen teachers over the centuries have produced one of the most extensive literatures of any religious system. On this matter, Suzuki himself cautions the western reader: "In spite of their claim that Zen is beyond expressions or explanations, the masters in China where it originated and in Japan where it is still flourishing have written voluminously on the subject" (1970, p. 1). Language and thinking are fundamentally neutral. The intention behind their use determines their negative or positive valence and impact. On this point, from a psychoanalytic perspective, Bion writes:

> It is too often forgotten that the gift of speech, so centrally employed, has been elaborated as much for the purpose of concealing thought by dissimulation and lying as for the purpose of elucidating or communicating thought.
>
> (1970, p. 3)

In terms of his endeavor to reveal the "emotional Truth" of the session, he advocates what he describes as:

> Therefore, the Language of Achievement, if it is to be employed for elucidating the truth, must be recognized as deriving not only from sensuous experience but also from impulses and dispositions far from those ordinarily associated with scientific discussion.
>
> (1970, p. 3)

At the same time, Bion recognizes the limits of language. He notes that language is intended to convey sensuous experience and that the data of psychoanalysis is nonsensuous. So, he doesn't refute language, he examines the underlying intention that is mobilizing how it is used. In a similar manner, Dōgen points to the limits of language, not its total refutation.

From the Zen perspective Dōgen's response to language questions our *relationship* to language, not language itself, and by extension, our relationship to thinking, our internal language. That is, it is not language or thinking itself that is problematic, as Fromm notes in his misguided orientation. Rather, from the Sōtō Zen perspective, it is our grasping, attachment, or overattachment to language that creates the problem. Language is just as much part of "reality" as is "silence." Zen promotes a "middle way" that is without attachment or aversion; without grasping or pushing away. The devaluation of language is as equally problematic as the overvaluation of language.

Fromm falls further into a dualistic mode by splitting thought—language and pre-reflective directly felt reality. For example, he writes that his agenda is to "rid myself of this social filter of language" (1960, p. 127). To this point, Wright argues:

> that regardless of how East Asians have understood the role of language in Zen experience, "we" are no longer justified in thinking that this kind of religious experience (or any other) stands altogether beyond the shaping power of language and culture.
>
> (1992, p. 113)

Concluding Thought

Nevertheless, these authors, despite their biases and limitations, opened the doors to a vast and enriching area of study and practice. In future studies, it would be fruitful to review Suzuki's works to identify and tease out additional parallels in Erich Fromm's writings on Zen. With this background in mind, the next chapter will review Suzuki's response to Dōgen and Sōtō Zen. An examination of Suzuki's ideological biases, contradictions, conflations, and the historical influences on his incomplete and negative depictions of Sōtō Zen practice will be instructive in elaborating the Sōtō Zen influence on the realizational perspective.

Notes

1. Note: To avoid confusion, from here on, "Suzuki" refers to D.T. Suzuki throughout the text. S. Suzuki will be used to refer to the influential Sōtō Zen teacher Shunryu Suzuki.
2. For elaboration, see K. Nishitani (1966).
3. For example, see Chapter Five, Section: "What is the Use of Understanding?"
4. For a detailed explication of the Bhavachakra from both views, see Modernist: C. Trungpa (1976), Traditionalist: T. Gyatso & J. Hopkins (2000).
5. For example, Koestler, A. (1960).
6. For an extensive review, see Fader, L. (1980).

References

Anderson, R. (1999). *Being Upright: Zen Meditation and the Bodhisattva Precepts*. Berkeley, CA: Rodmell Press.
Bion, W. (1970). *Attention and Interpretation*. London: Karnac.
Bleandonu, G. (1994). *Wilfred Bion: His Life and Works. 1897–1979*. London: Free Association Books.

Bobrow, J. (2010). *Zen and Psychotherapy: Partners in Liberation*. New York: W.W. Norton.
Cooper, P. (2010). *The Zen Impulse and the Psychoanalytic Encounter*. London: Routledge.
Cooper, P. (2019). *Zen Insight, Psychoanalytic Action: Two Arrows Meeting*. New York & London: Routledge.
Dōgen, E. (1243a). *Hensan*. In: Nishijima & C. Cross (Trans.), *Master Dogen's Shobogenzo, Book 3* (pp. 207–214). London: Windbell Publications, 1997.
Evans-Wentz, W. (1927). *The Tibetan Book of the Dead; or the After-death Experiences on the Bardo Plane*. London: Oxford University Press, 1960.
Evans-Wentz, W. (1954). *The Tibetan Book of the Great Liberation or the Method of Realizing Nirvana through Knowing the Mind*. Oxford: Oxford University Press, 1968.
Fader, L. (1980). Arthur Koestler's Criticism of D.T. Suzuki's Interpretation of Zen. *Eastern Buddhist*, 13(2):46–72.
Faure, B. (1993). *Chan Insights and Oversights: An Epistemological Critique of the Chan Tradition*. Princeton, NJ: Princeton University Press.
Franck, F. (Ed.) (1982). *The Buddha Eye: An Anthology of the Kyoto School*. Bloomington, IN: World Wisdom Inc.
Fromm, E. (1941). *Escape from Freedom*. New York: Henry Holt & Co.
Fromm, E. (1950). *Psychoanalysis and Religion*. New Haven, CT & London: Yale University Press.
Fromm, E. (1967). Memories of Dr. D.T. Suzuki. *Eastern Buddhist*, 2(1):86–89.
Fromm, E., Suzuki, D. T. & DeMartino, R. (1960). *Zen Buddhism and Psychoanalysis*. New York: Harper & Brothers.
Harrington, A. (2016). Zen, Suzuki, and the art of psychotherapy. In: Y. Fehige (Ed.), *Science and Religion, East and West* (pp. 1–33). London & New York: Routledge. https://www.routledge.com/Science-and-Religion-East-and-West/ Fehige/p/book/9781138961364
Heine, S. (2008). *Zen Skin, Zen Marrow: Will the Real Zen Buddhism Please Stand Up?* Oxford & New York: Oxford University Press.
Horney, K. (1945). *Our Inner Conflicts*. New York: W.W. Norton.
Iwamura, J. (2010). *Virtual Orientalism: Asian Religions and American Popular Culture*. Oxford: Oxford University Press.
Jung, C. (1931). Forward to the Second Edition. In: R. Wilhelm, *The Secret of the Golden Flower* (pp. xiii–xv). New York: Harcourt Brace & Co. 1962.
Jung, C. (1935). The Tibetan book of the dead: Psychological commentary. In W. Y. Evans-Wentz (Ed.), *The Tibetan Book of the Dead*. London: Oxford University Press, 1964 (pp. xxxv–lii).
Jung, C. (1949). Foreword. In: D. T. Suzuki (Ed.), *Introduction to Zen Buddhism* (pp. 9–29). London: Rider & Co., 1949.
Kapleau, P. (1965). *The Three Pillars of Zen*. New York: Harper & Row.
Kelman, H. (1960). Psychoanalytic thought and eastern wisdom. In: A. Molino (Ed.), *The Couch and the Tree: Dialogues in Psychoanalysis and Buddhism* (pp. 72–79). New York: North Point Press, 1998.
Koestler, A. (1960). *The Lotus and the Robot*. London: Hutchinson & Co.
Leighton, D. (2008). Zazen as an enactment ritual. In: S. Heine & D. Wright (Eds.), *Zen Ritual: Studies in Zen Buddhist Theory and Practice* (pp. 167–184). New York: Oxford University Press, 2008.
Lopez- Corvo, R. (2005). *The Dictionary of the Work of W.R. Bion*. London: Karnac.
Lopez-Corvo, R. (2006). *Wild Thoughts Searching for a Thinker: A Clinical Application to W.R. Bion's Theories*. London: Karnac.

Magid, B. (2002). *Ordinary Mind: Exploring the Common Ground of Zen and Psychotherapy.* Somerville, MA: Wisdom Publications.

McDaniel, R. (2015). *The Third Step East: Zen Masters of America.* Richmond Hill: The Sumeru Press.

Merton, T. (1967a). D.T. Suzuki: The man and his work. *Eastern Buddhist,* 2(1):3–9.

Merton, T. (1967b). *Mystics & Zen Masters.* New York: Farrar, Straus and Giroux.

Merton, T. (1968). *Zen and the Birds of the Appetite.* New York: New Directions.

Moncayo, R. (1998). True subject is no-subject: The real, imaginary, and symbolic in psychoanalysis and Zen Buddhism. *Psychoanalysis and Contemporary Thought,* 21:383–422.

Moncayo, R. (2012). *The Signifier Pointing at the Moon: Psychoanalysis and Zen Buddhism.* London: Karnac.

Suler, J. (1993). *Contemporary Psychoanalysis and Eastern Thought.* Albany: State University of New York Press.

Suler, J. (1995). In search of the self: Zen Buddhism and psychoanalysis. *Psychoanalytic Review,* 82:407–426.

Suzuki, D. T. (1949). *Introduction to Zen Buddhism.* London: Rider & Co.

Suzuki, D. T. (1961). A reply from D.T. Suzuki. *Encounter,* 17 (October):56–58.

Suzuki, D. T. (1970). Self the unobtainable. *Eastern Buddhist,* 3(2):1–8.

Suzuki, S. (1970). *Zen Mind, Beginner's Mind.* New York: Weatherhill.

Uchiyama, K. & Okumura, S. (2014). *The Zen Teaching of Homeless Kodo.* Boston, MA: Wisdom Publications.

van der Braak, A. (2020). *Reimagining Zen Buddhism in a Secular Age.* Leiden & Boston, MA: Brill\Rodopi.

Watts, A. (1932). *An Outline of Zen Buddhism.* London: The Golden Vista Press.

Watts, A. (1948). *Zen.* Stanford: James Ladd Delkin.

Watts, A. (1957). *The Way of Zen.* New York: Pantheon Books.

Wienpahl, P. (1965). Review. *Philosophy East and West,* 15(1):81–82.

Wilhelm, R. (1931). *The Secret of the Golden Flower.* New York: Harcourt Brace & Co., 1962.

Wright, D. (1992). Rethinking language in Zen experience. *Philosophy East and West,* 42(1):113–138.

Wright, D. (1998). *Philosophical Meditations on Zen Buddhism.* Cambridge: Cambridge University Press.

Chapter 5

D.T. Suzuki and Dōgen

The previous chapter presented an examination of D.T. Suzuki's incomplete depiction of Zen Buddhism characterized by sectarian biases and an extreme iconoclasm. His work has been misinterpreted by the western reader as expressing antinomian leanings, a point he criticizes in his later writing (1970). This chapter examines his response to Dōgen's explication of Sōtō Zen as an example of the interplay of these tendencies. While Suzuki's body of work is too extensive to review in its entirety and would not be relevant to the present context, the material presented in this chapter is focused specifically on his response to Dōgen and Sōtō Zen. This focus emphasizes Suzuki's ideological biases, contradictions, conflations, and incomplete depictions of Sōtō Zen practice in relation to the Sōtō influence on the realizational perspective.

In terms of the larger picture, my intention is not to ascertain "superior" or "inferior" brands of Zen or to stress differences over similarities. Differences, similarities, and identities all exist to varying degrees between and within various Zen sects. As a living and evolving tradition that at times over its history, as with any religious tradition, Zen has become enlivened and revitalized, sometimes in novel ways that reflect the interests and unique personalities of different teachers. However, they occur within the context of a highly defined and structured religious context. Rather, I hope to clarify and highlight my point that Suzuki's explication of Zen Buddhism does not represent the whole tradition. His specifically Rinzai orientation, modified by his deep immersion and internalization of western philosophy, religion, and science, as discussed in the previous chapter, is limited by a sectarian and an apologist view as well as by the historical and cultural contexts that his work emerged from and how it was presented to the North American reader.

Sparse Representation

In his extensive writings, Suzuki doesn't have much to say about Dōgen or the Sōtō School beyond passing notations and somewhat ambivalent critiques. He typically refers to Dōgen in brief pieces of information (1949, 1953, 1955).

For instance, in an edited collection of his writings, he simply notes, "The Sōtō School was introduced into Japan by Dōgen, A.D. 1233, who went over to China early in the thirteenth century and was duly authorized by his master Tendo Nyojo" (1955 p. 20). He also makes scattered and very brief historical notations without elaboration or further discussion, such as "Zen was in those days represented by Eisai (1140–1215) and Dōgen (1200–1253)" (1953, p. 365).

His response to Dōgen, one might accurately say, was quite ambivalent. Despite his modernist approach to explicating Zen for the western reader, his response to Dōgen is clearly to be biased on the side of traditional sectarian criticism. For instance, he contrasts Dōgen's *shikantaza* practice with the influential Japanese Zen teacher Bankei (1622–1693). Suzuki considered the latter as "one of the great Zen masters of modern Japan." He continues with a devaluation of *shikantaza* that he describes as a form of "silent contemplation" and as "artificial" (1972, p. 176).

Historical Antecedents: Unbalanced Critique

Hongzhi (1091–1157), a prolific writer and advocate of silent illumination, as noted in Chapter Three, cogently and clearly points out that the components of *mokusho*, *shamatha* (calm abiding), and *vipashyana* (insight) are equally integral aspects of the practice. One simply cannot be present without the other. Regarding insight, Hongzhi clearly informs the student to engage in active "investigation," a term he uses repeatedly. In this regard, silent illumination, as Byrne asserts, is "more dynamic than is commonly perceived" (2019, p. 175). This point is clearly lost on its sectarian critics.

It is clear in terms of his criticism of Dōgen's *shikantaza* that Suzuki follows in a long line of critics going back to the highly influential Dahui Zonggao (1063–1135) and other prominent Linji (Rinzai) teachers in China.[1] Typically, these criticisms are highly selective and completely ignore the insight aspect of *mokusho* practice. These critics target the silent aspect exclusively by focusing on excerpts from the complete texts on silent illumination, which of course, when taken out of context, support their critiques. For example, Hongzhi writes in part:

> [You should engage] in the great rest and the great cessation so that white mold starts growing at the corners of your mouth and grass growing out of your tongue; in this way you become completely emptied out, washed sparkling clean, polished to a bright shine.
>
> (Schlütter, 2008, p. 151)

This selective targeting of out of context sections of text certainly supports critiques that *mokusho* and by extension *shikantaza* are nothing but quietist practices.

Doctrinal Differences and Their Impact on Practice

Suzuki's critique of Dōgen and the Sōtō School can be examined both from the interrelated perspectives of doctrine and practice. An outline of the major conceptual and doctrinal difference between the two sects will help clear up misunderstandings regarding Zen and the relationship between Zen and psychoanalysis when viewed from a realizational perspective.

Doctrinally, *mokusho* and *shikantaza* support and express the Caodong (Sōtō) doctrine of our already existent realization in contrast to the Linji portrayal of enlightenment as a unique and discrete event that occurs at a specific time.

Schlütter presents compelling evidence that connects the critique of *mokusho* as a specific example of the large-scale attempt to completely discredit the Caodong sect and its doctrinal stance. He writes, "... that not only the teachings but also the lineage of the Caodong tradition was challenged by forces within the Linji tradition in what would seem to be attempts to undermine its authority" (2008, p. 123).

Suzuki appears to carry this tradition of criticism forward into the modern era through his writings in which he both ignores and criticizes Dōgen and the Sōtō school. Not unlike his predecessors, Suzuki's critique of Dōgen's *shikantaza* similarly exemplifies this incomplete analysis and distorted presentation of silent illumination, which historically served sectarian agendas.

Similarly, although Suzuki acknowledges that "We cannot deny that there are many good points in Sōtō, which ought to be carefully studied" (1949, p. 111), "these good points" are noticeably missing from Suzuki's text. At the same time, he expresses a distinct devaluation of Sōtō Zen in contrast to the Rinzai school and notes, "but as to the living of Zen there is perhaps greater activity in the Rinzai, which employs the *kōan* system" (p. 111). The implication that Sōtō Zen is characterized by lesser activity functions as a reference to the critique that *shikantaza* is nothing but a quietist practice equivalent to "cold ashes and dry wood" (Schlütter 2008, p. 126) or in terms of Hongzhi's silent illumination, Dahui argues:

> Literati often have [the problem of] busy minds. So today, in many places, there is a kind of heretical silent illumination Chan ... they teach them to be like' cold ashes or dry wood,' or like a 'strip of white silk,' or 'like an incense pot in an old shrine,' or 'cold and somber" (P. 126). [And that] it could lead people to sit immovable in the ghostly cave under the black mountain until they get calluses on bones and buttocks, and saliva dripping from their mouths.
>
> (p. 127)

From There to Here: Expressive Practice

A major source of conflict and the resulting critique of silent illumination stems from the Caodong view that enlightenment and delusion are simply abstract constructs and therefore they do not really exist outside of the mind. This presents a problem for the Linji tradition. The *kōan*, as promoted by Dahui, functions to create a sudden bursting forth into enlightenment.

As I note elsewhere (Cooper, 2019), religious practices, such as *shikantaza* in the case of the Sōtō sect and *kanna-zen* (*kōan* contemplation) with respect to the Rinzai sect, are direct expressions of core religious beliefs. Stated briefly, Dōgen's radical nondualism describes practice and realization as operating together in the very moment of sitting. Hence, he describes practice as expressive or as an "enactment ritual" (Leighton, 2008, p. 167) of our original enlightenment, not as an instrument employed temporarily to reach realization at some future point in time that is characterized as a unique state of mind occurring at a specific moment. From this perspective, there is no sudden bursting forth at a defined moment in time. From this point of view, an instrumental approach ironically devalues the present moment, which, as an aside, from Bion's perspective, as we will explore in Chapter Eleven, "Bion and Dōgen: Realizational Practice, Emotional Truth," is the only moment of importance. In this regard, Dōgen emphasizes the activity and relationships in the moment-to-moment engagement in all the activities of our lives and in our relationships with others.

Understandably, in defense of the Linji tradition, Suzuki views Dōgen's conception of *shusho ichinyo* (practice/realization oneness) as muddled, confusing, and incomplete. He argues, "That there is no way that just sitting ... can avoid being mere Silent Illumination, taking that designation in a pejorative sense" (1976, p. 4). However, Suzuki's "pejorative sense" is based on an incomplete understanding of the practice, as noted above. Ironically, his critique of a perceived quietist and gradualist orientation in Dōgen's practice, as Faure (1993) notes, could easily be applied to his instrumental or facilitative depiction of *kanna-zen*.

While *shikantaza* is certainly more passive than *kanna-zen*, it is clearly not a quietist practice that leads to "dead wood and ashes," as Suzuki would have the reader believe. Further, we do not have to rely exclusively on Dōgen to find references to the dual mode of calming and insight that characterizes silent illumination. For example, in a detailed review of the history of the practice, Yen quotes the 7th century Chan master Yongjia Xuanjue (665–713), who notes, "Having forgotten all involvement, one is silent and still, yet divine wisdom by nature is incisively penetrating" (in: Yen, 2001, p. 140). Yen concludes his review by noting:

> At the same time this does not imply that the mind becomes dark and incognizant. Quite the contrary it is the distortions of deluded and conditional thinking that are silenced, with this silence, the mind's innate wisdom shines unobstructed, perfect clear and luminous.
>
> (p. 142)

From Here to There: Facilitative Practice

In contrast to Dōgen, from the Rinzai perspective, Suzuki conceives practice as facilitative or as a means to an end in terms of the achievement of specific preferred psychological states such as *satori*. This facilitative orientation finds expression in the title of his book *The Zen kōan as a Means of Attaining Enlightenment* (1994). Elsewhere, for example, he writes, "Without the attainment of satori no one can enter the truth of Zen" and "Satori is the raison d'etre of Zen without which Zen is no Zen" (1949, p. 95).

In sharp contrast to D.T. Suzuki's Rinzai perspective, consider the popular Sōtō Zen priest Shunryu Suzuki's relationship to *satori*. In his Preface to his popular book *Zen Mind, Beginner's Mind* (1970), Huston Smith tells this amusing but poignant story that highlights this doctrinal difference:

> Whereas Daisetz Suzuki's Zen was dramatic, Shunryu Suzuki's is ordinary. Satori was focal for Daisetz, and it was in large part the fascination of this extraordinary state that made his writings so compelling. In Shunryu Suzuki's book the words satori and kensho, its near-equivalent, never appear.

Smith continues:

> When, four months before his death, I had the opportunity to ask him why satori didn't figure in his book, his wife leaned toward me and whispered impishly, "It's because he hasn't had it"; whereupon the Roshi batted his fan at her in mock consternation and with finger to his lips hissed, "Shhhh! Don't tell him!" When our laughter had subsided, he said simply, "It's not that satori is unimportant, but it's not the part of Zen that needs to be stressed."
>
> (1970, p. 9)

It should be noted that this whole business of *satori* has been questioned. For instance, Shephard (1995) writes:

> Descriptions of satori are often vague, making this experience easy to claim by persons far less accomplished than Suzuki. To his credit, the Japanese savant is reported to have been unimpressed by outpourings of the Beatniks Jack Kerouac and Allen Ginsberg; the occasion was a meeting they gained with him in New York. These innovators believed they understood Zen; others were in strong doubt on such points.
>
> (p. 187)

It is sectarian differences such as these that influence D.T Suzuki's thinking and evaluation of Dōgen's Zen.

This distinction between expressive and facilitative practices requires further elaboration to clarify the link between doctrine and practice. Beginning with some brief comments from the doctrinal perspective, Suzuki describes *shikantaza* and Dōgen's nondual conception of practice/enlightenment as lacking because, as he notes, Dōgen's discussion requires a missing delineation. In sharp contrast to the radical nondualist orientation of the Sōtō position, Suzuki further argues that practice and enlightenment are separate. He comments that enlightenment falls into the realm of philosophy, not practice.

Suzuki's perception reflects two very different underlying doctrinal assumptions: Dōgen's conception, as I noted above, of practice as expressive and nondualistic or *shusho ichinyo* (practice/realization oneness) in contrast to Suzuki's dualistic assumption that informs a facilitative or goal-oriented practice, such as concentrating one's efforts on solving a *kōan* to the exclusion of all other possible perceptual input, as I noted above, by placing a high value and emphasis with the goal to achieve *satori*, a preferred psychological state. Dōgen is clearly not interested in isolated and preferred psychological states. Rather, he emphasizes what he describes as authentic practice that fuels a continuous actional stance informed by wisdom and compassion as they are expressed in all relationships. Commenting on Dōgen's emphasis on action, Nishijima contrasts his approach from philosophy:

> Dōgen, through the Buddhist dialectic, wants to lead us away from thoughts based on belief in spirit and matter. [And] Dōgen recognized the existence of something that is different from thought; that is, reality in action. Action is completely different from intellectual thought and completely different from the perceptions of our senses. So Dōgen's method of thinking is based on action.
>
> (1994, p. xv)

Such inter-sectarian perspectives have led Heine, through what he describes as an "intertextual analysis," to introduce his illuminating discussion regarding Dōgen's use of the *kōan* by asking, "Is it [*kōan*] a psychological device that defeats language or a literary tool that fosters textuality?" (1994, p. 4). Of course, any answer would depend on internalized doctrinal preconceptions, which I have noted, can be either conscious or unconscious.

These doctrinal distinctions also impact the different uses of the *kōan* by these two Zen systems. Suzuki views *kōan* practice as a method devised to short-circuit and purge thinking and language, which from this position are viewed as obstacles to realization. Suzuki views the *kōan* as the alpha and omega of Zen that accounts for its effectiveness and its uniqueness. He writes:

> The systematization of kōan is, therefore, the one thing that is most characteristic of Zen. It is this that saves Zen from sinking into trance, from becoming absorbed in mere contemplation, from turning into an exercise

in tranquillization ... Satori is attained in the midst of this activity and not by suppressing it, as some may imagine.

(1949, p. 111)

For Suzuki, based on this core assumption, *kanna-zen* (*kōan* concentration) practice engenders a radical psycho-perceptual shift that cuts through and transcends dualistic consciousness, language, and conceptual thinking with the goal of engendering a state of realization beyond words, beyond thought. Yen offers the following details regarding the use of the *kōan*:

> In the past, as today, gong'an [kōan] have proven an effective approach to Chan training. Originally, they were used throughout all branches of Chan, including the Chinese Caodong (Sōtō) school, which is often mistakenly thought to give its attention solely to the practice of "silent illumination" (*mozhao*) or Dogen's teaching of "just sitting, nothing more" (*shikantaza*). In time, however, their use became increasingly identified with the Linji (Rinzai) line.
>
> (2001, p. 123)

In contrast, Dōgen exploits and expands the polysemous quality of language in extremely radical, novel, and creative ways. By doing so, he acknowledges the role that language and thinking play in the realizational process, which he views, as continuous and relational. In this manner, he views language and thinking as supportive rather than as an obstacle to the Zen realizational process. In this way, the *kōan* functions to support the practitioner's understanding in dialog with the teacher and fellow practitioners in terms of how realization is expressed in our actional and relational life.

He elaborates his position in *Katto*, "The Complicated" or "Entangling Vines" (1243e). The "complicated" refers to language. Dōgen argues that language itself disentangles the practitioner from language. He writes:

> In general, although sacred beings all aim to learn the cutting of the roots of the complicated, they do not learn that cutting means cutting the complicated with the complicated, and they do not know that the complicated is entwined with the complicated. How much less could they know that the succession of the complicated continues by means of the complicated? Few have known that the succession of the Dharma is the complicated itself. No one has heard so. No one has said so. Could many have realized so in experience?
>
> (Nishijima & Cross, 1997, pp. 35–36)

In short, language and thought do not obscure experience; rather, they are the experience of the expression of experience. It is the practitioner's relationship to these processes and the intention behind their use, whether conscious or unconscious, that determines, to use Bion's warning, "... that the language was elaborated as much for the achievement of deception and evasion as for truth" (1970, p. 3).

Suzuki's stance runs counter to the Sōtō perception of practice as a "ritual enactment" and an "expression" of our beginningless and endless enlightened mind. *Zazen*, practiced as an enactment ritual, was not unique to Dōgen but derives from the Chan influence on his own training with Tendo Nyojo in China. As Peter Hershock observes, for instance, "As it would come to be understood in Chan, Buddhist practice does not consist of a method for arriving at an end of liberation but a method for its actualization and demonstration" (2014, p. 58).

In this manner, by establishing an artificial dichotomy between *kanna-zen* and *shikantaza* on a practice basis, D.T. Suzuki's writing leaves the false impression that the two schools are completely distinct, thus overlooking similarities and identities. Contemporary scholars question this view.[2]

This simple black and white distinction between *kanna-zen* and *shikantaza* as exclusive and definitive markers or identifiers that distinguish between the Rinzai and Sōtō sects is not so cut and dry as it appears at first glance.

It is worth noting that Suzuki was not alone in his view of Dōgen's Sōtō Zen as "anti-*kōan*." The Sōtō sect as a whole was involved in perpetrating this group anti-*kōan* characterization of the Sōtō tradition. For example, *Shinji Shobogenzo*, Dōgen's 300 *kōan* collection without commentary, was suppressed for centuries.

Further, the intention behind promoting these different practices and the use they are put to requires elaboration. For example, while Dōgen was a fierce critic of the influential Rinzai teacher, Dahui, and his use of the *wato* (turning or cutting word or phrase of a *kōan*) to promote spiritual realization, they both shared a common agenda to revitalize the living religion. For instance, speaking of Dahui, who revitalized the use of *kōan* in the 12th century in China and by Dōgen in the 13th century in Japan, Heine notes that despite Dōgen's harsh critique of Ta-hui:

> ... they were equally eager to restore a lost sense of spontaneity and vitality to the kōan tradition, so that these leaders of Chinese Rinzai and Japanese Sōtō cannot be appropriately understood as standing for monolithic ideologies that somehow existed in polarized and antithetical fashion.
>
> (1994, p. 13)

Heine concludes that modern scholarship:

> ... helps to clarify an understanding of the kōan's importance in his teachings in a way that compels a rethinking and re-evaluation of the unfolding of the entire kōan tradition, the history of which has generally been told without reference to Dōgen's approach.
>
> (1994, p. 7)

I would add that Suzuki's writing, considering the lack of serious attention given to Dōgen, described above, clearly exemplifies this point.

Dōgen's relation to the *kōan* tradition, for instance, was far more complex than Suzuki's depiction that Dōgen promulgated a complete rejection of the *kōan* and an insistent and exclusive emphasis solely on *shikantaza* practice. Dōgen was not critical of the *kōan*. Quite the contrary, he makes constant use of the *kōan* throughout his writings to exemplify and support his doctrinal points. He frequently offers radical reinterpretations and critiques of standard *kōan* commentaries, often at odds with conventional interpretations. His commentaries and interpretations consistently articulate and support his religious vision. He typically would stand a conventional meaning/interpretation on its head, especially regarding reversing critiques of *zazen* practice as well as shifting from a naturalistic view that rejects practice or a facilitative or instrumental view of practice as a tool to his distinct expressive view of practice.[3]

Further, he reinterprets *kōans* that advocate or suggest hierarchies, such as between one party in the dialog being depicted as an enlightened being and the other characterized as an ignorant monk. For example, consider his commentary on the dialog between Shibi Xuansha and a nameless monk in *Ikka Myoju*, One Bright Pearl (1239b). Here is the dialog.

What Is the Use of Understanding?

Some years after attaining the way, Xuansha instructed his students, saying:

> "The entire world of the ten directions is one bright pearl."

Once a monk asked him:

> "I heard that you said, 'The entire world of the ten directions is one bright pearl.' How should I understand this?"

Xuansha said:

> "The entire world of the ten directions is one bright pearl. What do you do with your understanding?"

The next day, Xuansha asked the monk:

> "The entire world of the ten directions is one bright pearl. How do you understand this?"

The monk said:

> "The entire world of the ten directions is one bright pearl. What do you do with your understanding?"

Xuansha said:

"I see that you have worked out a way to get through the demon's cave on the black mountain."

(Tanahashi 2012, Kindle location, 2457–2468)

"What's the Use of Understanding?" The Ignorant Monk

This dialog is quite terse, simple, and straightforward. In the text of *Ikka Myoju*, Dōgen leaves it open to interpret for ourselves. There are a number of possible interpretations, just as for Dōgen there are many unique expressions of the one reality. The question becomes, "how do you see it?" "What is the use of understanding?" conveys several different meanings.

Traditional Interpretation

In this interpretation, the monk didn't understand Xuansha's statement. In this dualistic view, the permanent unchanging transparent and perfect pearl that is free from defilement is hidden within. In this regard, it is separate and thus becomes the "object" of our seeking, just as in the facilitative view of practice *satori* becomes an object of our seeking. This seeking creates a subject-object separation and leads to attachment and aversion. In practice, this creates pressure and the effort to acquire preferred states of mind. From this vantage point, the monk is deluded by the causes and conditions of his life and "sees" from a perspective that is defiled by the "dust" of thinking and the intellect.

Continuing with the pearl image from this dialog, this dust that covers the pearl is our karmic way of discriminative thinking and judgment-making based on our preferences. In other words, we can say that from this viewpoint, the pearl is colored by the Three Poisons: delusion, attachment, and aversion. Intellectual understanding becomes viewed as the function of this dust. It covers the pearl and prevents the practitioner from seeing the pearl directly. The monk asked: how can he use intellectual understanding to really see this true subject that hears, sees, and experiences all things? But the pearl was beyond his conditioned, judging mind. Discriminative thinking hides it. In this interpretation, the pearl is the real subject of seeing, hearing, and thinking rather than the monk. The idea is that we search for it through practice. This approach to *zazen* is instrumental or facilitative. It is also nihilistic as it negates the intellect. The problem is not the intellect. It's the overuse of the intellect that obscures intuitive knowing.

Alternative Traditional View: The Monk Got It!

From this alternative to the traditional point of view, the monk had the same realization as Xuansha. This view, while coming to a different conclusion, characterizes the monk as fully realized before Xuansha even asked the question.

However, this interpretation advocates a critique of language. His question was really asking why, if this bright pearl is one with the ten-direction world and beyond intellectual understanding, did Xuansha need to say anything at all using language? In other words, dialog would just cause more discursive thinking and intellectual understanding to arise in the monk and obscure realization, so don't ask. In this regard, the "dust" of thinking is still a problem. Although both are viewed as being on equal footing, the bottom line is that an underlying dualism remains through the view that thinking is an obstruction and a problem that requires elimination. One might argue that the monk asked the question to examine Xuansha's understanding and intention. To say such a thing was already to bring the present reality that is beyond discrimination into discrimination. Why did Xuansha do such a foolish thing? This orientation, while viewing the monk and Xuansha as both realized, not unlike the first interpretation, also veers off in a nihilistic direction in terms of the monk's implied critique of language and thinking processes. As we will see below, Dōgen views talking and silence on equal terms.

Dōgen's Interpretation

Dōgen shifts the narrative structure of the dialog to articulate a very different meaning. His commentary leans toward this second interpretation; however, with an important and significant difference. Dōgen views this dialog between Xuansha and the monk, not as a realized master teaching an ignorant and deluded student, but as two realized beings sharing their realization, each in their own unique way. According to Dōgen, both, master and monk, understood that despite the fact that reality is beyond thinking, they nonetheless express and demonstrate this reality using words. This is typical of Dōgen's creative way of turning traditional teachings around.

"What is the use of understanding?" raises an important question: "What good is *samadhi* concentration or *prajna* wisdom, if we don't demonstrate our understanding in our lives?" Dōgen argues that from the very first, the monk is not asking a question as is described in the first interpretation and he is not challenging Xuansha as is implied in the second interpretation. Rather, both Xuansha and the monk are sharing and expressing their realization together. Dōgen's view of Xuansha's response "The entire ten direction world is one bright pearl, what is the use of understanding it?" conveys a very different meaning than is described in the two previous views. "What is the use of understanding?" from Dōgen's perspective is not a question. It is a statement and an expression of *Immo* or suchness, as will be elaborated in Chapter Eight, "Dōgen's Expression of Suchness." In his interpretation, Xuansha and the monk are clearly equals and are playing with each other. They are both bodhisattvas working for our benefit. The dialog is repeated the next day with the roles reversed. Xuansha asks the monk's question from the previous day and the monk responds with Xuansha's answer from the previous day. From Dōgen's radically nondualistic perspective, we could say that Xuansha and the monk are two unique beings that sharing realization together represent the two oscillating aspects of the one reality, expressing the identity of the relative and the absolute. Both the monk and Xuansha knew that they were using words and understanding to share this reality beyond thinking, discrimination, and language.

Xuansha concludes by saying, "I know that you are making a livelihood inside a demon's cave in the black mountain." In marked contrast to the two previous traditional interpretations, "the black mountain" and the "demon's cave" are not viewed by Dōgen as metaphors for being lost in delusion. Rather, he views the total darkness as a metaphor for nondiscrimination, or nonduality, the absolute, and "making a livelihood" refers to, using revisioned discrimination or understanding in relation to how we live our lives. So again, we have both aspects of reality, the relative and the absolute, expressed in this dialog. Xuansha praises the monk and asserts that the monk is vigorously living and freely using discrimination within the reality of beyond discrimination. Dōgen acknowledges the authenticity of the monk's response and realization by noting, "Even though it seems that the monk is playing with conditioned intellect in speaking these words, they are the clear manifestation of 'Great Activity,' which is just the Great Standard itself" (Nishijima & Cross, 1994, p. 41).

In conclusion, from Dōgen's point of view, both thinking and language are equally just as much the reality of the moment as is not thinking and silence. They are simply and fully alternative expressions of the One Bright Pearl. This "cartwheel" interpretation represents typical Dōgen. He transmits the teachings in a highly creative way through an alternative reading of traditional stories, which he deconstructs, sometimes word-by-word. He then reconstructs the stories to convey his unique message. In this case, he doesn't exclude language or write it off as "dust" that must be "wiped away" through practice. He doesn't view language in a dualistic way as an obstacle to realization. For Dōgen, language is an equal aspect of One Bright Pearl.

Interestingly, the first traditional interpretation that views Xuansha's enlightened comment and the monk's ignorant lack of deep understanding continues in the interpretations of contemporary Sōtō Zen commentators. As for Nishijima's commentary regarding the monk's simple repetition of Xuansha's words as recorded in *Shinji Shobogenzo*, Dōgen's *kōan* collection serves as an example of how the significant overlap between the traditional interpretations rooted in the Rinzai tradition can remain unconsciously embedded in the minds of Sōtō teachers. Nishijima writes:

> This imitative answer was rejected completely... He was trapped in the dark world of the intellect and was very far from seeing the brilliant pearl. [Nishijima concludes that the monk] "had not attained an intuitive understanding of it. It had not penetrated his bones and marrow. He was making his efforts but was still thrashing around in the dark."
> (M. Luetchford & J. Pearson, Eds., 2003, p. 23)

"Thrashing around in the dark," which is obviously viewed negatively in this commentary, refers to the Ghost Cave on the Black Mountain. However, Dōgen understands the Ghost Cave as a metaphor for nonduality, as noted above, and also as representing *samsara*, the relative world, and the place where activities and relationships occur. This is where we work from. In contrast, the contemporary Sōtō Zen teacher and Dōgen scholar Shohaku Okumura offers the following very different commentary:

> Actually what Dōgen writes here is not about a teaching of Xuansha's that he repeats to a monk who doesn't see the reality. According to Dōgen, both of them understood that the reality is beyond thinking, and yet they nonetheless discussed how to express and show this reality using words. This is typical of Dōgen's creative way of reading traditional teachings.
>
> (2017, p. 21)

How do you understand "What is the use of understanding?" How does it apply to your life? Are these three understandings mutually exclusive or do they interact in ever-evolving permutations dependent on causes and conditions?

Intention

It would be profitable to ask, "What was the intention and underlying relationship to *kōan* practice and study, which, as noted, stems from very different relations to language and thinking, as well as differing religious goals and the methods for achieving them, as exemplified in the three *kōan* interpretations above?" For instance, Dōgen's critique of Ta-hui's use of the *wato* as a means of defeating reason, exhausting thinking, and subverting language is at odds with his understanding and use of language. Based on this intention and practice goal to inhibit and derail language, Dōgen viewed *kanna-zen* as limited and misguided.

Dōgen constantly refers to *Genjokōan*, "Reality Here and Now," the presently lived real-life manifestation of the *kōan* in daily life and which he clearly prefers to *kōan* contemplation and which is a central point in his teachings.

D.T. Suzuki's Flawed Critique

Based on the differing core doctrinal assumptions between these two points of view, Suzuki's critique is flawed from the outset. Suzuki overlooks the insight aspect of *mokusho* (silent illumination) and thus perceives it as exclusively a quietist practice. Further, because he erroneously conflates Dōgen's *shikantaza* exclusively with quietist practices, his critique is rooted in erroneous foundation.[4] Briefly restated, "In silence there is illumination; in illumination there is silence—the two cannot be separated" (Yen 2008, p. 63).

Dōgen was also, along with Dahui and others, fiercely critical of quietist practices, which he described, for example, as "withered trees and dead ashes." For example, Bielefeldt summarizes a series of strong comments leveled by Dōgen that demonstrate the consistency of his critique of quietist practices throughout his writings:

> "In his Shobogenzo *tashin tsu*, he explicitly warns against the practice of "cutting off considerations and forgetting objects." In the *hotsu mujo shin*, he criticizes the ignorant monks of Hinayanist leanings who neglect the aspiration for Bodhi and advocate "suspending considerations and freezing the mind."
> And further:
> In a similar vein, in his *Zazen shin*, Dōgen dismisses the "stupid illiterates" (orokanaru zuzan), so common in Sung, who think that zazen aims at a state of peace and calm attained through mental vacuity ... that are nothing but "models for reverting to the source ... vain programs for suspending considerations and freezing in tranquillity.
> (1988, p. 136)

It should be quite clear, considering the emotional strength of Dōgen's consistently critical remarks that his *shikantaza* is not intended as a quietist practice as is suggested by Suzuki.

At the core of Suzuki's critique is his depiction of Dōgen's teachings on practice as "confusing," because he does not clearly define the differences between the various phrases he uses to point to *zazen*. Further, Suzuki argues that Dōgen does not clarify the distinctions between "zazen as a means" and "zazen as an end." I think that Suzuki's critique exemplifies the distinction between the Sōtō notion of *zazen* as enactment and expression, which renders realization as an active and ongoing, ever-evolving experience and the Rinzai notion of *zazen* as a tool to reach the goal of realization as a specific state of mind described as *satori*. Dōgen doesn't speak of practice/realization in terms of "means and end." That is clearly Suzuki's core assumption. For instance, Suzuki writes:

> On the plane of the identity (or nonduality) of practice and realization, both zazen as the means (practice) and zazen as the end (realization) may possibly be called non-dual. But when our chief object lies in explanation, it is best to have this difference well defined. The dispute between Kanna Zen and Silent Illumination Zen comes on the whole from not making this distinction. It can be said that *"taza-ism"* places weight on philosophy and overlooks the psychological or practical side. The nonduality of "practice and realization are nondual" belongs to philosophy. This non-duality alone is not enough.
> (1976, p. 7)

From a practice perspective, as noted above, D.T. Suzuki conflates the Chan practice of *mokusho* or silent illumination with Dōgen's *shikantaza*, which is questionable to begin with because he also describes *shikantaza* as "unique to Dōgen." For example, Suzuki writes, "in works like *Zazenshin* we see a contemplation of the Silent Illumination type, and the dynamic aspect of the reciprocal interrelation between one thing and another, the aspect of discrimination in non-discrimination, rather tends to be obscured" (1976, p. 13).

It is this flawed conflation that serves as a basis for his critique of Dōgen's practice. For example, Suzuki notes, "And yet the odour of Silent Illumination that accompanies Dōgen's kind of sitting is not easily removed" (1976, p. 16). He continues, and asserts that this tendency, which has been described by Hakuin as "sitting still and silent like a withered tree and holding on to the death" and "Dōgen's Zen a faint shadow of inactivity and stagnation is visible" (p. 16).

In terms of the value (devaluation) placed on thinking in terms of historical precedents that contributed to this confusion and resulting conflation of silent illumination and *shikantaza* with a quietist agenda are addressed in Chapter Thirteen, "Thinking's Bad Rap."

Heine stresses this point from a perspective that emphasizes Dōgen's radical nondualism. He writes, "For Dōgen, any apparent distinction between the polarities of thought and thoughtlessness, means and end, or dynamism and quietude is overcome by the refutation of deficient views that fail to reflect the unremitting practice of zazen" (2020, p. 93).

For centuries, many Zen teachers have strived to expose and correct this erroneous instrumental and "quietist" view of *zazen* that persists in many quarters in the present. I believe that the stagnation that Suzuki refers to does indeed occur among individuals who unfortunately misunderstand the realizational aim of *shikantaza* practice.

I believe that it is on the basis of these historical precedents that informed Suzuki's critique of Dōgen's *shikantaza*, as is evidenced in his comments in a 1976 article that appeared in two parts in *Eastern Buddhist*, "Dōgen, Hakuin, Bankei: Three Types of Thought in Japanese Zen" Part I and Part II.

In this offering, Suzuki proposes to examine three different approaches and understandings of realization and three approaches to engendering the experience of realization. He describes Dōgen's approach as deriving from the Sōtō School in China, but, as I mentioned above, he considers Dōgen's elaboration of the practice of *shikantaza* as unique to his system.

Suzuki raises the question that in a subtle way implies a critical tone regarding Dōgen's conception of Zen practice because he is basically questioning the usefulness of *shikantaza* practice, which, as noted, he refers to in a clearly pejorative way as "*taza*-ism" (1976, p. 7).

However, I would argue that Dōgen clearly describes *shikantaza* as the most primary and unfiltered expression of suchness, and in this regard, based on the all-pervading nature of suchness coupled with his all-inclusive choiceless awareness, he has no need to distinguish between practice and realization. He does, however, distinguish between Bodhidharma's wall-gazing—which he connects to his *shikantaza*—and *shuzen* (learning meditation) in his first written communication upon his return to Japan from his pilgrimage to China in *Fukanzazengi* written in 1227. He writes, "The zazen I speak of is not learning meditation. It is simply the Dharma-gate of repose and bliss. It is the practice/realization of totally culminated enlightenment" (in: Waddell & Abe, 2002, p. 4). With this comment, he at once masterfully distinguishes his practice from the quietist *shuzen* practice, asserts his radical nondualism through an expressive practice, oriented in the subitist, or "sudden enlightenment" tradition in contrast to a goal-oriented practice, and at the same time, he aligns himself, his practice, and his teachings with the orthodox lineage harking back to Bodhidharma and the historical Buddha.

Concluding Comments

With the above points in mind, it seems quite clear that D. T. Suzuki artificially divides the Rinzai and Sōtō schools. He bases his argument on the distinctions between *kanna-zen* conceptualized as a tool and *shikantaza* which he erroneously characterizes as a quietist practice. He then criticizes Dōgen's supposed lack of clarity. For instance, he writes: "Once we speak of practice and reality we are compelled to give thought to each of them" (1976, p. 7).

Suzuki's biases, such as in this example, are coupled with a lack of serious and comprehensive scholarship and explication of East Asian Zen Buddhism, particularly in terms of his writings targeted for the western audience. This bias and resulting omission resulted in a glaring lack of substantive discussion of the Sōtō school in his voluminous writings. Faure asks, for instance, "... why were the obvious shortcomings of Suzuki's Zen apparently invisible to Suzuki himself and to his many Western followers?" (1993, p. 54). Alan Watts, who was an ardent follower of Suzuki's teachings, eventually addresses the limitations of Suzuki's writings on Zen. In the Preface to his popular book *The Way of Zen*, he writes:

> But as yet no one—not even Professor Suzuki—has given us a comprehensive account of the subject which includes its historical background and its relation to Chinese and Indian ways of thought. The three volumes of Suzuki's *Essays in Zen Buddhism* are an unsystematic collection of scholarly papers on various aspects of the subject, enormously useful for the advanced student but quite baffling to the general reader without an understanding of the general principles. His delightful Introduction to Zen Buddhism is rather narrow and specialized.
>
> (1957, pp. 7–8)

Nevertheless, while Suzuki left the reader blind to the treasures offered by Dōgen and the Sōtō school, he opened the doors to Zen for countless westerners. His influence exerted an unquestioned impact into the developing interest in Zen Buddhist thought among interested psychoanalysts and on the popular culture of the time. With this background in mind, the next chapter will examine more recent contributions to the Zen and psychoanalytic conversation.

Notes

1 For a comprehensive and thoughtful analysis, see M. Schlütter (2008).
2 See S. Heine (1994), for a comprehensive and thoughtful analysis of this issue.
3 The tile-polishing *kōan* serves as an excellent example and receives a detailed analysis by S. Heine (1994, pp. 215–216) and C. Bielefeldt (1988, pp. 141–143).
4 For a detailed description of *mokusho*, see Chapter Three, *Mokusho*: "Silent Illumination: Open to Whole Being."

References

Bielefeldt, C. (1988). *Dogen's Manuals of Zen Meditation*. Berkeley: University of California Press.
Bion, W. (1970). *Attention and Interpretation*. London: Karnac.
Byrne, C. (2019). Verses of silent illumination: Hongzhi Zhengjue's poetic vision of Caodong Zen. *International Journal of Buddhist Thought & Culture*, 29(2):171–205.
Cooper, P. (2019). *Zen Insight, Psychoanalytic Action: Two Arrows Meeting*. New York & London: Routledge.
Dōgen, E. (1227). *Fukanzazengi*. In: N. Waddell & M. Abe (Trans.), *The Heart of Dōgen's Shobogenzo* (pp. 1–6). Albany: State University of New York Press, 2002.
Dōgen, E. (1239b). *Ikka Myoju*. In: Tanahashi (Trans.), *Treasury of the True Dharma Eye: Zen Master Dōgen's Shobo Genzo* (Kindle location 2457-2468). Boston, MA & London: Shambhala.
Dōgen, E. (1243e). *Katto*. In: Nishijima & C. Cross (Trans.), *Master Dogen's Shobogenzo, Book 3* (pp. 35–41). London: Windbell Publications, 1997.
Faure, B. (1993). *Chan Insights and Oversights: An Epistemological Critique of the Chan Tradition*. Princeton: Princeton University Press.
Heine, S. (1994). *Dōgen and the Koan Tradition: A Tale of Two Shobogenzo Texts*. Albany: State University of New York.
Heine, S. (2020). *Readings of Dōgen's Treasury of the True Dharma Eye*. New York: Columbia University Press.
Hershock, P. (2014). *Public Zen, Personal Zen*. Lanham, MD.: Rowman & Littlefield.
Leighton, D. (2008). Zazen as an enactment ritual. In: S. Heine & D. Wright (Eds.), *Zen Ritual: Studies in Zen Buddhist Theory and Practice* (pp. 167–184). New York: Oxford University Press, 2008.
Luetchford, M. & J. Pearson (Eds.) (2003). *Master Dogen's Shinji Shobogenzo: 301 Koan Stories*. London: Windbell Publications.
Nishijima, G. & Cross, C. (1994). *Master Dogen's Shobogenzo, Book 1*. London: Windbell Publications.
Okumura, S. (2017). Lecture on the chapter of *Shobogenzo Ikka-myoju*. *Dharma Eye*, 28:18–31.
Schlütter, M. (2008). *How Zen Became Zen: The Dispute Over Enlightenment and the Formation of Chan Buddhism in Song Dynasty China*. Honolulu: University of Hawaii Press.
Shepherd, (1995). *Minds and Sociocultures, Vol. One*. Cambridge: Philosophical Press.

Smith, H. (1970). Preface. In: S. Suzuki (Ed.), *Zen Mind, Beginner's Mind* (pp. 9–11). New York: Weatherhill.
Suzuki, D. T. (1949). *Introduction to Zen Buddhism.* London: Rider & Co.
Suzuki, D. T. (1953). *Introduction to Zen Buddhism: Third Series.* London: Rider & Co.
Suzuki, D. T. (1955). *Studies in Zen.* New York: Dell Publishing, 2013.
Suzuki, D. T. (1970). Self the unobtainable. *Eastern Buddhist*, 3(2):1–8.
Suzuki, D. T. (1972). *Living by Zen.* Lew Beach, Maine: Samuel Weiser, 1994.
Suzuki, D. T. (1976). Dōgen, Hakuin, Bankei: Three types of thought in Japanese Zen. *Eastern Buddhist*, 9(1): 1–17.
Suzuki, D. T. (1994). *The Zen Koan as a Means of Attaining Enlightenment.* Rutland, VT: Charles E. Tuttle Co., Inc.
Watts, A. (1957). *The Way of Zen.* New York: Pantheon Books.
Yen, S. (2001). *Hoofprints of the Ox.* Oxford. Oxford University Press.
Yen, S. (2008). *The Method of No Method: The Chan Practice of Silent Illumination.* Boston, MA & London: Shambhala.

Chapter 6

A Zen Wave
Review

Authors who discuss Bion's theories and technical recommendations in relation to Buddhist practices and principles represent a diverse range of viewpoints, opinions, interests, and orientations, including Adams (1995); Alfano (2005); Bobrow (2002, 2004, 2007, 2010); Christensen and Rudnick (1999); Christensen, L. (1999); Cooper (1998, 1999a, 1999b, 2000, 2001a, 2001b, 2002a, 2002b, 2004a, 2004b, 2014a, 2014b, 2019, 2020); Eaton (2019); Epstein (1984, 1988); Harrison (2006); Krynicki (1980); Lopez-Corvo (2005, 2006); Mendoza (2010); Moncayo (1998, 2012); Morvay (1999); Pelled (2007); Rubin (1985, 2009); and Suler (1993, 1995); Zhang (2019).

These authors include psychoanalysts who make passing references to Buddhist thought and practice; psychoanalysts who study and practice Buddhism in varying degrees ranging from the occasional practitioner to the deeply committed formal student and ordained and transmitted Buddhist teachers, who are also experienced psychoanalysts and psychoanalytic educators, as well as psychotherapists who draw from psychoanalytic theories, but are not practicing or trained psychoanalysts.

A diverse variety of Buddhist perspectives, ranging from specific schools of Buddhism, find representation, including Zen: Adams (1995); Alfano (2005); Bobrow (2004, 2007); Cooper (2010, 2019); Lopez-Corvo (2003, 2006); Suler (1993, 1995); and Zhang (2019); Theravada Buddhism, including: Epstein (1984, 1988); Pelled (2007); and Rubin (1985, 2009); and Tibetan Buddhism, Mendoza (2010). Additionally, some authors draw from a variety of orientations that include both western and eastern wisdom traditions in their discussions such as Harrison (2006) and Nichol (2006).

These articles reflect a wide range of interests, orientations, complexity, and depth. Examples include broad-based discussions such as Adams work on what he describes as "revelatory openness" (1995, p. 463). Other authors emphasize Bion's work as a focal point of intersection between Buddhist thought and practice with psychoanalysis. For instance, Harrison speaks of "nondual therapy and western psychotherapy, focusing on Bion's work as a central pivot" (2006, first unnumbered page). Alfano writes in the context of what she describes as "traversing the caesura" (2005, p. 223). Bobrow (2002) from a Zen perspective and Mendoza

(2010) from a Tibetan viewpoint draw comparisons between Buddhist emptiness and Bion's O and K. Epstein (1984, 1988), Pelled (2007), and Rubin (1985, 2009) draw technical comparisons between Theravada Buddhist mindfulness meditation and psychoanalytic listening. Nichol (2006), Symington and Symington (1996), and Lopez-Corvo (2005, 2006) discuss Bion's technique and ideas with direct reference to Buddhist thought. For example, Symington and Symington (1996) draw comparisons between the Buddhist notion of "nonattachment" and Bion's technique of sitting without memory, desire, or understanding (1967, 1970). Lopez-Corvo draws comparisons between Bion's O and what he describes as the Zen notion of "origin" (2005, 2006). Bobrow (2004) draws attention to convergences and divergences between Buddhism and psychoanalysis. Eaton emphasizes the experiential aspect of reading Bion in terms of "... some of the way that his ideas inform the way that I listen as a psychoanalyst" in relation to "... an enlargement of the analyst's imagination" (2019, p. 53). While this article is not a comparative or integrative study, as a reader I cannot help but feel the implicit influence of Eaton's Buddhist practice winding its way subtly through his writing. One exception where he explicitly notes the openness that Bion's listening stance shares with Buddhist mindfulness practice.

Bobrow (2004) and Cooper (2000, 2014a) address the overall neglect of the unconscious dynamics and related ramifications for deeper understanding of the identities, similarities, and differences between Zen and psychoanalysis. Zhang's (2019) largely academic article speculates on the possible influence of Alan Watts' book *The Way of Zen* (1957) might have influenced Bion's later theories based on Bion's extensive footnotes that appear in the margins of his copy of the book.

Despite the diversity of Buddhist orientations, such as Southeast Asian Theravada Buddhism, Tibetan Buddhism, and Zen, referred to above, this review focuses on articles drawing from a Zen orientation, with an emphasis on Dōgen's "radical non-dualistic perspective" (Waddell & Abe, 2002, p. 59).

Articles that emphasize other traditions will be cited where relevant. This emphasis is intended to avoid conflating, obfuscating, and confusing or muddling fundamental and often subtle differences that exist among and between various Buddhist traditions, which are reflected and evidenced in approaches to practice described from the perspectives of differing sects. Similarly, while considerable research has been conducted from both cognitive behavioral and neuropsychological orientations, the ensuing discussion draws exclusively from a psychoanalytic perspective for comparable reasons.

Based on a review of the above-cited articles, it is clear that Bion's mandates have drawn a wide range of responses and avenues of exploration. As I see it, this diversity of response verifies the infinite possibilities evolving and blossoming through unsaturated space that he advocates and points to repeatedly and consistently in his writings and demonstrates the highly subjective nature of all experience. This wide-ranging variety of responses include total dismissal, criticism, idealization, and what lies in-between.

One might wonder about the unconscious forces that influence these various responses. For instance, in an article on meditation and psychoanalytic listening that begins with, in my opinion, the erroneous premise that psychoanalysis does not explicate specific instructions for attention training, Rubin criticizes Bion. He writes:

> The desire to have no desires (or memories or understanding) is another desire and does not "empty" the mind but keeps it full of, and occupied with, the thought of (the importance of) being without desires" (1985, p. 605). [And] Freud (1900) and Bion, for example, focused on the obstructions to facilitating it—what not to do.
>
> (2009, p. 94)

From this perspective, a point of view that emphasizes technique without considering the relation between theory and practice, or that practice functions as a manifestation of underlying core assumptions, Bion's mandates come to be viewed as negative and therefore "lacking." This appraisal might be accurate when read from an exclusively pragmatic and technical perspective, which is clearly the emphasis of the cited article.

However, when considering the theoretical underpinnings of Bion's technical advice, a very different response emerges. For instance, Grotstein emphasizes the positive aspects of Bion's directives by noting:

> Thus, all that Bion is really saying is "Do not prejudice the analysand's associations with ritualized routines of saturated anticipations; that is, do not project into them. Allow them to become incubated in the purity and virginity of your openness.
>
> (2000, p. 691)

Specific didactic instructions on how to listen would, from Bion's perspective, saturate the analyst's psychic space. That is exactly what Bion addresses with his concluding remarks in his highly condensed article "Notes on Memory and Desire" (1967). He writes:

> The theoretical implications can be worked out by each psychoanalyst for himself. His interpretations should gain in force and conviction – both for himself and his patient – because they derive from the emotional experience with a unique individual and not from generalized theories imperfectly 'remembered.'
>
> (1967, p. 19)

In contrast to authors who focus exclusively on technical comparisons between Buddhist meditation and psychoanalytic listening, some authors address the influence of intention (Bobrow, 2004; Cooper, 2014b). For instance, Bobrow addresses the multi-textured layering of any technique by questioning the motivation or intention at play. He writes:

> It is not just the technique of attention that is at play but how and to what ends it is used. "Noting" feelings in mindfulness meditation can be done in a mechanical, detached, even obsessional manner, without engaging them at all.
>
> (2004, p. 22)

Some Threads and Themes

In what follows, I would like pull on some of the diverse threads available in the literature.

Attachment/Nonattachment

Directly related to the Middle Way Buddhist orientation to experience, that is, without attachment or aversion, referred to above, Symington and Symington compare Bion's evolution of spontaneously arising memories with the Buddhist concept of *Nirodha*, which they define as "...the cessation of thirst for all that is transient" (1996, p. 169). They note that this thirst engenders *dukkha* or attachment to the transient aspects of the world and as a result engenders suffering. Further, they point out that "Dukkha has often been translated as 'suffering', but this is not correct. Dukkha means rather that attachment to the transient aspects of this world that brings about suffering" (p.169). They then clarify that:

> While attachment is typically associated with material things, it also refers to our internal world and how we cling to beliefs, thoughts, feelings, values, attitudes and in a word, any internal state that might emerge.
>
> (p. 169)

This clarification creates a connection to the psychoanalytic process and particularly to psychoanalytic listening and to Bion's reference to John Keats' notion of "Negative Capability." They observe that:

> ... it is also attachment to inner imaginative impressions and it is our clinical observation that these hidden attachments have a much greater pull over the psyche than outer physical things. To describe this state of mind after which the analyst must strive Bion uses the term Negative Capability, a term coined by Keats.
>
> (p. 169)

As an aside, regarding this point, Bion quotes Keats who writes, "I mean Negative Capability, that is, when a man is capable of being in uncertainties, mysteries, doubts, without any irritable reaching after fact and reason" (Bion, 1970, p. 125).

The Symingtons continue to describe the spontaneously arising memories that when unfettered by attachment, emerge through reverie as "extremely relevant" (p. 169). Bion distinguishes between forced memories and memories that emerge spontaneously. He reinforces this distinction to avoid confusion by describing the latter as "evolutions." While Bion's language might be rather strong and demanding, perhaps drawing on hyperbole to make his point, he is suggesting that we keep the psychic space unsaturated and free from preconceptions in order for "negative capability" to operate in as unobstructed manner as possible. However, it should be noted that Bion is not suggesting that the analyst empty the mind of everything, which I believe is quite a misreading of Bion's intention.

Revelatory Openness

Adams (1995) asserts that "psychoanalysis, existential phenomenology, and the great spiritual traditions are kindred disciplines devoted to discovering, exploring, and living in accordance with the depth dimensions of existence by evoking a radical openness to what is" (pp. 463–464). In this regard, Adams places both disciplines on equal footing. Consistent with a series of articles that emphasize the Theravada Buddhist practice of *vipassana* or mindfulness meditation (Epstein, 1985, 1988; Rubin, 1985, 2009; Speeth, 1982), Adams draws descriptive similarities between *vipassana* and Freud's technique of evenly suspended attention. Adams views both attentional strategies as "consonant practices." From the perspective that he describes as "revelatory openness," Adams makes reference to Bion's recommendations, which he describes in a highly positive manner as "radical" (p. 464) and "astonishing" (p. 475). He notes that Bion (1970) goes further than Freud by "making an astonishing recommendation to therapists, namely, to rid themselves of memory, desire, and understanding" (p. 475).

The point here is that he places both meditation and psychoanalytic listening on equal footing in terms of accessing a depth beyond surface, ordinary, everyday reality. This is in sharp distinction to articles that characterize Buddhism as adjunctive or lacking and psychoanalysis as deficient as is suggested by some authors. However, one implication with Adams' formulation is that it can be read or misread as promulgating the view that there are two (or more) separate realities, which, in my reading, clearly does not appear to be Adams' intention. Although not clearly articulated in this article, it is implied that the shift from discursive thinking to intuition implies a shift in perception, not a shift in realities. That is, the practitioner's relationship to reality shifts as the result of using what both Bion and Zen teachers describe as intuition (*prajna*) or what Adams describes as "a privileged mode of awareness, namely, revelatory openness wedded with the clarity of unknowing" (p.464). Adams views Bion's mandate as a shift from what Bion describes as what is:

> ... normally known as reality" [that is] the patient's habitual, conventional, and defensive sense of self and world; and that which the psychoanalyst seeks, through openness and unknowing (in the service of transformation), is a revelation of the deeper dimensions of the patient's self and world.
>
> (p. 476)

Traversing the Caesura

In the context of what she describes as "traversing the caesura," Alfano (2005) offers a highly sensitive clinical study that integrates Zen and psychoanalytic object relations thinking. She views "negative capability" as a key ingredient and underlying principle that supports Bion's mandate to relinquish memory, desire, and understanding. Alfano finds the source of negative capability in psychoanalysis as originating with Freud. She writes:

> Freud (1923), anticipating Bion by some forty-four years, recommends that analysts avoid "reflection," "expectations" and "memory."
> (p. 239).
>
> Bion understands negative capability as a mind that tolerates not knowing and remains open and receptive to the intuition of "O" evolutions by relinquishing "memory, desire, and understanding."
>
> (1967, p. 272)

Taking the queue from Bion and from Zen practice, Alfano speaks from her direct experience as a Zen practitioner and as a psychoanalyst and elaborates four capacities that, from my vantage point, demonstrate the mutual interpenetration of the core Buddhist notions of emptiness and dependent co-arising, which she describes in psychological terms as a "generative, bidirectional relationship between the conscious and unconscious, unconscious and unconscious, and between different self-states within and between analyst and analysand. These four capacities are mental flexibility, negative capability, unconscious reception, and intuitive capacities" (2005, p. 223).

Transcendent Attunement

Alfano's description of transcendent attunement requires elaboration because it describes clearly, succinctly, and convincingly her central personally experienced integration of Zen and psychoanalytic practice from a realizational perspective. Alfano demonstrates experientially how these capacities contribute to what she describes as: "transcendent attunement," a process "closely related to reverie" (p. 227). She notes:

> This is a disciplined, yet unselfconscious attentive process within the analyst, which has a counterpart within the analysand, in which boundaries between self and other and between somatic and psychic perception are temporarily dissolved.
>
> (p. 227)

And:
> A fluid state of being in which occurs a transient and nonpathological suspension of duality between self and other and that constitutes an atemporal mode of experiencing.
>
> (p. 223)

Alfano continues:

> Further, transcendent attunement can be thought of as occurring while in a state of reverie. This does not imply a regressive or pathological loss of boundaries, but rather a more fundamental relatedness, in which dualism of subject and object is itself transcended. We fleetingly enter a domain in which experience is neither subject nor object, neither located in time nor space, yet not outside of it. In these transitory moments it might be said we are nondualistically attuned.
>
> (p. 228)

What stands out is Alfano's integration of the fundamental Buddhist principles of the identity of the one and the many. Dōgen describes this distinction/identity as "Oneness and discrimination," which he notes needs to be constant and in balance. For instance, Kim notes: "This nondual 'oneness'" is generally expressed within Buddhism, as I have already noted, in terms of "neither identical nor different" (2004, p. 130).

Alfano, in psychological terms, clearly describes a balance that accounts for both emptiness ("suspension of duality") and dependent co-arising ("bi-directional relationship," "caesura"). She also renders her understanding in a clinically useful form by describing a technique for engendering this balance through her use of "intuitive capacities," or what Zen practitioners describe as *prajna*, or what the Zen philosopher Thomas Kasulis describes as "pre-reflective experience" (1981, p. 75). In her inclusion and elaboration of the role of somatic experiences as a fundamental and basic aspect of intuition, in the spirit of Dōgen, she elaborates a radical nondualism, and in a novel way, she extends the range of intuitive capacities. She writes:

> I found myself in a receptive somatopsychic state of being, as if the whole of me was a breathing, porous echo chamber attuning to my analysand's

> unconscious affective communications. I recognized that this form of somatopsychic reverie occurred while I was in a fluid mode of being, in which there was a transient suspension of duality between myself and my analysand. In a sense, my own self-conscious subjectivity was temporarily transcended.
>
> (p. 224)

Alfano accounts for the identity of relative and absolute, the interpenetration of oneness and distinction with the caution that:

> It is crucial to bear in mind that these capacities and the methods of reverie and transcendent attunement are an integral whole, just as psyche and soma are an integral whole, and cannot be thought of as discrete elements that exist apart from one another.
> (p. 226)
> This points to the need to allow for the elemental flow of primary process to inform and vitalize the domain of conscious life.
>
> (p. 226)

As an integral whole, these capacities fluctuate between foreground and background of experiencing and in the psychoanalytic context that Alfano describes, serve to exemplify Bion's general and abstract notion of O and K capacities, or stated in more experiential terms, as shifts between discursive and intuitive modes of functioning.

Mystical Dimensions and the Incommunicado Core

Drawing from the poet William Blake, Bobrow (2002) speaks from the foundational Zen agenda of questioning our inflated and reified views of self in relation to being with and listening to the patient in the context of Bion's mandate and his formulation of O. He writes:

> We might say that as our capacity for truth deepens, as self-preoccupation, constricted perception, and the need to defend any self recede, O—or Heaven—becomes available in the most ordinary phenomena: a wild flower, a weed, a laugh, a tear.
>
> (p. 66)

In this manner Bobrow makes solid connections between the foundational Buddhist principles of form and emptiness with Bion's O and K and points the reader back toward the function of intuition as a facilitator of religious truths and realization. He thus extends Bion's mandates beyond technical matters and emphasizes their realizational function. This is significant as unlike authors who have secularized Buddhism, by pulling on technical threads from the larger fabric of their religious tradition, Bobrow maintains Zen's basic religious fabric.

Bobrow (2002) explores aspects of the mystical dimensions of the psychoanalytic process, some rooted in Bion and Winnicott, through the lens of Zen. He draws connections between Zen, Winnicott, and Bion in relation to the "incommunicado core." He notes that, "This may relate to Bion's (1967) view of the relation between sensory experience and the mystical dimension" (2002, p. 64). Bion notes the interference of sensuous experience in intuiting psychic reality. He writes, "awareness of the sensuous accompaniments of emotional experience are a hindrance to the psychoanalyst's intuition of the reality with which he must be at one" (1967, p. 17). Speaking from the Zen Buddhist perspective, in contrast to Bion, Bobrow implies that sense-based experiences are fundamentally neutral and:

> ... it is rather the use we put them to. All the senses, including the sixth one, can be allies in the joint search for and creation of analytic truth, especially when we are not "chasing out through the five senses" as Meister Eckhart called it.
>
> (p. 64)

This orientation points to the significance of nonattachment described above with reference to Symington and Symington's connections between the Buddhist concept of *Nirodha* and psychoanalytic listening. Additionally, and this is as I see it, a key point of integration between Zen and Bion's psychoanalysis is that the issue becomes one of the relationships that occurs and of the actions that are taken. For instance, from the Zen perspective, the practitioner takes the "middle-way" free from attachment and grasping or aversion and pushing away. In other words, as Bobrow notes, this means:

> Rather, in cultivating a wide, inclusive and non-judgmental awareness—presence of mind, body and emotions—the analyst's unconscious attachments to narrow, constricting, and repetitive versions of memory, desire, and understanding, and his identification with and need to defend them recede. Direct, intuitive knowing can occur.
>
> (2002, p. 64).

Buddhist Emptiness and Bion's O

Mendoza (2010) compares Bion's notion of O with Buddhist emptiness with the intention to demonstrate "... the realization in the consulting room of his [Bion's] injunctions" (p. 305). Unfortunately, he does not provide any clinical material to exemplify the abstract aspects of his discussion or to demonstrate any clinical usefulness.

He observes: "In the Dharma it is the realization of emptiness which comprises wisdom, just as in Bion it is the evolution of O that comes into K" (p. 308). Mendoza describes the teachings on emptiness as "philosophically, spiritually and experientially mind-changing and life-changing" (p. 307). He attempts to use the realization of emptiness to promote psychic change in the clinical setting. In this regard, Mendoza employs a realizational view. However, Buddhist emptiness does not stand alone and only makes complete sense in terms of the related fundamental principle of dependent co-arising, as elaborated in Chapter Seven "Emptiness and Dependent Co-arising" (also Cooper, 2014b). The latter parallels the psychoanalytic notion of totalistic countertransference (Cooper, 1999b). The mutuality of these foundational Buddhist concepts is expressed succinctly, cogently, and tersely in the *Heart Sutra*, which is a key Buddhist teaching. It is paraphrased as "emptiness is form and form is emptiness; emptiness is no other than form, form is no other than emptiness." This relates directly to Bion's technical mandates. That is, the formless, intuited O evolves into thought and language and finds expression, which Bion describes as K. Unfortunately, the literature on psychoanalysis and Buddhism all but completely neglects dependent co-arising, thus promoting an incomplete picture of Buddhist soteriology that risks a dip into an unfortunately all too prevalent misinterpretation of Buddhism as nihilistic extremism such as exemplified by Alexander (1931). Bion's depiction of O→K within his own unique symbol system takes account of both. Dōgen, as discussed in Chapter Seven, through his radical nondualism, expresses the interpenetration of emptiness and dependent co-arising when he speaks of *"embodied* emptiness" (Kim, 2007 p. 45). O to K evolutions highlight a relationship. That is, Bion's emphasis is on the relationship between subject and object. With this being said, the comparison with Buddhist emptiness and Bion's O might be better demonstrated by examining the relationships that exist between emptiness and dependent co-arising and the relationship between O and K with no aspect excluded in his typically radically nondualistic way, thus avoiding the trap of being seduced by emptiness. Dōgen doesn't limit emptiness to its deconstructive function that cuts through every reification or delusional reification, as described by Mendoza. Dōgens radical nondualism by definition includes deconstruction/reconstruction, being/nonbeing, emptiness/form. Similarly, he doesn't limit emptiness to "mind only," as Mendoza suggests. He writes: "It is not the vacuum but the way we see things only as mental phenomena, appearances to mind, not as they exist in themselves" (2010, p. 314). As the Buddhist philosopher Gadjin Nagao notes, "Thus emptiness is intended to be an expression of true being" (1989, p. 4), not simply a perceptual error that is limited to the mind. Within deconstruction is also reconstruction. This is the "empty and form" of the *Heart Sutra* cited above. Emptiness can only be realized in form. Form is the embodiment of emptiness. The point to keep in mind is that Buddhist realization is not limited to ineffable experience, only known experientially through *prajna* (intuited wisdom or Bion's "intuition of 'O'") but is also "embodied" and known conceptually and linguistically.

Lopez-Corvo's References to Zen

The following critique exemplifies some of the problems associated with psychoanalytic writers who make spurious references to Zen. Lopez-Corvo (2005, 2006), who is a well-respected, close, and sensitive Bion reader, makes several references to Zen Buddhism in relation to Bion's thought, in particular with reference to Bion's notion of O. These references include a full entry in *The Dictionary of the Work of W.R. Bion* (2005) and which are further elaborated in a latter work in 2006. This creates a problem because his knowledge and understanding of Zen might be assumed by the reader who is not familiar with basic Buddhist concepts and terminology, to hold the same high degree of insight and scholarship as his understanding of Bion's ideas. However, his comments are highly speculative and misinformed through the use of spurious references and through conflation or confusion. For example, he cites the German philosopher Eugen Herrigel's influential book *Zen and the Art of Archery* (1953) as a primary source for his knowledge of Zen, despite the fact that Herrigel's "Zen training" has been largely refuted. For instance, Yamada (1981), who has offered an exhaustive, detailed, and well-documented research on the historical relationship between archery, Zen, Herrigel, and his archery teacher Awa Kenzo (1880–1939), clearly and convincingly demonstrates that Kenzo was not a Zen teacher. Yamada writes: "… it is practically impossible to detect any Zen elements in Awa's teaching. Surprisingly, it appears that Awa never practiced Zen even once in his life" (2001, p. 11). Further, Yamada cites Sakurai (1981, p. 223) who he notes "conscientiously studied Awa's life, wrote that, 'No evidence can be found that Kenzo ever trained with a Zen priest'" (Yamada, p. 11). Yamada places the confusion in a cultural context and concludes that:

> Awa did use the expression "bow and Zen are one" (*kyuzen itchimi*). Nonetheless, he did not expound archery (kyðdõ) or his *shadõ* as a way leading to Zen. Regardless of how Herrigel acquired that impression, today when many Japanese have the same misunderstanding we should not place the blame on Herrigel. Rather, the responsibility must be placed squarely on our own Japanese scholars who have failed to clarify the difference between the arts of Japan and Zen.
>
> (p. 11)

There has been a wealth of accurate, clearly written, and easily accessible material on Zen authored by legitimate contemporary Zen masters, as well as an explosion of classical texts available in translation for the contemporary reader. Additionally, there has been a rapidly expanding and evolving literature that attempts to articulate the integration of Zen and psychoanalysis written by psychoanalysts who actively study and practice Zen since the early offerings that Lopez-Corvo cites became available. This literature, cited above, would be readily available to Lopez-Corvo by 2005 and 2006, the dates of his publications.

Additionally, numerous articles are available by psychoanalysts who are seriously involved in Zen study and practice that present Zen accurately. However, he has completely neglected this rich source of valid information regarding Zen within the psychoanalytic domain. This problem is not unique to Lopez-Corvo and has been addressed by Finn (2011) and Moncayo (2012). For instance, Finn notes: "Some authors in the Buddhist psychoanalytic dialogue write as though they alone had come to observe the intersection of the two psychologies" (2011, p. 420). Mendoza's comment exemplifies Finn's observation when he writes:

> My paper does not base itself on the growing body of work linking Buddhist concepts with psychoanalysis, but on a personal experience of involvement in both disciplines. It derives from actual qualified teaching given in the lineage of oral transmission and capable of the insight that such a process of discipleship can evoke.
>
> (2010, p. 305)

Given the level of misinformation in the referenced titles, it's no wonder that he writes: "I have tried to understand Zen Buddhism for years" (p. 305). Thus, he acknowledges the evolving literature on Buddhism and psychoanalysis, but stands apart from it, deferring to his own personal experiences as a student of Buddhism.

The problem for the psychoanalytic reader is that Lopez-Corvo is a highly gifted and attuned Bion reader. This inadvertently lends a false credibility to his inaccurate discussion of Zen Buddhism, particularly among psychoanalytic readers who have had no exposure to Zen practice or study. I am reminded of the commentary on the Zen koan, "Chao Chou's Three Turning Words," Case 96 in the *Blue Cliff Record*: "When one person transmits a falsehood, 10,000 people transmit it as truth" (Cleary & Cleary, Trans., 1992, p. 526). As a result of ignoring the available literature, there is a failure to extend and expand the integration of these two disciplines in terms of a cohesive and incremental development. The result is a disjointed literature that lacks continuity.

Influence: Valid/Invalid

It is tempting to make connections between Zen and psychoanalysis. Perhaps there is a sense of enthusiasm and excitement for teasing out the various connections and influences. This has been the case in studies that lead to hasty comparisons that overlook significant differences. The following study that addresses purported influences serves as a case in point.

Zhang (2019) discusses the hypothesized influence that Alan Watts had on Bion's later theories based on a close and careful reading of Bion's handwritten notations in his personal copy of Watts' *The Way of Zen* (1957). Zhang concludes: "I argue that the material generated from his personal copy of *The Way of Zen* is genuinely informative about the connections between Buddhism and

Bion's own psychoanalytic theorizations" (p. 352). Zhang carefully qualifies his position by noting that:

> Due to the uncertainty over dating, it is impossible to establish with certainty whether Bion's readings on Zen actively initiated any of his own new theorizations. Given his use of 'O' and 'K' in the annotations, such formulations must certainly pre-date the reading, or, at least, the reading during which the annotations were made.
>
> (p. 352)

Despite this sober caution, Zhang continues: "However, it does seem likely that the encounter with Watts's book (and possibly others like it) at least influenced his thinking on psychoanalysis. Bion usually did not annotate books as extensively as he did *The Way of Zen*" (p.352).

Zhang's original approach to the conversation between Zen and Bion's psychoanalysis has merit. It creates new avenues of exploration in the incremental development of this growing literature. That is, how do specific Buddhist teachings and practices influence the development of psychoanalytic theory and practice? For example, my own immersion in Sōtō Zen study and practice has led me to resonate with Bion's approach as well as how I read psychoanalysis. However, Zhang's conclusion tends to be quite a generalization from Watts' naturalist and antiestablishment misinterpretation of Zen and Bion's psychoanalysis, which can be misleading. It would be more accurate to conclude that, based on the evidence that Zhang presents so meticulously, Bion might have been influenced by Watts' *misinterpretation* of Zen with his anti-practice, antiestablishment, and anti-cognitive biases that, as described in Chapter Four "Precursors: Suzuki Review," he inherited from Suzuki's biased presentation of Zen to the West.

For instance, in contrast to Suzuki and Watts, Bion does not refute language or intellect. He simply argues that these processes are not the way to collect the specifically nonsensuous psychoanalytic data, which relies on the psychoanalyst's capacity for intuition and reverie. For Bion (and for Dōgen), language is fundamentally neutral as are other experiences. The relation to language is important. Bion makes this clear in the opening of *Attention and Interpretation* (1970), where he states: "It is too often forgotten that the gift of speech, so centrally employed, has been elaborated as much for the purpose of concealing thought by dissimulation and lying as for the purpose of elucidating or communicating thought" (1970, p. 3). In this manner, he raises the influence of intention, which is ruled by both conscious and unconscious factors.

Review Conclusions

Bion's mandates have drawn a wide range of responses. This diversity of response verifies the infinite possibilities evolving and blossoming through the unsaturated space that both Bion and Dōgen advocate. They clearly point to the highly subjective nature of all experience: the wide-ranging variety, including total dismissal, criticism, idealization, and what lies in-between. This diversity seems to validate Bion's point: "Memory is always misleading as a record of fact since it is distorted by the influence of unconscious forces" (1967, p. 17). One might fruitfully ask: "What unconscious forces influence these various responses?" "What preconceptions are at work?" "How do they influence our experience?"

Eigen, for example, addresses the role of unconscious preconceptions with the following cautions:

> It is difficult to overestimate the role unconscious omniscience plays in deadening the capacity to experience. If one knows what is going to happen ahead of time, one does not have to experience it.... Our sense of knowing has a way of spreading through our mental field and acting like an anesthetic. What we know may lead to or block the new; it may heighten or dull experience.
>
> (1993, pp. 245–246)

Connecting Thread

One proposed connecting thread centers on how the various threads that these authors pull on can be interwoven into a multi-textured tapestry that, as mentioned, I describe as a "realizational model." If we consider Bion's emphasis on relationships that exist, we can also extrapolate to the Buddhist notion of the middle way that is responding to all experiences with an open mind, unobstructed by preconceptions, without attachment or aversion, what in Zen parlance is known as "taking the backwards step." In this way, both Bion and Dōgen are directing us to be more engaged in the present in their own differing albeit overlapping ways. In conclusion, Shunryu Suzuki's advice holds the same relevance as Bion's insistence to sit free from memory, desire, and understanding by noting: "If your mind is empty, it is always ready for anything; it is open to everything. In the beginner's mind there are many possibilities; in the expert's mind there are few" (1970, p. 21).

References

Adams, W. (1995). Revelatory openness wedded with the clarity of unknowing: Psychoanalytic evenly suspended attention, the phenomenological attitude, and meditative awareness. *Psychoanalysis and Contemporary Thought*, 18:463–494.

Alexander, F. (1931). Buddhistic training as an artificial catatonia. *Psychoanalytic Review*, 18:129–145.

Alfano, C. (2005). Traversing the caesura: Transcendent attunement in Buddhist meditation and psychoanalysis. *Contemporary Psychoanalysis*, 41:223–247.

Bion, W. (1967). Notes on memory and desire. In: J. Aguayo & B. Malin (Eds.), *Wilfred Bion: Los Angeles Seminars and Supervision* (pp. 133–149). London: Karnac, 2017. [Originally published in: Bion, W. (1967). Notes on memory and desire. The *Psychoanalytic Forum*, 2: 272-3, 279-80.]

Bion, W. (1970). *Attention and Interpretation*. London: Karnac.

Bobrow, J. (2002). Psychoanalysis, mysticism, and the incommunicado core. *Fort Da*, 8:62–71.

Bobrow, J. (2004). Presence of mind. *International Journal of Applied Psychoanalytic Studies*, 1:18–35.

Bobrow, J. (2007). The disavowal of the personal in psychoanalytic training. *Psychoanalytic Review*, 94:263–276.

Bobrow, J. (2010). *Zen and Psychotherapy: Partners in Liberation*. New York: W.W. Norton.

Christensen, A. & Rudnick, S. (1999). A glimpse of Zen practice within the realm of countertransference. *American Journal of Psychoanalysis*, 59:59–69.

Christensen, L. W. (1999). Suffering and the dialectical self in Buddhism and relational psychoanalysis. *American Journal of Psychoanalysis*, 59:37–57.

Cleary, T. & Cleary, J. C. (1992). *The Blue Cliff Record*. Boston, MA: Shambhala.

Cooper, P. (1998). The disavowal of the spirit: Wholeness and integration in Buddhism and psychoanalysis. In: A. Molino (Ed.), *The Couch and the Tree: Dialogues in Psychoanalysis and Buddhism* (pp. 231–246). New York: Farrar Straus/Northpoint.

Cooper, P. (1999a). Sense and non-sense: Phenomenology, Buddhist and psychoanalytic. *Journal of Religion and Health*, 35(4): 351–370.

Cooper, P. (1999b). Buddhist meditation and countertransference: A case study. *American Journal of Psychoanalysis*, 59:71–85.

Cooper, P. (2000). Unconscious process: Zen and psychoanalytic versions. *Journal of Religion and Health*, 39(1):57–69.

Cooper, P. (2001a). The gap between being and knowing in Zen Buddhism and psychoanalysis. *American Journal of Psychoanalysis*, 61(4):341–362.

Cooper, P. (2001b). Clouds into rain. *Journal of Religion and Health*, 40(1):167–184.

Cooper, P. (2002a). Between wonder and doubt: Psychoanalysis in the goal-free zone. *American Journal of Psychoanalysis*, 62(2):95–118.

Cooper, P. (2002b). The Pervasion of the object: Depression and unitive experience. *Psychoanalytic Review*, 89:413–439.

Cooper, P. (2004a). The Abyss becoming well: Psychoanalysis and reversals in perspective. *Psychoanalytic Review*, 91:157–177.

Cooper, P. (2004b). Oscillations: Zen and psychoanalytic versions. *Journal of Religion and Health*, 43(3):233–243.

Cooper, P. (2009). Oscillations reload. In: D. Mathers, M. Miller & O. Ando (Eds.), *Self and No-Self: Continuing the Dialogue Between Buddhism and Psychotherapy* (pp. 217–230). London: Routledge.

Cooper, P. (2010). *The Zen Impulse and the Psychoanalytic Encounter*. London: Routledge.

Cooper, P. (2014a). Taste the strawberries. *American Journal of Psychoanalysis*, 74:147–161.

Cooper, P. (2014b). Zen meditation, reverie, and psychoanalytic listening. *Psychoanalytic Review*, 101:795–813.

Cooper, P. (2019). *Zen Insight, Psychoanalytic Action: Two Arrows Meeting*. New York & London: Routledge.

Cooper, P. (2020). Realizational perspectives: Bion's psychoanalysis & Dōgen's Zen. *American Journal of Psychoanalysis*, 80:37–52.

Eaton, J. (2019). Between emotion and evolution. In: A. Alisobhani & G. Cortorphine (Eds.), *Explorations in Bion's "O" Everything We Know Nothing About* (pp. 53–60). London & New York: Routledge.

Eigen, M. (1993). *The Electrified Tightrope*. Northvale, NJ: Jason Aronson.

Epstein, M. (1984). On the neglect of evenly suspended attention. *Journal of Transpersonal Psychology*, 16(2): 193–205.

Epstein, M. (1988). Attention and psychoanalysis. *Psychoanalysis and Contemporary Thought*, 11:171–189.

Finn, M. (2011). Review: *The Zen impulse and the psychoanalytic encounter*, by Paul C. Cooper. *Psychoanalytic Review*, 98:419–420.

Grotstein, J. (2000). Notes On Bion's "memory and desire." *Journal of the American Academy of Psychoanalysis*, 28:687–694.

Harrison, J. (2006). Bion's O—An open gate between eastern and western psychotherapy. Retrieved from http://www.simplymeditate.org/?p=57

Herrigel, E. (1953). *Zen and the Art of Archery*. New York: Vintage Books.

Kasulis, T. (1981). *Zen Action, Zen Person*. Honolulu: University of Hawaii Press.

Kim, H. (2004). *Eihei Dōgen: Mystical Realist*. Boston, MA: Wisdom Publishers.

Kim, H. (2007). *Dōgen on Meditation and Thinking: A Reflection on His View of Zen*. Albany: State University of New York Press.

Krynicki, V. (1980). The double orientation of the ego in the practice of Zen. *American Journal of Psychoanalysis*, 40(3):239–248.

Lopez- Corvo, R. (2005). *The Dictionary of the Work of W.R. Bion*. London: Karnac.

Lopez-Corvo. (2006). *Wild Thoughts Searching for a Thinker: A Clinical Application to W.R. Bion's Theories*. London: Karnac.

Mendoza, S. (2010). The O of emptiness and the emptiness of O. *British Journal of Psychotherapy*, 26:305–320.

Moncayo, R. (1998). True subject is no-subject: The real, imaginary, and symbolic in psychoanalysis and Zen Buddhism. *Psychoanalysis and Contemporary Thought*, 21:383–422.

Moncayo, R. (2012). *The Signifier Pointing at the Moon: Psychoanalysis and Zen Buddhism*. London: Karnac.

Morvay, Z. (1999). Horney, Zen and the real self: theoretical and historical connections. *American Journal of Psychoanalysis*, 59:25–35.

Nagao, G. (1989). *The Foundational Standpoint of Madhyamika Philosophy*. Albany: State University of New York Press.

Nichol, D. (2006). Buddhism and psychoanalysis: a personal reflection. *American Journal of Psychoanalysis*, 66:157–172.

Pelled, E. (2007). Learning from experience: Bion's concept of reverie and Buddhist meditation: a comparative study. *International Journal of Psycho-Analysis*, 88(6):1507–1526.

Rubin, J. (1985). Meditation and psychoanalytic listening. *Psychoanalytic Review*, 72:599–614.

Rubin, J. (2009). Deepening psychoanalytic listening: The marriage of Buddha and Freud. *American Journal of Psychoanalysis*, 69:93–105.

Suler, J. (1993). *Contemporary Psychoanalysis and Eastern Thought*. Albany: State University of New York Press.

Suler, J. (1995). In search of the self: Zen Buddhism and psychoanalysis. *Psychoanalytic Review*, 82:407–426.

Suzuki, S. (1970). *Zen Mind, Beginner's Mind*. New York: Weatherhill.
Symington, J. & Symington, N. (1996). *The Clinical Thinking of Wilfred Bion*. London: Routledge.
Waddell & Abe. (2002). *The Heart of Dōgen's Shobogenzo*. Albany: State University of New York Press.
Watts, A. (1957). *The Way of Zen*. New York: Pantheon Books.
Yamada, S. (2001). The myth of Zen and the art of archery, *Japanese Journal of Religious Studies*, 28:1–30.
Zhang, Y. (2019). Wilfred Bion's annotations in *The Way of Zen*: an investigation into the practical encounters with Buddhist ideas. *Psychoanalysis and History,* 21(3):331–355.

Part Three
The Definite and the Infinite

Chapter 7

Emptiness and Dependent Co-Arising

This chapter provides an understanding of the basic Buddhist principles of *śūnyatā* or emptiness and the complementary concept of *pratītyasamutpāda*, or dependent co-arising. Along with the material discussed in the next two chapters, this chapter will contribute to the necessary groundwork for understanding assimilation and accommodation processes examined in Chapter Ten, "Assimilation and Accommodation," in order to explore the process of cultural transmission and cross-fertilization between Buddhism and western psychology, with specific emphasis on the interrelation between psychoanalysis and Zen Buddhism.

Mahayana Buddhism, of which Zen is a form, is rooted in *śūnyatā*, the school's foundational teaching. That is, all phenomena lack an inherent essence. "Emptiness" refers to the negation of a "self" that exists separately and independently of causes and conditions. However, it is important to keep in mind that this understanding of reality is not a form of nihilism, which is avoided through the equally important core notion of *pratītyasamutpāda*.

The historical Buddha's insight into the truth of emptiness functions as a clarification of dependent co-arising. Similarly, an understanding of dependent co-arising clarifies emptiness. No separate independent self means the realization of the fundamental interconnection, oneness, and identity of all being. Hence, the Zen paradox of the identity of the one and the many. We are uniquely separate and simultaneously connected. This is the nature of reality. Together with *śūnyatā*, *pratītyasamutpāda* constitutes what the Buddhist philosopher Gadjin Nagao (1989), for instance, describes as the foundational cornerstones and the nexus of Mahayana Buddhist ideology and practice. This identity of emptiness and dependent co-arising also expressed as the identity of being and nonbeing serves as the core teaching of Mahayana thought. The intertwining of being and nonbeing and the mutually interacting and constantly oscillating dynamic from being to nonbeing and from nonbeing to being is intertwined within both being and nonbeing. With these points in mind, here is a brief description of these terms.

śūnyatā—Emptiness

The Sanskrit term for emptiness is *śūnyatā*, translated in Japanese as *kū*, which also functions as the Japanese term for sky, space, or air. Other translations of *śūnyatā* include nothingness, nonexistence, nonreality, voidness, boundlessness, and illusion. Infinite becoming functions as an alternate depiction of *śūnyatā*, which acknowledges that reality and experience are in constant motion. Nishijima and Cross also emphasize experience and activity. They note: "But the real philosophical meaning of *śūnyatā* is emptiness; the bare, bald, naked, raw, or transparent state, that is, the state in which reality is seen as it is" (Nishijima & Cross, 1996, p. 10, f. 44).

When received and filtered through the unquestioned lens of western preconceptions, *śūnyatā* has been frequently and completely misunderstood. For instance, a nihilist orientation engenders a view of emptiness as a lack, interpreted as "nothingness" or "nonexistence." Emptiness has also been described as a "void" or "voidness." Thus, emptiness becomes reified into an object or a psychic location that contains contents that become emptied out from or as a location that one may courageously dive into. One implication of viewing emptiness as a psychic space or a "container," as is typical psychoanalytically, would be that the container is saturated. This would preclude, as Salvatti notes, "the emptiness necessary to create new meaning" (2019, p. 76). In both views, the fundamental teaching, expressed as "emptiness is form; form is emptiness" in the *Heart Sutra*, the basic text of the Mahayana emptiness tradition, becomes overlooked. Further, the notion of "no self" is taken literally rather than as a shorthand for the notion that as Buddhist emptiness teachings assert, there is no inherently existing permanent self that exists separately from causes and conditions. Dōgen, for example, is highly critical of this misunderstanding, which he examines and attempts to correct in the *Bussho* (Buddha nature) chapter of *Shobogenzo* written in 1241. The key point here is his use of the term "Being without" or "*Mu*," which refers to the negation that something exists. In this context, *mu* refers to the nonexistence of a permanent and eternal self or essence and is represented by a Chinese character that represents a piece of paper above a flame. Commenting on the Fifth Patriarch of Zen in China Zen Master Daiman, in *Bussho*, "Buddha Nature," Dōgen writes:

> the Fifth Patriarch says, "The buddha-nature is emptiness, so we call it being without." This clearly expresses that "emptiness" is not nonexistence. To express that the buddha-nature is emptiness, we do not say it is half a pound and we do not say it is eight ounces, but we use the words "being without." We do not call it "emptiness" because it is void, and we do not call it "being without" because it does not exist; because the buddha-nature is emptiness, we call it "being without." So real instances of "being without" are the standard for expressing "emptiness," and "emptiness" has the power to express "being without." This emptiness is beyond the emptiness of "matter is just emptiness." [At the same time,] "matter is just emptiness"

describes neither matter being forcibly made into emptiness nor emptiness being divided up to produce matter. It may describe emptiness in which emptiness is just emptiness. [He concludes by noting] This being so, the Fourth Patriarch and the Fifth Patriarch pose questions and make assertions about the buddha-nature being without, about the buddha-nature as emptiness, and about the buddha-nature as existence.

(Nishijima & Cross, 1996, p. 10)

Thus, Dōgen denies the interpretation that *śūnyatā* describes nothingness, nonexistence, or something unreal. Rather, *śūnyatā*, according to Dōgen, describes absolutely real existence and is not a negation of real existence. Being without expresses real existence.

With Dōgen's critique and clarification in mind, here is a concise, clear, and comprehensive definition of emptiness provided by the Tibetan Buddhist scholar Jeffrey Hopkins:

Phenomena are empty of a certain mode of being called 'inherent existence', objective existence', or 'natural existence'. This 'inherent existence' is not a concept superimposed by philosophical systems but refers to our ordinary sense of the way that things exist-as if they concretely exist in and of themselves, covering their parts. Phenomena are the things which are empty of inherent existence, and inherent existence is that which phenomena are empty. Emptiness or, more properly, *an* emptiness is a phenomenon's lack of inherent existence; an emptiness is a negative or utter absence of this concrete mode of being with which we are so familiar.

(1983, pp. 9–10)

This "inherent existence" that Hopkins describes, which all phenomena are "empty" of, refers to the illusion of a permanent and separate essence or self that exists separately from causes and conditions, such as an immortal soul that exists before and beyond our physical and mental being, a belief posited by many religious systems. In contrast to this view, described and criticized by Dōgen as the Senika heresy, all existence, without exception, arises in a context that is subject to causes and conditions.[1]

Ignorance

Simply stated, ignorance, or *avidya*, is the active resistance to the realization of the empty nature of our existence. Empty of what? Empty of a substantial, permanent, and separate essence or "self" that exists separately from causes and conditions. However, through *avidya*, we posit a separate and permanent sense of self, and this, according to Buddhism, is where our suffering begins because as soon as we posit a separate sense of self, we create a subject and object dichotomy, and as soon as we create this dichotomy, attachment and aversion arise and become enacted in the form of fear, envy, hate, and aggression. We want to hold on to what we have, and through greed and aggression, we want and often attempt to accumulate what others have. This process, to varying degrees, is all-pervasive and occurs on an individual level as well as on a global level, which explains the underlying causes of theft, vandalism, nationalism, racism, exploitation of women and children, holocaust, and war. This issue finds visual expression on the Buddhist *Bhavachakra*, Wheel of Life and Death. The Wheel is composed of a series of concentric circles. The center or hub includes a pig, a snake, and a bird. The pig represents *avidya* or this active unconscious not knowing that I mentioned. Out of the mouth of the pig, we see the snake representing aggression because it will strike without warning. We also see the bird, which represents fear or aversion because a bird will fly off at the least stimulus perceived as a threat or provocation. So, to summarize, the active not knowing described by Buddhists as ignorance is delusion because it blinds us and prevents us from realizing the essential truth of our existence, which is that all phenomena are empty, without a permanent essence, and emerge through causes and conditions. Now, I mentioned that *avidya* as active not-knowing stems from the reality of the emptiness of being.

It will be helpful to understand dependent co-arising, the complementary concept to emptiness. These two concepts, as I noted, constitute the foundational standpoints of Mahayana Buddhist doctrine. All teachings and practices derive from these two concepts regardless of the sect and the diverse forms of expression that the many schools of Mahayana Buddhism, such as Zen or Tibetan Buddhism, articulate. It is important to keep in mind that the goal of practice and understanding is focused on only refuting *inherent existence*, not all existence. To refute all existence would only lead to extreme nihilism. On the other hand, asserting a permanent, solid, or separate existence reflects an absolutist view. Realizing emptiness experientially refutes both extremes of nihilism and absolutism. This is what is referred to as the middle way. Through realizational practice, these two extremes are experientially identified, which engenders the experience of valid, relative, or empirical existence. It is only the sense of inherent existence that becomes dissolved.

The pervasive nature of ignorance finds expression in reified notions of the psychoanalytic unconscious conceptualized by Freud. Symington and Symington describe this phenomenon clearly:

> There is another pitfall about using the term 'unconscious'. It is visualized as if the unconscious is a thing, so that people use phrases such as 'it was banished into the unconscious' as if the latter was a locality in the mind.
>
> (1996, p. 9)

Pratītyasamutpāda—Dependent Co-Arising

Emptiness is extremely important in Zen thought and practice. However, emptiness does not describe the full point of view of Mahayana thought. The complementary notion of *pratītyasamutpāda* or dependent co-arising is equally critical and central. Nagao, for example, observes: "Together, emptiness and dependent co-arising constitute an emptiness in which dependent co-arising is empty and a dependent co-arising in which that which is empty dependently co-arises" (1989, p. 19).

pratītyasamutpāda refers to the notion that all existence arises contextually subject to causes and conditions. Thus, all phenomena, hence, all experience, exist relatively or empirically, but not inherently, absolutely, eternally, or independently. Zen practitioners refute absolute or ultimate existence but accept relative or empirical existence. Nothing arises independently. This relationship finds clear and poetic expression Buddhism in the writings of Nagarjuna, the 2nd-century founder of middle way Buddhism. He writes:

> Just as in a dream, happiness and suffering depend on dream objects and upon awakening these objects are known not to actually exist, likewise any phenomenon which arises in dependence should be known not to exist in the manner of its appearance.
>
> (Komito, 1987, p. 82)

Notice that Nagarjuna does not completely write off all existence. Rather, he questions the way phenomena appear to us through the lens of *avidya*. The Zen expression "coming down from the mountain cave and going into the marketplace," for instance, exemplifies the importance of relative existence and relationships. The middle way acknowledges both aspects of reality and cautions against getting caught in one at the expense of awareness of the other through dualistic thinking or through negation attributed to *avidya*.

Dependent co-arising conveys a sense of mutuality in terms of how phenomena arise. What arises is cocreated in a context. This sense of mutuality functions in contrast to what can be described as "empty," non-differentiated, and not existing, or what Bion describes in terms of the psychoanalytic encounter as "at-one-ment."

Differentiation or separateness on the other hand implies uniqueness, separateness, otherness; discrimination between self and other; and distinction between subject and object; from which Bion notes that K (knowledge) develops from experience and finds expression through language. In the case of psychoanalysis, the latter depends on which theories and life experiences the analyst has internalized and brings to bear on the situation.

In conclusion, regardless of whether either dependent co-arising or emptiness serves as a relative entry point to realizational understanding, ultimately, the two are identical. Both define each other. As noted above, the *Heart Sutra* asserts: "Form is emptiness; emptiness is form." Ultimately, reality, as noted, lacks inherent existence or any independent self or essence. Regardless of approaching realization through the notion that all phenomena arise dependently on causes and conditions or through the realization that reality is empty, the bottom line from the Mahayana standpoint is the lack of independent, permanent, inherently existing, or eternal selfhood.

Implications for Psychoanalysis

The realizational approach to psychoanalysis informed by Buddhist practice and experience includes an understanding of the dependently co-arising context and how this context influences the psychoanalytic encounter. How does the encounter manifest in the form of the mutual impacts that are exerted by both analyst and analysand on each other? It is from this perspective that these core Buddhist concepts become integrated with psychoanalytic theories of transference and countertransference with both conscious and unconscious dimensions.

It is tempting to draw comparisons between Buddhist emptiness and Bion's "O."

There are certainly identities. However, such comparisons exclude the importance of dependent co-arising. From the perspectives of *śūnyatā* and/or *pratītyasamutpāda*, both the analyst's experience and the analysand's experience can be understood as interrelated and arising dependently within the context created in the dyad. This nonjudgmental response is consistent with Dōgen's more all-inclusive stance described above and points directly to the fundamental Buddhist notion of *pratītyasamutpāda*, which, not unlike a totalistic understanding and use of countertransference (Racker, 1957), views all phenomena as contextual. This fundamental principle, with few exceptions, has been left out of the Buddhist and psychoanalytic conversation (Cooper, 1999b).

From a practical point of view, this fundamental Buddhist principle can contribute to the analyst's understanding and response to psychoanalytic listening. That is, reverie, for example, does not belong exclusively and solely to the analyst, but emerges in the dependently co-arising context of the treatment situation. Both the analyst and analysand contribute consciously and unconsciously to the internal and external experience of the analytic situation. Both analyst and analysand are simultaneously separate and connected. In this regard, the analytic situation is a lived experiential manifestation of the mutually interacting operation of emptiness and dependent co-arising that finds expression in the unsolvable Buddhist paradoxical construct of the identity of the one and the many and the simultaneity of identity and difference. The interacting participants are both one and two; both not one and not two. Ogden captures this basic Zen notion from a psychoanalytic perspective in his paraphrasing and extending of Winnicott's depiction that there is no mother without a baby and no baby without a mother. Ogden writes:

> ... we must live with the paradox (without attempting to resolve it) that there is no such thing as an analysand apart from the relationship with the analyst and no such thing as an analyst apart from the relationship with the analysand. At the same time, from another perspective, there is

obviously an analyst and an analysand who constitute separate physical and psychological entities.

(1997b, p. 720)

Similarly, from this radically nondualistic perspective, this observation can extend to internal experiences such as the analyst's reverie, noted above, and help to keep in mind that consciousness and unconsciousness are also dependently co-arising. Thus, reverie is considered a link between conscious and unconscious. That is, the analyst can make use of seemingly unrelated inner experiences such as what might be initially or superficially viewed as distractions to listening as dependently co-arising through the emerging causes and conditions between the analyst and the analysand and an important aspect of psychoanalytic listening and objective information about the patient's inner life.

Note

1 For a detailed explication and critique, see E. Dōgen (1231), *Bendowa* In: N. Waddell & M. Abe Eds. (2002, pp. 7–30).

References

Cooper, P. (1999b). Buddhist meditation and countertransference: a case study. *American Journal of Psychoanalysis*, 59:71–85.
Dōgen, E. (1241). *Bussho*. In: G. Nishijima & C. Cross (Trans.), *Master Dogen's Shobogenzo, book 2* (pp. 1–32). London: Windbell Publications, 1996.
Hopkins, J. (1983). *Meditation on Emptiness*. Boston, MA: Wisdom Publications.
Komito, D. (1987). *Nagarjuna's "Seventy Stanzas" A Buddhist Psychology of Emptiness*. Ithaca, NY: Snow Lion Publications.
Nagao, G. (1989). *The Foundational Standpoint of Madhyamika Philosophy*. Albany: State University of New York Press.
Nishijima, G. & Cross, C. (1996). *Master Dogen's Shobogenzo, Book 2*. London: Windbell Publications.
Ogden, T. (1997b). Reverie and metaphor: some thoughts on how I work as a psychoanalyst. *International Journal of Psycho-Analysis*, 78:719–732.
Racker, H. (1957). The meaning and uses of countertransference. *Psychoanalytic Quarterly*, 26:303–357.
Salvatti, A. (2019). Writing and transmission in Bion. In: A. Alisobhani & G. Cortorphine (Eds.), *Explorations in Bion's "O" Everything We Know Nothing About*. (pp. 31–38). London & New York: Routledge.
Symington, J. & Symington, N. (1996). *The Clinical Thinking of Wilfred Bion*. London: Routledge.
Waddell & Abe, (2002). *The Heart of Dōgen's Shobogenzo*. Albany: State University of New York Press.

Chapter 8
Dōgen's Expression of Suchness

In this chapter, the Chinese Chan concept of *Inmo*, or suchness, is defined and discussed in relation to Dōgen's *shikantaza* (just sitting) practice along with parallels to Bion's clinical recommendations to relinquish memory, desire, and understanding (1967, 1970). Dōgen advocates a radical nondualistic perspective. That is, as Dōgen emphasizes, the task of the Zen practitioner involves realizing the presently existing unitive nature of reality and then acting upon this unitive realization in the everyday world of duality and multiplicity. This orientation raises the question as to how Zen practice effects the practitioner's mode of being in the world in general and specifically, with respect to this discussion, what impact Zen Buddhist study and practice might have on the psychoanalytic encounter. This nondualistic orientation finds clear expression, especially in terms of a nonjudgmental sense of presence in Dōgen's discussion of *Inmo* or suchness.

Inmo Defined

Inmo is a colloquial Chinese expression that means "Just this," "That which is it," or "The Matter that is It." The Chinese Chan teacher Yunyan Tansheng (780–841) asserts suchness as "Just this is it!" All these alternate translations are ways of pointing to and expressing the ineffable reality, which, as I discussed in the previous chapter, Bion simplifies through his use of "O."

In a parallel to Bion's use of "O" to depict or attempt to name this ineffable reality or at least to note it, the Zen narrative relies on interrogatives such as "what," "where," and "who" to acknowledge and express the unnamable essence of any experience. From the perspective of suchness, these interrogatives are meant as declarative statements that point toward the ineffable truth of reality that is essentially unsayable. For example, the influential sixth ancestor of Zen in China Hui-neng (638–718) exclaims when greeting a new arrival at his monastery. Hui-neng asserts, "What is it that thus comes?" Hence, the statement "What is this!" functions as a declarative, not as a question, and might be better understood as "Just this is it!" (Leighton, 2000, p. 33), or as Dōgen describes in actional terms as: "What use is there going off here and there to practice?" (Waddell & Abe, 2002, p. 2). The antidote is to stay in the present, just as it is, without grasping and without pushing away.

This is it! It is not some other way, not something that is not happening now, whatever that may be. "This" expresses ultimate reality that goes beyond explanation; also, there is no need to explain it. It is not necessary. It is like saying "hand me that." We both know what "that" is, so there is no need to name it. In this regard, the matter which is it is very concrete. Dōgen often uses concrete images to explain it. We need to keep in mind that reality is reality and doesn't care what you call it. This is it, no matter what we think about it, no matter how we feel about it, no matter how you desire it to be.

Inmo functions as a fundamental unifying concept for Dōgen that he refers to throughout his extensive writings. In the opening paragraph of *Fukanzazengi*, "Universal Promotion of the Principles of Zazen" (1227), his first writing upon his return from a four-year pilgrimage in China, Dōgen writes: "If you wish to attain suchness, you should practice suchness without delay" (Abe & Waddell, 2002, p. 3). In the same piece, he discusses suchness in actional terms in a comment that distinguishes his form of *zazen* from meditative absorption by asserting:

> The Zazen I speak of is not learning meditation. It is simply the Dharma-gate of repose and bliss. It is the practice-realization of totally culminated enlightenment. It is things as they are in suchness.
>
> (p. 4)

And:
> Devote your energy to a Way that points directly to suchness.
>
> (p. 6)

Fifteen years later, he devotes a full chapter titled *Inmo*, "Suchness" (1242), included in his master work *Shobogenzo* (Treasury of the True Dharma Eye) to a discussion of this pivotal notion.

We come to Zen practice and to psychotherapy hoping to get somewhere else or to become someone else, but who and where would that be? We are already here, now! Just this is it! It is truly amazing; it is remarkable, this moment, just this moment is it. I am it. You are it. We are it! Now! We are Buddha nature, whether we, as the *Lotus Sutra*[1] notes, like it or not, believe it or not, care or not. This is it! Realization is just this is it! How remarkable! How amazing! Really, yet at the same time, so very ordinary. How did we get here? Dōgen tells us in *Inmo* that there is a natural spark or intention to be it, to realize it, because we already *are* it.

He opens *Inmo* by quoting "Great Zen Master Kokaku," who asserts: "If you want to attain the matter that is it, you must be a person who is it. Already being a person who is it, why worry about the matter that is it?" (Nishijima & Cross, 1996, p. 119). Dōgen then adds these comments to clarify this point. He writes:

> In other words, those who want to attain *the matter which is it* must themselves be *people who are it*. They are already *people who are it*: why should

they worry about [attaining] *the matter which is it* (emphasis in the original quote). He makes the point that directing oneself straight for this supreme truth of bodhi by describing the present as "it."

(p. 119)

Even though everything rises and falls, vanishes, never to return, *Bodhicitta* (enlightened mind) is present. This impulse to awaken the "Zen impulse" (Cooper, 2010, p. 1) will happen to everyone, whether we respond to it or not. *Bodhicitta* emerges from a deep appreciation of impermanence, and you might have noticed that impermanence becomes more obvious as you continue to practice. So, Dōgen argues that the simple *intention* to raise *Bodhicitta* is already verification of suchness. Just sitting, just this, being as it is. There is nothing to wait for; it's already as it is. Dōgen admonishes the student not to devalue the present moment by thinking that realization is somewhere or sometime else. When we devalue the present moment, we devalue our lives. So, Dōgen tells us not to worry. He notes that even worry is just this is it! In his radical nondualism, nothing is excluded. He writes:

> Remember, it happens like this because we are "people who are it." How do we know that we are "people who are it"? We know that we are "people who are it" just from the fact that we want to attain "the matter that is it." Already we possess the real features of a "person who is it"; we should not worry about the already present "matter that is it." Even worry itself is just "the matter that is it," and so it is beyond worry. Again, we should not be surprised that "the matter that is it" is present in such a state. Even if "it" is the object of surprise and wonderment, it is still just "it." And there is "it" about which we should not be surprised. This state cannot be fathomed even by the consideration of buddha, it cannot be fathomed by the consideration of the mind, it cannot be fathomed by the consideration of the Dharma world, and it cannot be fathomed by the consideration of the whole universe. It can only be described "Already you are a person who is it: why worry about [attaining] the matter that is it?" Thus, the "suchness" of sound and form may be "it"; the "suchness" of body and-mind may be "it"; and the "suchness" of the buddhas may be "it."
>
> (Nishijima & Cross, 1996, p. 120)

In his discussion of *Inmo*, Dōgen uses circular logic, a common feature in his writing, to make his point. Initially, he quotes Kokaku, as noted above, to repeat, "If you want to attain the matter that is it, then you must be a person who is it. Since you are a person who is it, why worry about attaining the matter that is it?" (p. 119). However, be reminded that he revises the original in actional not static or reified terms in *Fukanzazengi*, where he writes: "If you wish to attain suchness, you should practice suchness without delay" (Waddell & Abe, 2002, p. 3). Now, in this section of *Inmo*, he turns it around into an expression of his radical nondualism: "How do you know you are a person who is it? Because you want to attain the matter that is it!" (Nishijima & Cross, 1996, p. 119).

One might understandably ask, Wow! Can it be that simple? Dōgen says, "Yes!" Just sit and *be* the matter that is it. Ego is such a trickster and complicates this whole business. Perhaps we would like to think that we understood, penetrated, and realized something complicated and otherworldly profound. As he notes: "We should not worry about the already-present matter which is it" and "We already possess the real features…" (p. 119). The real features refer to the activity of *Bodhicitta*, which is realized in its most pristine form in the practice of *shikantaza*, or as Dōgen describes, *"shinjin datsuraku,"* dropping off body and mind, which he refers to in terms of realizing that body and mind are ultimately not really "me." With minimal personal reflection, it is easy to realize through personal experience that the body has constantly changed and continues to change over our lifetime. No one can escape this reality, which is ultimately the same for everyone. Similarly, we know that mind changes from moment to moment.

For Bion, this is O, the lived narrative in evolution. We may alter or influence the evolution of the narrative at any point by drawing attention to what he describes as a "selected fact." However, we must keep in mind that this intervention is also part of and not separate from the ongoing evolution, which raises the clinical question: "what is the impact of the intervention on the evolution?" When you sit in *shikantaza*, this ongoing evolution, which is in constant motion, becomes immediately obvious. This helps us to understand why Dōgen distinguishes his *zazen* from "learning meditation," quoted above. *Shikantaza* is not a concentration method where the practitioner tries to achieve and maintain one preferred state of mind or tries to get somewhere else. The freedom that *shikantaza* affords makes it abundantly clear that what we call mind is fundamentally impermanent. Dōgen emphasizes this point in terms of practice in *Fukanzazengi*:

> You should therefore cease from practice based on intellectual understanding, pursuing words and following after speech, and learn the backward step that turns your light inward to illuminate yourself. Body and mind will drop away of themselves and your original face will manifest.
> (Abe & Waddell, 2002, p. 3)

Another way to think about or to understand this seemingly paradoxical situation is that Dōgen's *shikantaza* practice and Bion's relinquishing memory, desire, and understanding engender a perceptual shift that makes more obvious something that is already present. Thus the "Middle Way" philosophy finds lived expression in Dōgen's *shikantaza* practice in terms of being with the rise and fall of all phenomena without grasping, without pushing away, and without seeking anything. This is *Inmo* realized and lived. We can easily be seduced by our fantasies, dreams, and wishes as well as our concerns and troubles. We can also attempt to avoid what feels unpleasant and seek what feels or what we imagine might be pleasant. In this regard, Bion notes that we speak to conceal just as much as to reveal truth.

The desire to obtain a goal, to be someone else, or to be somewhere else intrudes into the capacity to maintain a neutral awareness of all experience without attachment or aversion. We have a tendency to push away what is uncomfortable or intolerable and to grasp at what is pleasant and enjoyable. *Shikantaza*, "just sitting" or "only sitting," functions as a choiceless and objectless, all-inclusive awareness that does not prioritize any specific object of concentration and remains free from any notion of goal or progress. In this way, we begin to form a different relationship to sense input and allow intuition into the foreground. This is *Inmo*, Just this is it!

Dōgen reinforces this entire teaching, this whole business of "already being a person of the matter that is it," by noting that even if we do worry about attaining the matter that is it, it is already the ever-present matter that is it. "Tag, you're it!" This point is so very important to Dōgen. He very much wants the student to get it. So much so that he again reinforces this teaching, playfully, in my opinion: "Don't be surprised!" He steps back and says: "Even if it is the object of surprise and wonderment, it is still just it. And there is it about which we should not be surprised" (Nishijima & Cross, 1996, p. 119).

He concludes this section by emphasizing his goal-free orientation toward *Inmo* by noting that we can't understand this through intellect, philosophy, or any other mental considerations. In a parallel with Bion's recommendation to free ourselves from sense-mediated data, Dōgen teaches that realization derives through intuited experience. It can only be described as "Already you are a person who is it: why worry about attaining the matter which is it?" This brings into focus Bion's aversion to memory, desire, and understanding.

Similarly, as with Dōgen, Bion emphasizes the present moment by describing memory and desire as interferences with present experiencing. In the opening sentence of *Notes*, he writes: "Memory is always misleading as a record of fact since it is distorted by the influence of unconscious forces" (in: J. Aguayo & B. Malin, 2013, p. 136).

He further develops this point in 1970:

> But memory depends on the senses. It is limited by the limitations of the senses and their subordination to the pleasure pain principle; memories are therefore fallacious and memory has the defects of its origin in functions of possessiveness and evacuation.
>
> (p. 30)

Bion here reminds the reader that our conditioned habits of mind, our defensive mode of being with ourselves and others operate unconsciously to foreclose the intuited experience of the depths through overreliance on sense data, which saturates the open psychic space where intuition operates in the present moment, in the moment that, as I noted, Dōgen describes as *"Inmo."* This interference obstructs the free and clear evolution of O.

Bion is also, albeit indirectly, saying that overreliance on the senses in conjunction with unconscious defensive processes prevents us from living wholly and fully because our being is split, especially, in this context, in terms of our intuitive capacities being split-off, repressed, or otherwise occluded from access. His mandate from this perspective is a call for and a technique for reclaiming our wholeness. This is also implied in the outcome that he describes later in this article in terms of the wholeness and fullness of each session. He writes: "'Progress' will be measured by the increased number and variety of moods, ideas and attitudes seen in any given session" (p. 137). Bion continues by asserting that "Desires interfere, by absence of mind when observation is essential, with the operation of judgement" and "Memory and desire exercise and intensify those aspects of the mind that derive from sensuous experience. They thus promote capacity derived from sense impressions and designed to serve impressions of sense" (p. 136). Chapter Thirteen, "Ada: A Clinical Study," serves as an example of the impact of study and practice with *Inmo* exerts clinically through a case vignette, which will help to unpack and explicate the abstract aspects of this discussion.

Note

1 See T. Kubo & A. Yuyama (2007).

References

Bion, W. (1967). Notes on memory and desire, In: J. Aguayo & B. Malin (Eds.), *Wilfred Bion: Los Angeles Seminars and Supervision* (pp. 133–149). London: Karnac, 2017. [Originally published in: Bion, W. (1967). Notes on memory and desire. *The Psychoanalytic Forum*, 2:272–273, 279–280.]

Bion, W. (1970). *Attention and Interpretation*. London: Karnac.

Cooper, P. (2010). *The Zen Impulse and the Psychoanalytic Encounter*. London: Routledge.

Dōgen, E. (1227). *Fukanzazengi*. In: N. Waddell & M. Abe (Trans.), *The Heart of Dōgen's Shobogenzo* (pp. 1–6). Albany: State University of New York Press, 2002.

Dōgen, E. (1242) *Inmo*. In: G. Nishijima & C. Cross (Trans.), *Master Dogen's Shobogenzo, Book 2* (pp. 119–128). London: Windbell Publications, 1996.

Kubo, T. & Yuyama, A. (2007). *The Lotus Sutra*. Moraga, CA: BDK America, Inc.

Leighton, D. (2000). *Cultivating the Empty Field: The Silent Illumination of Zen Master Hongzhi*. Rutland, VT: Tuttle.

Waddell & Abe, (2002). *The Heart of Dōgen's Shobogenzo*. Albany: State University of New York Press.

Chapter 9

Bion's Use of "O" and "K"

This chapter provides a review and definition of Bion's use of what he designates as "O" and "K." Two concepts that are central to his later theories and clinical applications. O represents a far-reaching revolution in Bion's earlier basically traditional Freudian and Kleinian psychoanalysis with its knowledge-based emphasis to his shift to a radical experience and truth-based psychoanalysis with a highly subjective eye toward the unique individual, the psychoanalyst, and the relationship between them. We could say that O functions as a sign that represents this radical shift and finds expression in his comment: "Psycho-analysis itself is just a stripe on the coat of the tiger. Ultimately it may meet the Tiger—The Thing Itself—O" (1991, p. 112).

This evolution in his thinking impacts both his theory and his practice of psychoanalysis. European psychoanalyst Rudi Vermote emphasizes the radical departure from Bion's earlier work during this period, which he refers to as "after the Caesura" (2019, p. 1). The focal point of this shift centers on his notion of O, which Reiner describes as Bion's "... most mysterious idea, representing absolute truth and the state of mind necessary to apprehend it. It is a place of experiential awareness rather than judgement" (2012, Kindle Loc. 221). In a similar vein, Salvatti notes that "In his new approach ... what matters is the reality of the session and what could be seized from it" (2019, p. 75).

O becomes the central pivot and reference point to many of his theories, including, for example, his notions of beta and alpha elements and functions, container and contained, and his practice guidelines that include intuition of O, the use of internal reverie as a source of psychoanalytic information; his technical mandate to relinquish memory, desire, and understanding; and his recommendation to cultivate, maintain, and tolerate an active not-knowing until a pattern emerges. Understanding O through emotional experience is crucial to understanding his theories and practice. Through the concept of O, Bion opens the space of psychoanalysis in infinite directions, which he describes as unique to each psychoanalyst, analysand, and to the relationship that develops during the psychoanalytic encounter, as he notes in his conclusion to "Notes on Memory and Desire":

> The foregoing is a brief account distilled from putting the precepts advocated into practice. The theoretical implications can be worked out – by

each psychoanalyst for himself. His interpretations should gain in force and conviction – both for himself and his patient – because they derive from the emotional experience with a unique individual and not from generalized theories imperfectly 'remembered'.

(1967, p. 19)

Reiner speculates that:

> One might view the metaphysical experience of O as the "selected fact" that organizes and helps make sense of Bion's theories.
> (Bion, 1962)

And:

> In terms of clinical work, Bion ascribed central importance to O as the foundation of psychoanalytic practice, the necessary psychoanalytic perspective upon which the success of analytic work depends.

(2012, Loc. 231)

Bion's Purpose

In the first of a series of lectures that Bion delivered to the psychoanalytic community in Los Angeles in 1979, Bion uses the experience of the recognition of anxiety to exemplify Kant's notion of "thing-in-itself" in relation to the psychoanalytic encounter. He argues that the language that psychoanalysts use to describe nonsensuous states, such as anxiety, is inadequate because it "is derived entirely from sensuous experience" (in: Aguayo & Malin, 2013, p. 2). He elaborates his point further:

> Now, I think that I can explain my point in this way: we are all of us without exception, quite sure that we know about the reality of anxiety. So much so that it doesn't strike us as odd. But, it hasn't got a smell, it hasn't got a shape, you can't see it, you can't hear it, it is not open to any of our physical senses. Nevertheless, the language that we talk is derived entirely from what one might call sensuous experience. One is therefore constantly using a very inadequate form of language to talk about something which is absolutely known to us, about which there can be no disagreement whatsoever.

(pp. 2–3)

Bion continues by reiterating his point: "We are most of us in agreement, and convinced about the reality of certain things which are simply not perceptible to the senses" (p. 3). Given this basic assumption, Bion's expressed concern centers on his observation that whatever we have to say about the experience is not the experience itself, it is what he describes as "secondary" (p. 3). However, he adds, "What we are concerned with is, however, the thing itself: the reality, the fundamental reality with which psychoanalysts have to deal with" (p. 3).

Given his concern for adequate and effective communication both within the analytic setting and between colleagues, Bion attempts to resolve this discrepancy between language and the ineffable, nonsensuous, unknowable reality of psychoanalytic experience or "the thing-in-itself," which he regards as absolutely necessary, through the use of "O." He writes:

> Since I don't know what reality is, and since I want to talk about it, I have tried to deal with this position by simply giving it a symbol "O" and just calling it "O", ultimate reality, the absolute truth. There are various phrases of this kind, which one can pick up from philosophy, from religion and so on, but meaning by that, the fundamental reality with which we are concerned—and which we have to talk about and deal with in terms which are not adapted to that use at all.
>
> (p. 3)

The Evolution of O in Bion's Thinking

Bion hints at O in *Elements of Psychoanalysis* through reference to Kant's "thing-in-itself" (*Ding an sich*). He writes: "I shall therefore close the discussion by assuming there is a central abstraction unknown because it is unknowable yet revealed in an impure form" (1963, p. 7). He adds, "From this definition it is clear that supposed psycho-analytical elements cannot be observed" (p. 7). He then references Kant, "In this respect it is not unlike Kant's concept of a thing-in-itself—it is not knowable though" (p. 7).

While Bion does not name this unknowable experience as O in this offering, he certainly points toward it as the center of his experiential and truth-based psychoanalysis: "It will be a 'central abstraction unknown because unknowable' but adumbrated in impure form, by its verbal representation" (p. 8). This Kantian influence leads Bion clinically to assert in *Transformations*, where O is explicitly stated: "The intense experience is ineffable but once known cannot be mistaken" (1965, p. 74).

Bion continues to further elaborate his use of O in *Transformations*. He writes:

> My theory would seem to imply a gap between phenomena and the thing-in-itself and all that I have said is not incompatible with Plato, Kant, Berkeley, and Klein, to name a few, who show to the extent to which they believe that a curtain of illusion separates us from reality.
>
> (1965, p. 147)

Regarding this "curtain of illusion" that he speaks of, Bion points to both conscious and unconscious influences:

> Some consciously believe the curtain of illusion to be a protection against truth which is essential to the survival of humanity; the remainder of us believe it unconsciously but no less tenaciously for that.
>
> (1965, p. 147)

Bion describes his use of O more clearly and definitively in *Attention and Interpretation*:

> It stands for the absolute truth in and of any object; it is assumed that this cannot be known by any human being; it can be known about, its presence can be recognized and felt, but it cannot be known.
>
> (p. 30)

The phrase "In and of any object" in the above quote (p. 30) points toward the infinite, all-pervasiveness of O. This would, by definition, include all language and all thought, in other words, what Bion alludes to by K, which will be discussed below.

O continues to thread its way through Bion's subsequent writing. For instance, in *Cogitations*, he writes:

> Many mystics have been able to describe a situation in which it is believed that there really is a power, a force that cannot be measured, or weighed or assessed by the mere human being with the mere human mind.
>
> (1992, p. 371)

Bion's technical mandate to relinquish memory, desire, and understanding increases the possibility of freeing up intuition engendering and experiencing at-one-ment. That is, when consciousness is dominated by memory, desire, and understanding and when sense-awareness and linear thinking are dominating, intuition remains covered over, if you will, and inaccessible. Actually, intuition is always operating, but can remain hidden in the background of perceptual experiencing and discursive thinking, thus interfering with at-one-ment or being O.

Cautionary Preface to Defining Bion's O and K

Bion was primarily interested in "openings." A clear-cut definition of O, which might become reified and internalized as a psychic space saturating preconception, would run counter to his agenda to remain open to the infinite possibilities potentially available during the psychoanalytic encounter. On this point, the psychoanalyst Thomas Ogden notes:

> Bion uses such terms as 'the thing in itself', 'the Truth', 'Reality' and 'the experience' to convey a sense of what he has in mind by O. But since Bion also insists that O is unknowable, unnamable, beyond human apprehension, these nouns are misleading and contrary to the nature of O.
>
> (2004, p. 290)

O can only be realized in the moment, according to Ogden, "... by allowing its meanings to emerge (its effects to be experienced) as one goes. The effects are ephemeral and survive only as long as the present moment, for no experience can be stored and called up again" (p. 291).

Rhode expresses this point clearly and succinctly in relation to the notion of psychoanalytic "cure." He writes:

> As the variable, 'O' activates a state of becoming unrelated to any claim to therapeutic progress or cure. From the mystical perspective nothing progresses or is cured. There is either an evasion or a recognition of 'O' by way of a becoming.
>
> (1998, p. 118)

These points should be kept clearly in mind as we approach any specific definition of Bion's use of O and K.

O and K Defined

Drawing from philosophy and specifically from Kant's notion of the ineffable "thing-in-itself," referred to above, Bion uses the symbol O to point to the ineffable, unknowable constantly evolving emotional Truth of the psychoanalytic encounter. O and K function for Bion as two distinct ways for experiencing and speaking about what he describes as the data of psychoanalysis.

As I understand it, O and K function to represent and to speak about the core experiential aspects of Bion's mandate to relinquish memory, desire, and understanding, as he begins to articulate, as if thinking out loud in his book *Transformations* (1965), and that he starts to describe in his brief but highly condensed article "Notes on Memory and Desire" (1967) and that he further elaborates in his book *Attention and Interpretation* (1970). In this regard, resistance is conceptualized as a resistance to the "becoming of O."

Buddhist Ignorance in Relation to O

Similarly, the Buddhist notion of *avidya* or ignorance functions as an active understanding of the process involved in resisting the truth of existence, which from the Zen perspective is conceptualized as an active not-knowing or ignoring of the truth represented in the Three Marks of Existence, which includes no inherently existing permanent self, the impermanence of all phenomena, and the truth of the resulting suffering through clinging to enjoyable experiences and pushing away hated experiences. These three conditions are described by Buddhists as the source of all suffering. They are represented visually as the pig, the snake, and the bird at the hub of the Buddhist *Bhavachakra*, The Wheel of Life and Death.

With relevance to both Buddhism and psychoanalysis, Bion describes this resistance as "The gap between reality and the personality, or, as I prefer to call it, the inaccessibility of O, is an aspect of life with which the analyst is familiar under the guise of resistance" (1965, p. 147).

However, as noted above, Bion conceptualizes resistance in terms of the Truth of O, which is a departure from traditional views of resistance, such as related to the manifestation of transference dynamics or as a defense against libidinal or aggressive drives. He writes:

> Resistance is only manifest when the threat is contact with what is believed to be real. There is no resistance to anything because it is believed to be false. Resistance operates because it is feared that the reality of the object is imminent. O represents this dimension of anything whatever – its reality.
> (1965, p. 147)

In this regard, Bion acknowledges the infinite dimensions inherent in psychic space. Thus, for Bion, the fundamental ground of psychoanalysis is O. This is a "groundless ground" (Braver, 2012, p. 194) that is constantly in motion and at once both empty and full. Bion (1970) uses O to keep the psychic space open and unsaturated with preconceived meanings. He is interested in an infinite expansion of meaning, which any specific definition would, from his point of view, inhibit or foreclose. The question from the realizational perspective becomes how does one define, understand, and experience O?

Bion describes his use of O as follows:

> I shall use the sign O to denote that which is the ultimate reality represented by terms such as ultimate reality, absolute truth, the godhead, the infinite, the thing-in-itself. O does not fall in the domain of knowledge or learning save incidentally; it can be 'become', but it cannot be 'known'.
> (1970, p. 26)

By asserting that "O can become," Bion is emphasizing the dynamic activity of O over the notion of O as a static object or distinct state of mind like a posited element to be discovered in the future, such as the Rinzai Zen notion of *satori*, posited as a fixed endpoint described in Chapter Five, "Suzuki and Dōgen." This is important in terms of understanding the dynamic, inclusive relationship between O and K as well as both Bion's and Dōgen's emphasis on the notion of a continuously evolving present. Bion adds:

> It stands for the absolute truth in and of any object; it is assumed that this cannot be known by any human being; it can be known about, its presence can be recognized and felt, but it cannot be known.
> (p. 30)

O as Personal Experience

I believe that we each come into our own unique experiential knowing of O through our own practice. This is so because the unique causes and conditions of each of our individual lives engender our own personal worldview. Here is an example of experiencing "O":

> In my experience O unfolds at times with clarity; other times ambiguously, hidden from awareness or quite obvious. Sometimes I completely miss it and forget about it, at other times I stumble over it, like stubbing my big toe on a chair leg in the dark; other times its so blindingly obvious that it can be embarrassing. Whether obvious or oblivious to me, O circles endlessly like the Zen enzo, a symbol and expression of emptiness and becoming; full and complete, yet translucent, almost transparent, simultaneously opening and closing; opening to new and unforeseen openings; opening to closings that transmute into new openings. All the while turning and being turned between delusion and realization; between somethingness and nothingness; all inclusive everythings, whole being Buddha nature; self, no-self; big Self, small self; a moment of encounter; the cosmic infinite everythingness. O points to a psychoanalysis free of fixed positions, formulas and preconceived techniques, and, to use a Zen phrase, O functions "to hold the empty space" so prone to becoming saturated, suffocated and closed down with meaning and old habit formations. All bringing the attention to the activity of Buddha nature realization manifesting in the practice of just sitting right now.
>
> (Cooper, 2019, p. 100)

Intention

What drives the intention that mobilizes the intuition of O? This intention is fueled by "F," Bion's notation for faith, that is, faith in the unknowable and ineffable truth of O. There is nothing complicated about this. It is a fundamental aspect of being, plain and simple, that he describes in actional terms as an experiencing capacity. In this regard, as Rhode notes, O is an empty function from which everything evolves and which is simultaneously the lived and the experienced evolution of everything. Nothing is excluded. From Rhode's perspective, O can be considered as a "sign," a "discontinuity," or an "empty device." As a sign, he describes the function of O as "… Bion's conception of a religious vertex on which the void originates signs" (1998, p. 53). Regarding the psychoanalytic encounter, the ongoing narrative, which for Bion approximates emotional truth, is the lived O of the session. This comment reflects Bion's tendency to strive for precision. Thus, his language is terse, direct, cogent, and right to the point. On this point, Eigen writes:

> He struggles to say exactly what he means, to see what he says and say what he sees. At the same time the very saying and seeing are parts of an ongoing process in which psychic life strives to (re)create itself. However, part

of Bion's elusiveness is not simply due to the incessant movement of the experiences (the experiencing capacity) he struggles with, but his success in often saying something one scarcely believes he is saying. One's difficulty as a reader is, finally, not Bion's abstruseness, but his nakedness. One does not want to hear or bear or believe in Bion's message.

(1985, p. 321)

It is our own resistance to lived truth that renders Bion incomprehensible. In this regard, resistance is conceptualized as resistance to the becoming of O. Bion notes that it is easier to know "about" than to being and experiencing.

"K"—Knowledge

In contrast or as a complement to O, Bion uses the notation K to point to what can be known though the senses and expressed through language. As such, K functions as his term for knowledge. He writes: "K denotes a complex idea, or a series of ideas, in its most simple and uncomplicated form" (1990, p. 11).

In this regard, K functions to contain and formulate what Bion describes as a "configuration" (1970, p. 55) and which functions to represent and communicate an approximation of the lived, ineffable, emotional experience of the realized O. On this point, in terms of the individual "mystic" within the context of organizational structures, he writes:

> The configuration that represents the relationship between the mystic and the institution can be recognized in, and be the representation of, the relationship between the emotional experience and the representative formulation (words, music, painting, etc.) designed to contain it. The same configuration can be seen in the relationship between the Dionysian emotional experience and the Apollonian representation. Direct access to the O of the mystic and the O of the Dionysian orgy is both contained and restrained by the religious dogmas substituted for them in the minds of 'ordinary' people.

(1970, p. 85)

K then refers to what Zen teachings describe as relative reality, the object of perception, and representative of O, and what can be known through the senses and discursive reasoning. He argues that when not the result of the evolution of O, K can function as a resistance that interferes with the realization of O, except when O evolves into K (O→K), which otherwise remains unknowable. K as a variable depends on one's point of view, or what he describes as a "vertex" or, as he writes, "vertices such as religious, aesthetic and scientific often represented in the world of reality by persons and their points of view" (1990, p. 11). K then, from the Zen point of view, describes relative or empirical reality, the object of dualistic perception, a unique expression of the absolute. In this regard, K functions as an expression that is representative of O. That is, O can be known nonsensuously through intuition but can only be approximated and represented through the senses, discursive reasoning, and verbal communication.

It is important to reiterate that Bion's phrase "in and of any object," quoted above, points toward the infinite, all-pervasiveness of O. This would—by definition—include all language and all thought, in other words, what Bion alludes to by K. The fact that O, as Bion notes, cannot be known, does not mean O is not present. Of course, from this perspective, O cannot be known in the usual sense-impression or cognitive meaning of knowing, because in unitive experiencing, as Dōgen notes from the Zen perspective, ultimately there is no subject/object separation.

For Bion, the knowing referred to by O is intuited through what he describes as "at-one-ment." Bion's technical mandate to relinquish memory, desire, and understanding increases the possibility of freeing up intuition and engendering and experiencing at-one-ment. That is, when consciousness is dominated by memory, desire, and understanding and when sense-awareness and linear thinking are dominating, intuition remains covered over, if you will, and inaccessible. Actually, intuition is always operating, but can remain hidden in the background of perceptual experiencing and discursive thinking. Bion's point regarding clinical impact can be summarized in terms of this question: "How do we talk about real life without being misleading or incomprehensible?" He argues that "… the analyst should always be talking about real life. No interpretation is any good unless it is reminiscent of real life" (1990, p. 12).

In Zen parlance we speak of "chopping wood and carrying water; eating when hungry and drinking when thirsty" to emphasize the real-life aspect of experience. It is captured beautifully, for example, in the Zen Master Joshu's answer to the monk who asked, "What is the meaning of Bodhidharma coming from the west?" Joshu answered, "The cypress in the garden." He was not going to engage in abstract philosophical speculation, just simply the lived here and now present of real-life experience. This point is captured beautifully in another encounter dialog, "Joshu's Wash Your Bowl," the 39th koan in the 13th-century koan collection *The Book of Serenity:*

> A monk asked Joshu, "I have just entered the monastery: please give me some guidance."
> Joshu said, "Have you had breakfast yet?"
> The monk said, "Yes I have eaten."
> Joshu continues, "Then go wash your bowl."
>
> (Cleary, T., 2005, p. 171)

In this regard, ineffable O can only be known and spoken about indirectly when the intuited lived experience of O evolves into K and spoken about. He cautions that language itself derives from sense-based experience and is also limited to K.

This core assumption and theoretical distinction between O and K and the related technique of relinquishing memory, desire, and understanding derive from a dualistic assumption rooted in Kant's notion of "Thing-in-itself", and, as I will discuss in Chapter Eleven, "Bion and Dōgen: Realizational Practice, Emotional Truth," represent a major difference with Dōgen's nondualistic assumptions. That is, for Bion, noumenon and phenomena are fundamentally separate. A posited unknowable essence cannot be known but, as Bion notes, only intuited. Bion writes:

> Restating this in terms of psycho-analytic experience, the psycho-analyst can know what the patient says, does, and appears to be, but cannot know the O of which the patient is an evolution: he can only 'be' it.
> (1970, p. 27)

In this manner, Bion "operationalized" the Kantian "Thing-in-itself" as noumenon for psychoanalytic purposes through his use of O and K and through his distinction between what can be experienced through intuition and what can be known through the senses. He thus transforms psychoanalytic realizations from static objects of knowledge to a fluid ongoing, evolving realizational experiencing, both beginningless and endless. Bion's realizational orientation is tersely if not poignantly expressed clinically in the following series of observations:

> Out of the darkness and formlessness something evolves.
> (1967, p. 136)
> It shares with dreams the quality of being wholly present or unaccountably and suddenly absent.
> (p. 137)
> What is "known" about the patient is of no further consequence: it is either false or irrelevant. If it is "known" by patient and analyst, it is obsolete.
> (p. 136)
> Otherwise the evolution of the session will not be observed at the only time when it can be observed—while it is taking place.
> (p.137)
> The psychoanalyst should aim at achieving a state of mind so that at every session he feels he has not seen the patient before. If he feels he has, he is treating the wrong patient.
> (p. 138)

It is from this perspective that Bion advocates the clinical practice of relinquishing memory, desire, and understanding as, for example, when he asserts most cogently, "Discard your memory; discard the future tense of your desire; forget them both, both what you know and what you want, to leave space for a new idea" (1980, p. 11).

For both Bion and Dōgen, this reality is not objectifiable, not conceptualizable, and not realized through thinking or through other sensory modalities, although O is always present, evolving and functioning in all experience, including K, whether realized or not.

References

Aguayo, J. & Malin, B. (2013). *Wilfred Bion: Los Angeles Seminars and Supervision.* London: Karnac.
Bion, W. (1963). *Elements of Psychoanalysis.* London: Karnac.
Bion, W. (1965). *Transformations.* London: Karnac.
Bion, W. (1970). *Attention and Interpretation.* London: Karnac.
Bion, W. (1980). *Bion in New York and São Paulo.* E. F. Bion, (Ed.). Perthshire: Clunie Press.
Bion, W. (1990). *Brazilian Lectures: 1973 São Paulo, 1974 Rio de Janeiro / São Paulo.* London: Karnac Books.
Bion, W. (1991). *A Memoir of the Future.* London: Karnac.
Bion, W. (1992). *Cogitations.* London: Karnac.
Braver, L. (2012). *Groundless Grounds: A Study of Wittgenstein and Heidegger.* Cambridge, MA: MIT Press.
Cleary, T. (2005). *The Book of Serenity.* Boston, MA: Shambhala.
Cooper, P. (2019). *Zen Insight, Psychoanalytic Action: Two Arrows Meeting.* New York & London: Routledge.
Eigen, M. (1985). Toward Bion's starting point: Between catastrophe and faith. *International Journal of Psycho-Analysis,* 66:321–330.
Ogden, T. (2004). An introduction to the reading of Bion. *International Journal of Psycho-Analysis,* 85:285–300.
Reiner, A. (2012). *Bion and Being: Passion and the Creative Mind.* London: Karnac.
Rhode, E. (1998). *On Hallucination, Intuition and the Becoming of "O."* Binghamton & Cluj: ESF Publishers.
Salvatti, A. (2019). Writing and transmission in Bion. In: A. Alisobhani & G. Cortorphine (Eds.), *Explorations in Bion's "O" Everything We Know Nothing About,* (pp. 31–38). London & New York: Routledge, 2019.
Vermote, R. (2019). *Reading Bion.* London & New York: Routledge.

Part Four

Realizational Perspectives

Chapter 10

Assimilation and Accommodation

Zen Buddhism's transmission to the west occurred during a time of major cultural transition. In the wake of World War II and the Korean conflict, for the United States, this transition coincided with the strong opposition to the Viet Nam war and the rise of the counterculture movement with its increasing interest in a variety of eastern ideas, religions, and practices such as yoga, Vedanta, and the focus of this exploration, Zen Buddhism. This transition involved the dependently co-arising inter-contextual interaction between both eastern and western cultural traditions and ideas that can be fruitfully viewed through the lens of the processes of assimilation and accommodation.

For the purposes of this offering, simply stated, by "assimilation" I am referring to the process of absorbing of new information. Accommodation in this context refers to the alterations in psychic structure that allow for the assimilated material to become integrated with and modify previously existing psychic structures. From the Zen perspective, the concept of "no fixed point," discussed in Chapter One, expresses this same process in more general terms.

From this perspective, this chapter examines the interacting processes of cultural accommodation and assimilation leading to American forms of Zen that have emerged and have become rooted in North American soil, as exemplified in the one-to-one psychoanalytic encounter as well as the overall psychoanalytic response to Zen Buddhism in terms of levels of acceptance and/or rejection. This process of assimilation and accommodation involves making connections between diverse, frequently contradictory elements of psychoanalytic theory and technique with Zen Buddhist religious principles, soteriological aims, and varied associated practices designed to actualize aims such as one-on-one encounters with a teacher, structured ritual practices, and meditation techniques. This process requires integrating these diverse elements into a multicolored tapestry of shared understanding. In this regard, speaking of Bion's O, Grotstein notes: "Bion's conception of O becomes the arch symbol for the collective mystique that wrapped itself around the elements of this collective mystery of knowing and being known" (2019, p. 19).

The Psychoanalytic Encounter

Within the one-to-one context of the psychoanalytic encounter assimilation and accommodation occur on both conscious and unconscious levels through the operation of intuitional and cognitive capacities with both mutually interacting linear and circular aspects. By this I mean that, on the one hand, there is an incremental and ongoing development in which new insights are built upon the foundations of preexisting building blocks, many of which become questioned, altered, or eliminated as a result of the process. At the same time, a process of refinement and integration occurs through circling repeatedly through previously integrated experiences. These capacities oscillate between foreground and background with either one or the other dominating consciousness at any given moment. For instance, the process of accommodation finds expression in Antonino Ferro's discussion of the "narrative derivative" (2002, p. 184), which functions as a clue as to how the analyst can accommodate to the analysand's internal experience as expressed in the analysand's narrative. He writes:

> But we can also consider the patient's communication as emerging from the immediacy of what goes on in the here and now—a real time response to the emotional impulse of the relational moment. This last perspective offers us the opportunity to modulate our interventions continually, so as to facilitate an expansion of the capacity to think.
>
> (p. 184)

In other words, according to Ferro, the patient is offering the analyst clues, sometimes more direct than at other times, into how to interact in a way that keeps the conversation fresh, open, and fruitful. In this manner, the attuned analyst assimilates the patient's views and makes accommodations that alter previous preconceptions about the patient that contribute to more attuned responses. In turn, the analysand will, over time, question and modify false perceptions of reality. Ferro's notion will be examined further below.

Bion conceptualizes these processes between individuals within the one-to-one psychoanalytic encounter, as described in the previous chapter, in terms of the "evolution of O," the emotionally intuited truth to K, conceptualized knowledge. Dōgen conceptualizes these processes on a nonexclusive, all-inclusive "cosmological dimension" in terms of "relative and absolute being" (Abe, 1992).

During the psychoanalytic encounter, assimilation and accommodation processes can be summarized as follows. Initially, the patient mostly talks and the analyst mostly listens; thus, cognitively and consciously the analyst takes in (assimilates) new information about the patient. At the same time, through the operation of internal reverie, the analyst is also receiving the patient's unconscious communications. One important way that psychoanalysis conceptualizes this unconscious communication process is through the controversial notion of projective identification, which has its origins in preverbal life. As an aside, given the controversy regarding projective identification, it will be helpful to summarize the various ways the term is understood. Thomas Ogden provides this succinct and clear description: "Projective identification is a psychological process that is at once a type of defense, a mode of communication, a primitive form of object relations, and a pathway for psychological change" (1993, p. 21). Regarding the latter, in terms of the dependently co-arising context of the realizational perspective, as Ogden notes, projective identification functions "... as a pathway for psychological change, projective identification is a process by which feelings like those that one is struggling with are psychologically processed by another person and made available for reinternalization in an altered form" (p. 21).

As these unconscious communications emerge into awareness through the analyst's intuitive capacities, they can then be transformed into cognitions and expressed through the mediation of language in the form of notations or interpretations. As will be demonstrated in Chapter Thirteen, "Ada: A Clinical Study," through a clinical vignette, the analyst's intuited understanding of the patient's experience can remain silently contained for the time being. The content of the analyst's response will be influenced by and mediated through language made available through the theories that the analyst has internalized. All the material that has been assimilated will contribute to the accommodations that are made in terms of how the analyst perceives, experiences, understands, responds to, and interacts with the patient. As mentioned above, Ferro conceptualizes this process of assimilation and accommodation in terms of "narrative derivatives," which he notes, "... act as 'carriers' towards the knowable by means of operations whereby a narrative fabric is woven" (2005, p. 2). It is through the narrative derivative Ferro informs the reader that:

> every patient tells us constantly how we must be and how we must comport ourselves in order to reach him; one of the possible ways of listening to what the patient tells us after an interpretation is to regard it as a comment on the interpretation itself ... but must be used in the analytic 'kitchen' in such a way that adjustments required can be made.
>
> (2009, pp. 167–168)

Simultaneously, the patient is also getting to know the analyst filtered through a combination of actual perceptions and unconscious preconceptions that influence perception. These perceptions are colored through unconscious preconceptions that are conceptualized psychoanalytically in terms of transferences. Over time, through the ongoing interactions between the analyst and the analysand, accommodations are made as preconceptions are brought into conscious awareness and questioned.

The Larger Picture

Extending these basic principles of assimilation and accommodation beyond the consultation room, a similar process occurs in relation to the interactions between psychoanalysis as a body of knowledge supported by a collection of diverse and often contradictory theories and Zen, a realizational system also supported by an extensive and diverse body of knowledge that interacts with methodologies geared toward actualizing its salvational goals. Over time, through training, study, and the experience of personal analysis, the analyst internalizes theory and practice in ways that contribute to what we may refer to as one's "analytic self." This contributes to the analyst's mode of being in the world. Now suppose the analyst becomes exposed to Zen. Suppose the analyst reads about it or begins to practice and study with a teacher, which, over time, has become more prevalent.[1] The analyst then will begin to assimilate new information, which will be rejected or accepted to one degree or another. In the latter case, the newly assimilated experiences and related material will be accommodated and integrated within existing structures as they become modified, based on the interaction between preexisting psychic structures and the assimilated material, which, in turn, influence the analyst's conception and response to the analytic encounter in both conscious and unconscious ways. Similar processes are occurring for the Zen practitioner who becomes interested in psychoanalysis. As a result, both psychoanalysis and Zen Buddhism continue to develop and evolve in new directions within the context of the host culture.

Through assimilation, new ideas and practices spill into and are both mediated and modified by existing internal structures and preconceptions. Many are unconscious. Assimilation involves projection, which colors and filters one's perception of what new material is being presented and what will be assimilated. In contrast, accommodation involves the deconstruction to varying degrees and reorganization of existing cognitive structures. These processes can be radical, for instance, such as in a major conversion that engenders a deconstruction or abandonment of many, if not all, preexisting structures. Alternatively, accommodations may be minimal. They may depend on the emotional attachment to the existing structures in relation to the emotional impact of new structures, both of which emerge contextually in a mutually dependent co-arising dynamic, as described in Chapter Seven.

Through accommodation, existing structures become transformed as the assimilated content is internalized and becomes integral to the resulting structural alterations. As a result, new forms emerge, such as is often described as "American Zen" or "Beat Zen," in terms of modifications to the mental health field in various versions of "contemplative psychotherapy," or as is exemplified in what I am elaborating psychoanalytically, in this offering as the "Realizational Perspective," as will be described in the next chapter. This orientation evolved and developed over time through a continuously evolving process of assimilation and accommodation, the result of the ongoing influence of study, practice, and deepening familiarity with both disciplines.

Within a context provided by a transitional period characterized by a radical questioning and reorganization of values and priorities, an evolution occurs. Through a process of simultaneous and mutual influence in the Zen and psychoanalytic narrative, the trend continues in the direction of movement from an objective, philosophical, intellectual, experience-distant, and speculative narrative, as exemplified in Fromm's work (1960), over time to a predominantly but not exclusive subjectivity, largely informed by experience, practice, and an emerging experience-near narrative. This shift in the Zen and psychoanalytic dialog began to unfold in new directions generated by individuals who are deeply immersed in both disciplines as psychoanalysts, psychoanalytic educators, ordained Zen Buddhist priests, and formally transmitted Zen teachers.

Shifts: Objectivity/Subjectivity

The Zen Buddhist scholar Peter Hershock describes these mutually interacting personal subjective/experiential influences, along with the larger societal and cultural changes and with equal relevance to psychoanalysis, as creating "The development of a deepening rift between what might be called objective/external and subjective/internal approaches to most accurately presenting Zen" (2014, p. xv). Similarly, this trend that Hershock describes regarding religious studies can be observed in the Zen and psychoanalytic dialog as well.

The cultural shift from a predominantly objective/scientific orientation to a subjective/experiential orientation is increasingly active in psychoanalysis, especially but not exclusively among practitioners who emphasize a realizational orientation. Psychoanalysis reflects and exemplifies this shift in terms, for example, of the movement over the course of its development and evolution from a "one-person" endeavor with its notions of pathology and cure to a two-person mutually influencing, contextually arising, dyadic context. This shift finds expression in the distinction that Bion makes between "sensuous and non-sensuous experience" (1970).[2]

This shift is also evident in Bion's emphasis on the uniqueness of the individual and the relevance of the psychoanalytic encounter to reality. For example, in response to a question regarding the uniqueness of psychoanalysis, during a series of seminars that he gave in New York City in 1977, he offers this response:

> What makes it unique is that there are two unique people in the room. The more respect one has for the individual the more obvious it is that there is no other "you" and no other "him" or "her". On the other hand, there is something wrong with an analysis which doesn't remind both the analysand and the analyst of real life. What is it about if it has no resemblance to the universe we live in—a universe of ideas and thoughts and feelings?
>
> (1980, pp. 18–19)

Bion, for example, in questioning "Medicine as a Model" tracks this movement from scientific objectivity to an experiential and subjective model for psychoanalysis notes:

> Most people think of psycho-analysis, as Freud did, as a method of treatment for a complaint. The complaint was regarded as similar to a physical ailment which, when you know what it is, has to be treated in accordance

with the rules of medicine. The parallel with medicine was, and still is, useful. But as psycho-analysis has grown so it has been seen to differ from physical medicine until the gap between them has passed from the obvious to the unbridgeable. [And] But the more we see of psycho-analysis the more the models become inadequate to define, report, or apply psycho-analysis. Differentiation has meant that models which were illuminating have become opaque and often misleading even to psychoanalysts.

(1970, p. 6)

Religious Expression

Examples of assimilation and accommodation from the religious domain find expressions, for instance, in the work of Rubin Hábito and Robert Kennedy. Hábito, a Jesuit priest, encountered Zen as a missionary in Japan where he was ordained and received dharma transmission from Yamada Koun, Roshi. The mutual influences of both his Catholic background and Zen Buddhism find expression in his books, *Living Zen, Loving God* (2004) and *Healing Breath: Zen for Christians and Buddhists in a Wounded World* (2006).

Robert Kennedy, a Jesuit and a psychoanalyst, also encountered Zen in Japan and, like Hábito, was ordained by Koun Roshi. His books *Zen Spirit, Christian Spirit* (1996) and *Zen Gifts to Christians* (2000), as these titles suggest, both authors offer a mixing together of the two traditions. Interestingly, as an aside, Kennedy serves a traditional Catholic Celebration of the Eucharist during his Zen retreats. Many of his attendees are Catholic nuns and monks.

The trend toward accommodation and assimilation is evident in each of these authors' work, fueled by the trend toward subjectivity and experience and away from objectivity and science. Psychoanalysis within itself and in relation to the influence of Zen reflects this shift in the larger culture. Alternatively, from this vantage point, the rise of objectivity and evidence-based behavioral therapies may, from this perspective, be viewed as a resistance to subjective and experiential trends that question preconceived beliefs and that emphasize relationships and actions. In this regard, these approaches can limit what may be assimilated and the extent to which accommodations will occur, which, for instance, has engendered an expanding "secular Buddhism," largely associated with the current mindfulness movement and mindfulness-based behavioral technologies.

Both Zen and psychoanalysis, when viewed from the realizational perspective, address this tendency to resist psychic change. For example, speaking of the resistance to Bion's later ideas, Australian analysts Joan and Neville Symington write:

Therefore the causal notions that underpin much of Freud's theory and practice and which are present in a deep-rooted way in the minds of many analysts obstruct the mind from arriving at comprehension of the development process.

(1996, p. 7)

They offer the following advice:
The reader needs to purge her mind as far as possible of these 'tenets' of psychoanalytic faith. Adherence to these theories will block understanding Bion's analysis of the analytic process [And] We believe, however, that if the reader tries to hold on to these Freudian 'tenets' she will not understand the work of Bion.

(p. 12)

Similarly, The Zen scholar Steven Heine, speaking of Dogen's scathing critique of the pre-Buddhist Senika belief in the existence and immortality of a "soul," notes: This belief:

… still lingers among Buddhist theorists and infects various forms of Zen thought. This predisposition becomes the foremost barrier to enlightenment, very difficult to displace and overthrown because the assumption of duality between this moment and eternity infuses everyday thought in ways that have devastating implications for the attainment of spiritual realization.

(2020, p. 124)

The deeply rooted resistance to questioning or relinquishing old carefully guarded and tightly held religious beliefs or theoretical principles, whether conscious or unconscious, engendered a negative reaction to Bion's later formulations. When his innovations in theory and practice contradicted or negated Klein's or Freud's theories, the critiques among the "faithful" were rationalized by questioning Bion's sanity.

Along similar lines but from a more philosophical perspective, Cobb and Ives (1990) present an article by the eminent Zen Buddhist scholar Masao Abe titled "Kenotic God and Dynamic Sunyata," which offers a detailed examination of Buddhist emptiness, a concept that in relation to dependent co-arising, forms the center of the Zen salvational endeavor, as discussed in Chapter Seven. Abe's discussion is followed by responses from prominent Jewish and Christian scholars. Abe's agenda centers on questioning reified and brittle notions of "God" in an endeavor to open these traditions into a deeper level of engagement through the Zen Buddhist understanding of emptiness. In this regard, the goal to successfully engender deepened engagement depends on the assimilation and accommodation of the Buddhist notion of emptiness.

From Dōgen Zen's actional and relational orientation, especially as elaborated by Kim (2004, 2007), it becomes clear that the clarity and realizational experiences that practice can engender, provide the practitioner with the option to question and change reified beliefs, values, and desires. As both Abe and Kim suggest, the individual can strive for outcomes beyond those that have influenced previous choices and actions. Both Zen and psychoanalysis create the opportunity to shift old habituated relational dynamics once they evolve into conscious awareness. In this regard, in terms of the relationship between the primary actional motivators, wisdom, and compassion, for example, Hershock notes:

> ... cultivating wisdom is thus a process, first, of realizing that relationality is more basic than "things" that are "related," and second, that deepening wisdom is inseparable from expanding compassion. In other words, Buddhist wisdom is relational transformation.
>
> (2014, p. 10)

Mind-to-Mind Transmission

A significant and central pivot regarding actional and relational dynamics finds expression in the Zen notion of "mind-to-mind transmission," a core teaching that distinguishes Zen Buddhism from other forms of Buddhism of the time and that can be paraphrased as "a special transmission outside of the teachings beyond words and letters that points directly to the mind and heart and that facilitates seeing one's true and realized nature" (my paraphrase). This orientation clearly highlights and prioritizes the lived relationship between student and teacher and finds clear expression in the Zen literature, such as in countless encounter dialogs, which Hershock, for example, describes as "... the skillfully embodied interaction of teacher and student" (2014, p. 25).

From a psychoanalytic perspective, it might be instructive to examine the role of unconscious communications that occur between individuals to understand how a student might internalize the teacher's values, interests, and ideas and how such internalizations contribute to the student's realizational and relational processes. For example, in terms of thinking, Kim describes the practice-engendered notion of "revaluated" or "revalorized" thinking (2007). In actional terms, realization generates a choice between ego-oriented actions and reactions generated by the "three poisons"—ignorance, attachment, and aversion—often appearing in the form of fear, hate, and aggression on the one hand, and on the other hand responding through wisdom and compassion. However, it must be kept clearly in mind that mind-to-mind thinking does not function as a substitute for thinking or for the expression of revalorized thinking through language. Dōgen makes a very sharp distinction between overattachment to language and language that functions as a lived expression of realization. For instance, Heine, in a discussion of Dōgen's poetry, writes:

> In contrast to some approaches in Zen, which regard verbal communications as unnecessary or inherently misleading, Dōgen does not reject or seek to abandon language. Rather, he views language as an inexhaustible reservoir of meaningful ambiguities, all of which are embedded and at times concealed in the words of everyday speech.
>
> (1997, p. 61)

And:
> ... all forms of oral and written communication – sutras, epistles, sermons, sayings, poetry and philosophy – are part of the continual unfolding of the awakened mind. Therefore, Dogen's view is that language is essential to the transmission of enlightenment. Not only does he deny the view that language is inherently misleading, but he insists that the experience of awakening can and must be symbolically disclosed.
>
> (p. 62)

From an individual and practice-oriented perspective, the shift from a goal-oriented or facilitative practice as demonstrated by the theory and practice of *shikantaza*, just sitting, expresses in actional and relational terms, the difference between ego-centered and compassionate action.[3]

The Zen Infusion

The Zen "infusion," if you will, into psychoanalysis has exerted a demonstrable impact. These impacts required and continue to require a psychoanalysis that is available and open to receive such impacts and a Zen that has been modified to make the influences accessible, as was discussed in terms of D.T. Suzuki's role in initiating this impact in Chapter Four, "Literature Review: Precursors."

The current psychoanalytic landscape continues to be quite diverse, ranging from extremely conservative and classical positions that from a "medical perspective" view anything that Buddhism has to offer as regressive and pathological, as suggested in the title of the 1931 article by Franz Alexander "Buddhistic Training as an Artificial Catatonia (The Biological Meaning of Psychic Occurrences)," to the more receptive view as is suggested in the recent book title *Zen and Psychotherapy: Partners in Liberation* (2010) by Joseph Bobrow, who is both a Zen Buddhist priest and a practicing psychoanalyst. The point here is that psychoanalysis in not a reified and concrete rigidly defined structure. Depending on what beliefs and theories have become internalized, the individual analyst might or might not be receptive to the infusion of Zen Buddhism.

The initially all-pervasive Oedipal conflict elaborated by Freud and his agenda to "universalize" a "scientific psychoanalysis" exemplifies this point. Freud's reductionist and universalist use of the Oedipus myth formed the background of his critique. Whatever did not fit or agree with his view, which was intended to present psychoanalysis as scientific, secular, and objective, bore the brunt of his critique. For instance, his view was that mystical experience, conceptualized as an oceanic feeling, was nothing more than a regression back to the womb.[4] This emphasis, as I see it, left Freud blind to culturally derived influences on his unconscious preconceptions. In turn, this agenda had an impact on his views and interfered with his ability to assimilate and accommodate to eastern realizationally oriented religious traditions. Thus, he failed to understand that Buddhism, as well as other eastern traditions developed and functioned through radically different cultural contexts and resulting preconceptions. For example, the Buddhist reductionist notions such as selflessness, emptiness, or what are described as the three poisons, which include primary ignorance, attachment, and aversion, engendered radically different religious forms and expressions and salvational methodologies than the western religious counterpart that characterized the prevailing Christian and Judaic god image as patriarchal, all-powerful, and otherworldly.

Buddhist Transferability

Buddhism, over its history of accommodation and assimilation as it spread to different cultures, demonstrates a consistent ability to flexibly translate and transform itself based on the receiving culture and the historical context. For example, regarding D. T. Suzuki and the Kyoto school, Faure notes that in communicating with western philosophy, "... they relied on Christian categories even when rejecting them" (1993, p. 53).

The question for future studies in the present context—the interpenetration of Zen Buddhism and psychoanalysis—may fruitfully be stated as: "What transformations in Zen are facilitating its adaptability and amenability to interested psychoanalysts?" "What transformations and variations in psychoanalysis have engendered receptivity to Zen among those psychoanalysts interested in Zen?" From a reverse perspective, we might profitably ask: "How have individuals who are deeply immersed in Zen practice and study, such as formally transmitted teachers and ordained priests, among the many psychotherapies available, become drawn to psychoanalysis and specifically to Bion's work?" In this regard, psychoanalysis has been increasingly viewed as a "psycho-spiritual process," which supports and enhances what originated as a religious journey rather than as Bion describes in his discussion of the widening gap between science and psychoanalysis, quoted above, as simply a "treatment for a complaint" (1970, p. 6). For example, early writers on the subject such as Fromm (1960), Horney (1945), and Kelman (1960) viewed Zen as an eastern form of psychoanalysis (Kaplan & Parsons, 2010, p. 123). This reality appears to be nurturing and supporting the psychoanalysis and Zen narrative.

However, at the same time, it is important to note that Zen Buddhism has not replaced or supplanted existing psychoanalytic structures, theories, or techniques. Rather, its development within psychoanalysis has gradually evolved into what we may describe, depending on one's vantage point, as a "subdiscipline." Within the larger framework of psychoanalysis, this evolving narrative critically questions and continues to alter scientific and objective psychoanalytic preconceptions while simultaneously embracing theoretical and practical aspects of the discipline that were already present and to a large degree accepted by mainstream psychoanalysis through its ongoing evolution independently of Buddhist influences. For example, the concept of "totalistic countertransference," pioneered by the Argentinian psychoanalyst Heinrich Racker (1957), which favors a subjective/experiential view of the psychoanalytic encounter and anticipated the shift from a one-person to a two-person psychoanalysis, fits well into the core Buddhist propositions of emptiness and dependent co-arising discussed in Chapter Seven.[5]

Perhaps as assimilation and accommodation processes continue to evolve, both psychoanalysis and Zen consisting of natural "threads" interwoven into the larger fabric of a truly integrated realizational psychoanalysis in a mutually reinforcing and continuously interacting dynamic will become increasingly integrated. These living and continuously evolving disciplines exert a mutual impact on each other in a manner that raises any number of questions to consider for future discussion. For example: Does psychoanalysis work gradually toward a "cure?" This perspective implies an "illness" to be overcome; a posited goal to be reached. How does the notion of "progress and cure" interact with the expressive and goalless notions of Sōtō Zen practice described as *mushotoku*, or no gaining mind?

Does psychoanalysis function to facilitate what I refer to as more "emotional elbow room?" Emotional elbow room generates an expanding and spontaneous, vibrant, confident, and creative expression of the lived present. Does this approach ignore the reality of mental illness?

Are these two orientations mutually exclusive? Bion clearly advocates the latter approach in his concluding remarks in his 1967 article "Notes on Memory and Desire." He writes:

> The pattern of analysis will change. Roughly speaking, the patient will not appear to develop over a period of time but each session will be complete in itself. "Progress" will be measured by the increased number and variety of moods, ideas and attitudes seen in any given session.
>
> (1967, p. 137)

This latter orientation put forward by Bion and others toward psychoanalysis parallels Dōgen's actional and relational orientation elaborated, for instance, by Kim (2004, 2007), as it refers more to an attitude, a relationship, and related actions, rather than to any specific or discrete mental event, state of mind, that may be described as a "diagnosis," "goal," or "cure."

I would argue that both of the above posited questions are occurring concurrently, each reinforcing the other in a mutually arising and interacting dynamic either occupying the foreground or the background of awareness. Bion is very emphatic about where he stands in terms of subjectivity and an experience-based psychoanalysis. He introduces his book *Attention and Interpretation* by asserting:

> I doubt if anyone but a *practising* psycho-analyst can understand this book although I have done my best to make it simple. Any psycho-analyst who is *practicing* can grasp my meaning because he, unlike those who only read

or hear *about* psycho-analysis, has the opportunity to experience for himself what I in this book can only represent by words and verbal formulations designed for a different task. They were developed from a background of sensuous experience.

(1970, p. 1)

Karma

This point can be developed further from the Zen perspective by considering the notion of *karma*, simply translated as "action" or "activity," and habit (karmic) formations or *samskaras* in Sanskrit. From this point of view, the activities, perceptions, and interactions with the environment that influence each individual's experiences results in a unique perception of reality. Over time, these influences develop into consistent, often unquestioned, habitual, and automatic ways of perceiving and interacting with one's internal world and in terms of how these perceptions influence our view of the external world and interpersonal relations.

Is the core Zen Buddhist belief in no inherently existing self; the false notion from the Buddhist perspective of a self that operates separately from causes and conditions tenable from a psychoanalytic perspective? If so, then how does this Zen view interact with the prevailing psychoanalytic view? What is the prevailing psychoanalytic view? What accommodations are made? For example, my own accommodation has been to gravitate toward areas of psychoanalysis that hold basic identities with the areas of Buddhism that I have gravitated toward. Similarly, I suspect that my psychoanalytic views have also influenced the beliefs and practices of Zen Buddhism that have attracted me. In this regard, I propose a mutually interacting and constantly evolving dynamic with both linear and circular dimensions and trajectories, an evolution, if you will, of $Aß \rightarrow B$ in contrast to a linear, one-directional cause and effect model $A \rightarrow B$. This model, as I have described previously, is consistent with Matte-Blanco's reconceptualization of the Freudian unconscious, where at the deepest levels everything mysteriously becomes everything else. In this example, the relation would be $A = B$, $B = A$ (Cooper, 2010). This conceptualization is also consistent with the basic Buddhist depiction of emptiness and dependent co-arising. Clinically, for example, this conceptualization has drawn me towards what may be described as a "crisscross" model of countertransference that integrates Freud's earlier understanding of countertransference from a one-person perspective as the analyst's "blind spot" that has nothing to do with the patient and requires resolution through the requisite training analysis and a "totalistic" (Racker, 1957) conception of countertransference that posits an interacting dynamic between both analyst and analysand. It is from this mutually interacting set of influences that I posit a mutual accommodation and integration described here, as I mentioned above, as the "Realizational Perspective."

Alternatively, another all too common resistance to accommodation has been and continues to be to maintain the prevailing secular view by picking and choosing techniques and teachings out of the larger fabric of Buddhism to absorb into and enhance the prevailing secular view of the therapeutic endeavor. This seems to dominate the professional landscape and what accounts for the rise in secular mindfulness, particularly regarding behavioral technologies. In this way, this approach bypasses what for the western mind, as I noted above, the seemingly unbelievable, unplausible aspects of the Buddhist tradition without subjecting such views to the test of personal experience and to the "catastrophic" changes that true accommodation can entail.[6] This approach leaves unquestioned any aspect of the Buddhist view and its potential impact that is not consistent with the prevailing view. Similarly, this approach ignores the opportunity to critically consider aspects of the western view that may be deemed unplausible from the Mahayana Buddhist perspective from which Zen emerged. That is, holders of the prevailing western psychological view can assimilate Buddhist practices while simultaneously maintaining a nonreligious view and no affiliation to any religious system. In fact, early western Zen writers insisted that Zen Buddhism is not a religion, anything but, which they described alternatively as a "perennial philosophy," "software for the mind," a "way of life," and so forth.

This brings us back to the questions I raised before. How do our internal preconceptions determine how anyone would answer any of these questions?

I believe that questions such as these as well as questions not yet asked must be constantly addressed through self-scrutiny, continued dialog, and experience to maintain the vitality, authenticity, and creative growth of both disciplines and most importantly, for the benefit of those who seek our assistance.

Notes

1 Bobrow, J. (2010); Cooper, P. (2010, 2019); Kennedy, R. (1984); Moncayo, R. (2012).
2 See W. Bion, 1970, Chapter Three: "Reality Sensuous and Psychic" pp. 26–54.
3 See Chapter Fourteen, "*Shikantaza*: 'Basic Fact of Sitting' Practice Session" for a detailed discussion and guided practice instructions.
4 See W. Parsons (1999) for a thorough explication and revisionist understanding of Freud's view.
5 For elaboration and supporting clinical material regarding this relationship, see P. Cooper, *The Zen Impulse and the Psychoanalytic Encounter*, Chapter 10 "Unitive Experience and the Pervasive Object" (2010, pp. 203–228).
6 See M. Eigen (1985) for an insightful explication of this point.

References

Abe, M. (1990). Kenotic God and dynamic sunyata. In: Cobb & Ives (Eds.), *The Emptying God: A Buddhist-Jewish-Christian Conversation* (pp. 3–65). Eugene, OR: Wipf & Stock Publishers.

Abe, M. (1992). Dōgen on Buddha Nature. In: S. Heine (Ed.), *A Study of Dōgen: His Philosophy and Religion* (pp. 35–76). Albany: State University of New York Press.

Alexander, F. (1931). Buddhistic training as an artificial catatonia. *Psychoanalytic Review*, 18:129–145.

Bion, W. (1967). Notes on memory and desire. In: J. Aguayo & B. Malin (Eds.), *Wilfred Bion: Los Angeles Seminars and Supervision* (pp. 133–149). London: Karnac, 2017. [Originally published in: Bion, W. (1967). Notes on memory and desire. The *Psychoanalytic Forum*, 2: 272–3, 279–80.]

Bion, W. (1970). *Attention and Interpretation*. London: Karnac.

Bion, W. (1980). *Bion in New York and São Paulo*. E. F. Bion (Ed.), Perthshire: Clunie Press.

Bobrow, J. (2010). *Zen and Psychotherapy: Partners in Liberation*. New York: W.W. Norton.

Cobb, J. & Ives, C. (1990). *The Emptying God: A Buddhist-Jewish-Christian Conversation*. Eugene, OR: Wipf & Stock Publishers.

Faure, B. (1993). *Chan Insights and Oversights: An Epistemological Critique of the Chan Tradition*. Princeton: Princeton University Press.

Ferro, A. (2002). Narrative derivatives of alpha elements: Clinical implications. *International Forum of Psychoanalysis*, 11:184–187.

Ferro, (2005). *Seeds of Illness, Seeds of Recovery*. London: Routledge.

Ferro, A. (2009). *Mind Works: Technique and Creativity in Psychoanalysis*. New York & London: Routledge.

Fromm, E., Suzuki, D. T. & DeMartino, R. (1960). *Zen Buddhism and Psychoanalysis*. New York: Harper & Brothers.

Grotstein, J. (2019). Bion crosses the rubicon. In: A. Alisobhani & G. Cortorphine (Eds.), *Explorations in Bion's "O" Everything We Know Nothing About* (pp. 17–30). London & New York: Routledge.

Hábito, R. (2004). *Living Zen, Loving God*. Boston, MA: Wisdom Publications.

Hábito, R. (2006). *Healing Breath: Zen for Christians and Buddhists in a Wounded World*. Somerville: Wisdom Publications.

Heine, S. (1997). *The Zen Poetry of Dōgen: Verses from the Mountain of Eternal Peace*. Boston, MA: Tuttle Publishing Co.

Heine, S. (2020). *Readings of Dōgen's Treasury of the True Dharma Eye*. New York: Columbia University Press.

Hershock, P. (2014). *Public Zen, Personal Zen*. Lanham, MD: Rowman & Littlefield.

Horney, K. (1945). *Our Inner Conflicts*. New York: W.W. Norton.

Kaplan, G. & Parsons, W. (2010). *Disciplining Freud on Religion: Perspectives from the Humanities and Social Sciences*. Lanham, MD: Lexington Books.

Kelman, H. (1960). Psychoanalytic thought and eastern wisdom. In: A. Molino (Ed.), *The Couch and the Tree: Dialogues in Psychoanalysis and Buddhism* (pp. 72–79). New York: North Point Press, 1998.

Kennedy, R. (1996). *Zen Spirit, Christian Spirit: The Place of Zen in Christian Life*. London: Continuum.

Kennedy, R. (2000). *Zen Gifts to Christians*. London: Continuum.

Kim, H. (2004). *Eihei Dogen: Mystical Realist*. Boston, MA: Wisdom Publishers.

Kim, H. (2007). *Dōgen on Meditation and Thinking: A Reflection on His View of Zen*. Albany: State University of New York Press.

Ogden, T. (1993). *Projective Identification and Psychotherapeutic Technique*. Lanham, MD: Jason Aronson Publishers.

Racker, H. (1957). The meaning and uses of countertransference. *Psychoanalytic Quarterly*, 26:303–357.

Symington, J. & Symington, N. (1996). *The Clinical Thinking of Wilfred Bion*. London: Routledge.

Chapter 11

Bion and Dōgen
Realizational Practice, Emotional Truth[1]

The Zen Buddhist priest Eihei Dōgen (1200–1253), the influential founder of the Sōtō Zen School in Japan, has been described as "... one of the most intellectually audacious monks associated with premodern Zen" (Hershock, 2014, p. 103). Similarly, the British psychoanalyst, Wilfred Bion (1897–1979), has been described as:

> a polarising figure. In part, paradoxically, I think it is because he represented wholeness ... representing a transcendent numinous state reflected the potential for a state of mental health and wholeness theretofore omitted from psychoanalytic discourse.
>
> (Reiner, 2012, Kindle location 123)

Symington and Symington in the introduction to their book on Bion's theories in relation to clinical technique note:

> Wilfred Bion (1897–1979) is considered a provocative and illuminating contributor to the debate on the nature of psychoanalysis. His understanding of the processes involved constitutes a radical departure from all conceptualizations which proceeded him.
>
> (1996, first unnumbered page)

Their shared highly experiential and in-the-moment emphasis finds expression from the Zen perspective and equally from the psychoanalytic perspective, as reflected in these two quotes:

> The experience of zazen undermines all definitions. It wears them out, empties and explodes them. Nothing remains but the absolute reality of lived experience, alone and complete.
>
> (Deshimaru, 2012, p. 99)

> Any psycho-analyst who is practicing can grasp my meaning because he, unlike those who only read or hear about psycho-analysis, has the

opportunity to experience for himself what I in this book can only represent by words and verbal formulations designed for a different task.

(Bion 1970, p. 1)

As these quotes indicate, Dōgen and Bion were both highly creative, brilliant, prolific writers and thinkers whose works share many areas of overlap, despite having lived in vastly different cultures, with a 700-year gap between them. They both exerted and continue to wield a radical impact on their respective disciplines. Their ideas stand independently on their own, yet, at the same time, they continue to contribute to the contemporary cross-fertilization between Buddhism and psychoanalysis.

However, despite the highly regarded philosophical and theoretical complexity, and sometimes enigmatic expression of their teachings, they both shared the practical agenda of strengthening and deepening a direct experiential realizational practice with an insistent emphasis on the experience of the ever-evolving present moment; Bion striving for the emotional truth of the session; Dōgen advocating authentic practice.

The lived, intuited experiences derived through practice serves as the core of their respective orientations. The direct experience of authentic practice animates their teachings and brings them to fruition for both Zen practitioners and psychotherapists in the 21st century.

This common ground in their orientations finds expression in the above opening quotes. They point directly to the shared emphasis on the highly subjective, personal, and experiential nature of both Zen Buddhism and psychoanalysis. The experiential nature of the realizational perspective serves as the fundamental converging point shared by both thinkers. It is this point of convergence that, despite major conceptual differences, renders "late Bion's" (Vermote, 2011, p. 1089) "epistemological" (Bleandonu, 1994, p. 141) writings so appealing to psychoanalysts and therapists who practice or draw from Zen Buddhist teachings despite the fact that Bion doesn't reference Buddhist thought or practice anywhere in his writings or that Dōgen's writings were written during the Japanese Kamakura period (1185–1333), centuries before Freud's original peregrinations into his nascent psychoanalysis. This convergence point can be arbitrarily elaborated based on these four major points that I describe as a realizational perspective and that provides a starting point for this offering. They include:

1. Primacy of experience rooted in the present moment;
2. Radical openness to unknowing;
3. Relationship between intuition and cognition;
4. Shift from an emphasis on static mind states to the fluidity of psychic functions and actional relationships.

It is within the structure provided by these four points that the realizational orientation will be elaborated.

There has been plenty of commentary from a psychoanalytic perspective on the practical application and underlying themes in Bion's brief article "Notes on Memory and Desire" (1967). For example, Ferro, 2005; Ogden, 2005; and Symington and Symington, 1996. I have elaborated various connections between Dōgen's Sōtō Zen and Bion's ideas previously (Cooper, 2010, 2019). In this present chapter, I plan to bring both to the table, sort of speak by offering an examination of the interaction between Dōgen's Zen and Bion's psychoanalysis with an emphasis on Bion's practical mandate to "relinquish memory, desire and understanding" and Dōgen's *shikantaza* (just sitting) with *mushotoku*, "no gaining mind" that for Dōgen serves as his recommended form of experience-based "thorough investigation" or "exploration" (*Hensan*, 1243a), or his "needle point" (1243b) into what Dōgen describes as the "true reality of all beings." For him this involves an ongoing and endless realizational process characterized by action and relationships rather than a goal-oriented quest to seek imagined end states or preferred and static states of mind such as "enlightenment" or *satori*. The primacy and significance of *shikantaza* for Dōgen finds expression in the title of *Zanmai O Zanmai*, "The Samadhi that is the King of Samadhis" (1244). He writes passionately, evocatively, and confidently that:

> To transcend the whole universe at once, to live a great and valuable life in the house of the Buddhist patriarchs, is to sit in the full lotus posture. To tread over the heads of non-Buddhists and demons; to become, in the inner sanctum of the Buddhist patriarchs, a person in the concrete state, is to sit in the full lotus posture. To transcend the supremacy of the Buddhist patriarchs' supremacy, there is only this one method. Therefore, Buddhist patriarchs practice it solely, having no other practices at all.
> (Nishijima & Cross, 1997, p. 281)

Similarly, Dogen's emphasis on the present moment is clearly and cogently expressed throughout his writings. For example, in *Bussho, Shobogenzo* (1241) Dōgen writes:

> Wanting to know the meaning of the buddha-nature mean, for example, "Really knowing the meaning of the buddha-nature just here and now."

And:

> "Should just reflect real time, causes and circumstances" means "Know causes and circumstances as real time, just here and now!"
> (Nishijima & Cross, 1996, p. 5)

In explicating the realizational perspective, I intend, to reflect on the cross-fertilization, identities, and differences between Bion's and Dōgen's recommendations with an emphasis on how Bion's thinking dovetails with Zen Buddhist foundational principles and practices as expressed in the scriptural tradition of Zen Buddhism and in the writings of psychoanalytic thinkers who have drawn from and extended Bion's work on technique as they converge and diverge within the context of the realizational perspective. In this way I hope to expand and extend both areas of enquiry. The practical significance that I intend to convey centers on the complaint by some commentators (e.g., Rubin, 1985) that Bion really doesn't provide the reader with a clearly articulated method for accomplishing his mandate, "to relinquish memory, desire and understanding," his recommended listening stance for the psychoanalyst, in his instructions, beyond his recommendation to tolerate not knowing until a pattern emerges and, of course, the requisite personal analysis that analytic candidates engage in during training, if not afterwards as well. This latter point seems to be disregarded in the available literature.

Rooted in the Kantian notion of the unknowable "thing-in-itself," which I will elaborate below, for Bion, this mandate is intended to cut through sense-based knowing with the goal of bringing our innate wisdom and intuition into the foreground and in touch with the ineffable emotional "T" (Truth) of the session that he describes simply as "O." Zen, over its long history does have the necessary tools both in its philosophy and in its practices to engender *prajna*, or experiential, intuitive knowing, or what the Tibetan translator Evans-Wentz (1927) describes as "quick knowing" of the lived and continuously evolving moment.

On the other hand, Bion's psychoanalytic orientation brings into the foreground the understanding and practical tools to address largely unconscious stumbling blocks encountered by the Buddhist practitioner from a perspective that contemporary Buddhist practitioners to a large extent seem increasingly amenable to, and which I hope to draw out with clarity for the benefit of both the psychotherapist and the Buddhist practitioner. With this orientation in mind, I will elaborate the four basic points that constitute the basis of the realizational perspective that I listed above.[2]

Primacy of Experience

Bion's theoretical formulations derive from his direct experiences occurring during the psychoanalytic encounter and circle right back to the psychoanalytic dyad. He makes this process explicit in his book *Transformations*, which, as he develops his theory, as if thinking out loud, he asserts as the basis of his notion of transformations as they evolve through the patient's process as experienced during each session (1965):

> I shall assume therefore that the material provided by the analytic session is significant for its being the patient's view (representation) of certain facts which are the origin (O) of his reaction. [And] In practice this means that I shall regard only those aspects of the patient's behaviour which are significant as representing his view of O. [And] I shall call on clinical experience to illustrate the next stage of this investigation.
>
> (1965, p. 15)

From this perspective everything that Bion has to say about psychoanalytic practice begins with and ends with his experience, as he notes, "because they derive from the emotional experience with a unique individual and not from generalized theories imperfectly 'remembered'" (1967).

Bion further elaborates this radical turn in his theoretical thinking and associated clinical approach that emphasizes direct experience in *Attention and Interpretation* (1970). He writes:

> Any psycho-analyst who is *practicing* can grasp my meaning because he, unlike those who only read or hear about psycho-analysis, has the opportunity to experience for himself what I in this book can only represent by words and verbal formulations designed for a different task.
>
> (p. 1)

Note the emphasis that Bion places on the word *"practicing."* He is setting up his argument that language is based in and designed to communicate sensuous experience, which is not in the realm of psychoanalytic experience, and not the subject of psychoanalysis, and in fact, language, according to Bion, clouds over the intuited awareness of psychoanalytic experience. However, he doesn't refute language or discard language, since ineffable experience, O, which can only be intuited experientially, becomes "known" through evolution into K, knowledge, which can then be communicated through language in the form of an interpretation or notation and, at best, approximates experience, both of the analysand and the analyst's intuition of the analysand's experience. The important point then becomes how close an approximation can be made. That is to say, to draw from Bion's (1965) notion of "transformations" (1965), there is an ongoing and paradoxical consciousness of the intuited (or perceived) reality of the moment, as well and as equally significant, the uniqueness of each individual's experience. For instance, to take a concrete example, two individuals will agree that a particular object of perception is a teacup. However, the actual experience of the cup is multi-determined by many internal and external factors such as past experiences, light, shadows, and vantage point. This point can be developed further from the Zen perspective by considering the notion of *"karma,"* simply translated as "action" or "activity," which become reified and internalized as *samskara* (habit [karmic] formations). From this point of view, the activities, perceptions, and interactions with the environment that influence each individual's experience, coupled with any preconceptions, result in a unique perception of reality. Over time, these influences develop into consistent habitual and automatic ways of perceiving and interacting with the world both internally and in terms of interpersonal relations. In this regard, an array of causes and conditions interact and influence the analytic encounter. Some are conscious and others interact unconsciously. One formulation that addresses this experiential fact is summarized in the various psychoanalytic theories of transference

134 Realizational Perspectives

and countertransference. The analyst's preconceptions in terms of how these theories are internalized will contribute to his/her preconceptions and influence what is said about the lived realizational experience itself. For example, perhaps a Kleinian would interpret the anxiety related to an unconscious phantasy; from a Kohutian perspective, perhaps the analyst would say something about the self-state of the patient. Ferro offers a series of "exercises" that captures this point clearly, succinctly, and playfully:

> After a transference interpretation, at the Monday session a patient says, 'Today, the motorway was terrible, I was being tailgated by a lorry and I was terrified because it was so close behind me.'
> *Analyst 1:* 'There is a part of you that in the absence of analysis persecutes you and you don't know how to escape this persecution.'
> *Analyst 2:* 'Perhaps at the last session I interpreted too much and my words were the lorry.'
> *Analyst 3:* 'This is a terrible experience, just like in the movie *Duel*.'
> *Analyst 4:* ***This*** is a terrible experience, just like in the movie Duel.'
> *Analyst 5:* 'So I should drive more slowly!'
> *Analyst 6:* 'Would it be impossible for you to drive faster?'
> *Analyst 7:* 'The lorry loomed like your father checking that you had done all your homework in the evening.'
> (2007, p. 180)

Then there are the multiply determined ways, based on the causes and conditions that create and reify internalized preconceptions, that would influence the many possible patient responses. Ferro continues by raising the following questions that all point to the immediate experience of the analyst, analysand, and the dependently co-arising context of the moment:

(a) Try to imagine how a patient (as you imagine him) would respond to each of these interpretations.
(b) Try to imagine how a patient nearing the end of analysis would respond to each interpretation.
(c) How would a severely paranoid patient respond?
(d) How would an obsessive patient respond?
(e) How would a phobic patient respond?.

(2007, p. 180)

Radical Openness to Unknowing

Both Bion and Dōgen orient themselves to a relinquishment or a coming to terms with the habitual dominance of cognition and linear rational thought processes in order to engender realizational truth. They both turn the emphasis on accumulating knowledge on its head and instead emphasize experiential authenticity and truth. For instance, Rhode, following Bion's lead, sums up the realizational orientation in terms of what he describes as a "mystical perspective," clearly, cogently, and succinctly in terms of the "gap":

> Some people seek to name and personify the gap, perhaps as a nameless dread. The continuum and any conceivable break in it begin to separate: the continuum transforms into the immanence of the natural world, while the break in the continuum gives utterance to a transcendental and supernatural order.
>
> (1998, p. 22)

Both Bion and Dōgen advocate being as open as possible to the infinite, ineffable, nonsensuous, immediately experienced present reality accessed through intuition. Dōgen addresses this orientation cogently and playfully, as elaborated in Chapter Eight, "Dōgen's Use of Suchness," in terms of *"Inmo"* (suchness, thusness, being-as-it-is) or to use Zen parlance, "That which is" or "Just this is it" (Leighton, 2015).

Dōgen uses the term *gūjin* (total exertion, total penetration)[3] to describe this sense of wholehearted openness to currently evolving experience. Alternatively, he uses the term *hensan*, or "thorough exploration" to convey this same intention. For instance, in terms of the immediacy of experience, in *Hensan* (1243a), Dōgen writes:

> Unless the truth of thorough exploration is actually manifest in the present, experience of the self is impossible and experience of the self is unsatisfactory; experience of others is impossible and experience of others is unsatisfactory; experience of "a person" is impossible, experience of "I" is impossible, experience of a fist is impossible, and experience of the eye is impossible—lifting the self by fishing the self is impossible, and rising up even before being fished is impossible. When thorough exploration is perfectly realized already, it is free of "thorough exploration".... Thus, we can conclude that the whole human being is mind, and the whole of mind is a human being. We investigate in experience the front and back of each such partial thought.
>
> (Nishijima & Cross, 1997, p. 211)

Influenced by D.T. Suzuki's Zen orientation, Karen Horney provides a poignant example of how this notion has influenced her approach to psychoanalysis. She uses the expression "wholeheartedness of spirit" to describe the analytic stance of total openness to the patient's ongoing currently manifesting experience. Horney (1945) quotes a Zen encounter dialog to explicate this orientation. She prefaces the story by commenting:

> It is interesting to note in this connection that in Zen Buddhist writings sincerity is connected with wholeheartedness, pointing to the very

conclusion we reach on the basis of clinical observation—namely, that nobody divided within himself can be wholly sincere.

(1945, pp. 162–163)

She then quotes the following Zen dialog:

Monk: I understand that when a lion seizes upon his opponent, whether it is a hare or an elephant, he makes an exhaustive use of his power; pray tell me what is this power?
Master: The spirit of sincerity (literally, the power of non-deceiving).

Horney then offers a quote from D.T. Suzuki in way of explanation:

Sincerity, that is, not-deceiving, means "putting forth one's whole being," technically known as "the whole being in action" … in which nothing is kept in reserve, nothing is expressed under disguise, nothing goes to waste. When a person lives like this, he is said to be a golden-haired lion; he is the symbol of virility, sincerity, wholeheartedness; he is divinely human.

(p. 163)

For Bion, unknowing begins with the primitive states of what cannot yet be represented psychically. He developed a theory of thinking that attempts to take account of what is not represented or differentiated and how transformations can be facilitated, or not be blocked by the analyst. That means sitting and tolerating not knowing until, as he notes, quoting the British poet and scholar John Milton, something is "Won from the dark and formless infinite" (1970, p. 88).

Not unlike Nangaku, who was encountered in Chapter One, after tolerating not knowing after his realization occurred through his direct experience of sitting for eight years, Bion notes that the analyst's lived experience of patiently sitting with the patient, in the not-knowing of the session until a pattern emerges, will have the result that:

His interpretations should gain in force and conviction—both for himself and his patient—because they derive from the emotional experience with a unique individual and not from generalised theories imperfectly "remembered."

(1967, p. 138)

From a Bionic perspective Vermote comments in terms of "… transformations in O, where losing oneself in awe of the infinite unknown can have a liberating and changing effect" (2017, p. 82). This orientation threads its way through writers speaking from a Bionic perspective (Eigen, 1998; Grotstein, 2007;

Lopez-Corvo, 2005, 2006; Rhode, 1998; Symington & Symington, 1996; Vermote, 2017).

Similarly, Dōgen notes in *Genjokoan* (1233):

> To carry the self forward and illuminate myriad things is delusion. That myriad things come forth and illuminate the self is awakening. Those who have great realization of delusion are buddhas; those who are greatly deluded about realization are sentient beings. Further, there are those who continue realizing beyond realization, who are in delusion throughout delusion. When buddhas are truly buddhas, they do not necessarily notice that they are buddhas. However, they are actualized buddhas, who go on actualizing buddha.
> (Aitken & Tanahashi, 1999, p. 35)

Intuition/Cognition

As described in Chapter Nine, "Bion's Use of "O" and "K," O points to the ineffable, essentially unknowable reality or Truth of the moment. O and K serve for Bion as two very different ways of understanding the psychoanalytic moment, which, he argues, is in constant flux. He distinguishes between experiencing and intuiting the unknowable data of psychoanalysis, which he notes as Transformations in O (T→O) and speaking about the known or Transformations in K (T→K). Bion (1970) uses O to keep the psychic space open and unsaturated with preconceived meanings.

Dōgen refers to the process that Bion describes as "intuition of 'O'" as "dropping off body mind." In his first treatise on meditation, *Fukanzazengi*, "Universal Principles of Zen Meditation" (1227), he argues, "No traps or snares can ever reach it" (Abe & Waddell, 2002, p. 6). This expression refers to discursive mind. The "backward step" that Dōgen refers to parallels Bion's use of the British poet John Keats' notion of "negative capability" (Bion, 1970, p. 125), which will be described below in the section on methodology. Dōgen therefore admonishes the student to:

> Cease from practice based on intellectual understanding, pursuing words and following after speech, and learn the backward step that turns your light inward to illuminate your self. Body and mind will drop away of themselves and your original face will manifest itself.
> (Waddell & Abe, 2002, p. 3)

Both Bion and Dōgen orient themselves to a relinquishment of an overreliance on, but not an abandoning of, cognitive linear thought processes and an opening into the infinite. Both are advocating being as open as possible to the infinite, ineffable, non-sensuous experience accessed through intuition. Bion points to the notion of "at-one-ment," which he notes, "No psycho-analytic discovery is possible without recognition of its existence, at-one-ment with it and evolution" (1970, p. 30).

Shift from Mind States to Functions (Stasis/Action)

Both Bion and Dōgen shift the emphasis away from static states of mind to relationships and functions. Vermote notes that Bion directed "... interventions from psychic content to psychic functioning" (2017, p. 76). That is, Bion directed his attention to the relationships between subject and object. For instance, he speaks of cycles of projection and introjection as nonsensuous unconscious forms of communication that impact both individuals in a relational dyad along with the resulting impacts such unconscious communications have on the object.

Bion speaks of "emotional experience" and observes, "An emotional experience cannot be conceived of in isolation from a relationship" (1962, p. 42). This actional/relational orientation finds contemporary expression in terms of the clinical setting by Ferro who, drawing from Bion, notes: "What matters is not only the patient's mode of functioning/dysfunctioning for it must always be seen in relation to the functioning/dysfunctioning of the analyst's mind" (2007, p. 52).

Similarly, Kim notes that the key to understanding Dōgen's technique centers on his "actional" orientation (2004, p. 54). Dōgen emphasized actional and relational functioning over static states of mind. Both Bion and Dōgen advocate being open to the unknown, ineffable experience as evidenced in their techniques. As noted above, Bion sitting free from memory, desire, understanding (1967, 1970); Dōgen sitting with *mushotoku* "no gaining mind" in *shikantaza* a form of meditation that Dōgen describes as "objectless, subjectless, formless, goalless, and purposeless" (Kim, 2004, pp. 62–63).

Basic Differences

The many insightful parallels between psychoanalysis and Buddhist thought that various writers have explored are interesting and useful. As described in Chapter Six, "A Zen Wave: Review," these articles contribute to the cumulative development and enrichment of the ongoing cross-fertilization of both disciplines. However, continued scrutiny reveals gaps in the apparent connections. The gaps become wider to the point of being seemingly unbridgeable. The problem that gets generated is the potential for biasing one "side" over the other. For example, making a spurious and simplistic identification of similarities on the one hand and on the other, making largely misinformed distinctions. Adding to this difficulty is the issue of perception, which Buddhists describe through the seemingly paradoxical notion of the identity of relative being and absolute being. Relative being, often referred in Zen parlance as the "10,000 things," addresses our uniqueness as individual beings in the world and the distinctions we encounter in everyday life. Absolute being refers to oneness or the inherently "empty" nature of reality. All existence is interconnected as "Whole Being" subject to causes and conditions. Paradoxically, we are simultaneously one and many. Applying this core Buddhist notion, the experience of reality becomes contingent on the ongoing perceptual shifts that oscillate between relative being and absolute being and in turn describes the unbridgeable gap as well as the identities between Buddhism and psychoanalysis. Typically, differentiation, hence, what appears as unbridgeable, from the Buddhist perspective, is associated with the intellect or cognitive processes; experiencing oneness tends to be associated with intuitive processes. Bion depicts O as Kant's "thing-in-itself" that has an absolute independent existence; existing as "noumenon" separately from sense objects. This is a fundamentally dualistic orientation between "sense and non-sense" (Cooper, 1999b). The dualistic tendency in this respect, from Bion's point of view, centers on the mind being split between memories, desires, or understandings and the experience of presence and a possible feeling of anxiety coupled with the attempt to disavow or split off any uncomfortable feelings. Bion advises that these anxious feelings are part and parcel of the experience of initially engaging in his method. He writes:

> If this discipline is followed there will be an increase of anxiety in the psychoanalyst at first, but it must not interfere with preservation of the rules. [And] This procedure is extremely penetrating. Therefore the psychoanalyst must aim at a steady exclusion of memory and desire and not be too disturbed if the results appear alarming at first. He will become used to it and he will have the consolation of building his psychoanalytic technique on a firm basis of intuiting evolution.
>
> (1967, pp. 18–19)

For instance, this situation can occur by actively or anxiously searching for a memory of something that was said in a previous session and losing awareness of what is presently occurring and experienced. On the other hand, remaining present with the not-knowing of the session free from any conceptual anchors can engender its own anxiety.

In contrast, Dōgen articulates a radical non-duality that includes both duality and non-duality. This paradoxical situation requires dualism to be included in order to posit a truly all-inclusive non-dualistic orientation. Dōgen's radical non-dualism is implied in his expressive and realizational approach to spiritual realization, which, for example, is clearly emphasized in *Bendowa*. For example, in terms of experience through practice, he writes:

> For enjoyment of this samādhi, the practice of [za]zen, in the erect sitting posture, has been established as the authentic gate. This Dharma is abundantly present in each human being, but if we do not practice it, it does not manifest itself, and if we do not experience it, it cannot be realized.
>
> (Nishijima & Cross, 1994, p. 1)[4]

However, Dōgen questions the relationship and the individual's perception of the relationship. Following traditional Mahayana Buddhist teachings Dōgen describes all existence as conditioned and lacking any absolute, separate, or "own" inherent existence. That is, there is no existence outside of conditioned existence. Thus, emptiness is interconnected with form, noumenon with phenomenon, sense with non-sense, and by extension, O with K.

Additionally, from this dualistic perspective, Bion strives to "purify" consciousness, hence "at-one-ment with O," by attempts to eliminate sense input. In this regard, any sense object would come to be viewed as what Buddhists would describe as an obscuration or an impurity. For example, the recommended antidote to the obscuration caused by greed is generosity. The antidote for hate is loving-kindness, and so forth. In contrast, Dōgen, from a non-dual perspective, exploits the intertwining of emptiness and form to foster realization without the need to maintain such distinctions or to apply antidotes. Dōgen's explication of the core notion of suchness or "That which is It," described above, and the related practice of *mushotoku*, meditation with no gaining mind, both exemplify this point from the dual orientation of philosophical and practice perspectives.

Further, these factors contribute to differentiation, and contribute to diversity in terms of how, for example, individual psychoanalysts think, as exemplified, as discussed in the literature review, the proliferation of a creative, multicolored palate with regard to how the relationship between Bion's psychoanalysis and Buddhism are expressed. In a parallel to Buddhist thought, as discussed above, Bion (1970) prefers the term "intuition" (p. 7) for experiencing "non-sensuous" (p. 18) reality and engendering "at-one-ment" (p. 30) with evolving O (p. 52).

Additionally, we can understand Bion's comment, in terms of Buddhist thought, as positing that the intellect gets in the way of experiencing what is really going on. However, one distinction to keep in mind is that, for Bion, psychic reality is non-sensuous, whereas for the Zen practitioner, sensuous (relative) realities and non-sensuous (absolute) realities are intertwined and ultimately one and the same reality. From the Buddhist perspective all phenomena are fundamentally empty of inherent existence. In this regard, while both maintain their uniqueness, from an absolute point of view there is no distinction. The moon serves as a symbol for realization in the Zen literature. For the Zen practitioner, the teacher can only point to the moon, but it is up to the student to see the moon personally. In this regard, both point to self-realization.

A Concluding Question

One pertinent question that serves as a conclusion to this discussion, based on the core notion of the identity of relative and absolute being might be stated as follows: "Can we approach the discussion regarding Buddhism and psychoanalysis creatively through a balance that acknowledges equally differences, similarities and identities without compromise?" By "without compromise" I mean without the filter of what Bion describes, as noted above, as preconceptions that oversaturate psychic space and result in the loss of the freedom to remain open to evolving experience. From a practice perspective for Bion, this demands not knowing, which is a state of mind that is free from the intrusions of "memory, desire or understanding" (1967, 1970). Similarly, as Dōgen advises, the practitioner develops and maintains the attitude of *mushotoku*, no gaining mind or with "beginner's mind" (S. Suzuki, 1970, p. 21). To conclude, as both Dōgen and Bion advise, this becomes an individual matter unique to each practitioner through identifying and working with reified and often unconscious preconceptions that when unacknowledged or left unidentified, contribute to blockages and that can create imbalances and that interfere with the creative and realizational impact of, to use the psychoanalytic situation as an example, what both individuals in the encounter bring to the situation.

Notes

1 This chapter is a revised and expanded version of P. Cooper (2020), "Realizational Perspectives: Bion's Psychoanalysis and Dogen's Zen." *American Journal of Psychoanalysis* 80:37–52, reprinted with the kind permission of Springer.
2 Hopefully, the reader will add and elaborate additional points over time.
3 See Cooper, 2010, for an explication and practical application of *gūjin*.
4 In this context, "Dharma" refers specifically to the Buddhist path as expressed in zazen, or seated meditation.

References

Aitken, R & Tanahashi, K. (1999). Actualizing the fundamental point. In: K. Tanahashi (Trans. & Ed.), *Enlightenment Unfolds: The Essential Teachings of Zen Master Dōgen* (pp. 35–39). Boston, MA: Shambhala.
Bion, W. (1962). *Learning from Experience*. London: Karnac. Northvale & London: Jason Aronson, Inc.
Bion, W. (1965). *Transformations*. London: Karnac.
Bion, W. (1967). Notes on memory and desire, In: J. Aguayo & B. Malin (Eds.), *Wilfred Bion: Los Angeles Seminars and Supervision* (pp. 133–149). London: Karnac [Originally published in: Bion, W. (1967). Notes on memory and desire. *The Psychoanalytic Forum*, 2:272–273, 279–280.]
Bion, W. (1970). *Attention and Interpretation*. London: Karnac.
Bleandonu, G. (1994). *Wilfred Bion: his Life and Works. 1897–1979*. London: Free Association Books.
Cooper, P. (1999b). Buddhist meditation and countertransference: a case study. *American Journal of Psychoanalysis*, 59:71–85.
Cooper, P. (2010). *The Zen Impulse and the Psychoanalytic Encounter*. London: Routledge.
Cooper, P. (2019). *Zen Insight, Psychoanalytic Action: Two Arrows Meeting*. New York & London: Routledge.
Deshimaru, T. (2012). *Mushotoku Mind: The Heart of the Heart Sutra*. Chino Valley, AZ: Hohm Press.
Dōgen, E. (1227). Fukanzazengi. In: M. Abe & N. Waddell (Eds.), *The Heart of Dōgen's Shobogenzo* (pp. 1–6). Albany: S.U.N.Y. Press, 2002.

Dōgen, E. (1231). *Bendowa*. In: G. Nishijima & C. Cross (Trans & Eds.), *Master Dogen's Shobogenzo, Book 1* (pp. 1–23). London: Windbell Publications, 1994.
Dōgen, E. (1233). *Genjokoan*. In: K. Tanahashi (Trans. & Ed.), *Enlightenment Unfolds: the Essential Teachings of Zen Master Dōgen* (pp. 35–39). Boston, MA: Shambhala, 1999.
Dōgen, E. (1241). *Bussho*. In: G. Nishijima & C. Cross (Trans. & Eds), *Master Dogen's Shobogenzo, book 2* (pp. 1–32). London: Windbell Publications, 1996.
Dōgen, E. (1243a). *Hensan*. In: Nishijima & C. Cross (Trans. & Eds.), *Master Dogen's Shobogenzo, Book 3*. (pp. 207–214). London: Windbell Publications, 1997.
Dōgen, E. (1243b). *Zazenshin*. In: G. Nishijima & C. Cross (Trans. & Eds.), *Master Dogen's Shobogenzo, Book 2* (pp. 91–106). London: Windbell Publications, 1996.
Dōgen, E. (1244). *Zanmai O Zanmai*. In: G. Nishijima & C. Cross (Trans. & Eds.), *Master Dogen's Shobogenzo, Book 2* (pp. 281–284). London: Windbell Publications, 1997.
Eigen, M. (1998). *The Psychoanalytic Mystic*. London: Free Associations Press.
Evans-Wentz, W. (1927). *The Tibetan Book of the Dead; or the After-death Experiences on the Bardo Plane*. London: Oxford University , 1960.
Ferro, (2005). *Seeds of Illness, Seeds of Recovery*. London: Routledge.
Ferro, A. (2007). *Avoiding Emotions, Living Emotions*. London: Routledge.
Grotstein, J. (2007). *A Beam of Intense Darkness: Wilfred Bion's Legacy to Psychoanalysis*. London: Karnac.
Hershock, P. (2014). *Public Zen, Personal Zen*. Lanham, MD.: Rowman & Littlefield.
Horney, K. (1945). *Our Inner Conflicts*. New York: W.W. Norton.
Kim, H. (2004). *Eihei Dōgen: Mystical Realist*. Boston, MA: Wisdom Publishers.
Leighton, D. (2015). *Just This is It: Dongshan and the Practice of Suchness*. Boston, MA: Shambhala.
Lopez- Corvo, R. (2005). *The Dictionary of the Work of W.R. Bion*. London: Karnac.
Lopez-Corvo, R. (2006). *Wild Thoughts Searching for a Thinker: A Clinical Application to W.R. Bion's Theories*. London: Karnac.
Nishijima, G. & Cross, C. (1997). *Master Dogen's Shobogenzo, Book 3*. London: Windbell Publications.
Ogden, T. (2005). What I would not part with. *Fort Da*, 11:8–17.
Reiner, A. (2012). *Bion and Being: Passion and the Creative Mind*. London: Karnac.
Rhode, E. (1998). *On Hallucination, Intuition and the Becoming of "O."* Binghamton & Cluj: ESF Publishers.
Rubin, J. (1985). Meditation and psychoanalytic listening. *Psychoanalytic Review*, 72:599–614.
Suzuki, S. (1970). *Zen Mind, Beginner's Mind*. New York: Weatherhill.
Symington, J. & Symington, N. (1996). *The Clinical Thinking of Wilfred Bion*. London: Routledge.
Vermote, R. (2011). On the value of 'late Bion' to analytic theory and practice. *International Journal of Psychoanalysis,* 92:1089–1098.
Vermote, R. (2017). "The sane and the insane psychotic": Attacks on linking revisited from Bion's later work. In: C. Bronstein & E. O'Shaughnessy (Eds.), *Attacks on Linking Revisited: A New Look at Bion's Classic Work* (pp. 75–86). London: Karnac.
Waddell & Abe. (2002). *The Heart of Dōgen's Shobogenzo*. Albany: State University of New York Press.

Part Five
Practice

Chapter 12

Thinking's Bad Rap

This brief *mondo* (question and answer dialog), cogently and tersely points to the role and importance of thinking in Zen practice:

> Once, when the Great Master Hung-tao of Yüeh Shan was sitting [in meditation], a monk asked him, "What are you thinking of, [sitting there] so fixedly?"
> The master answered, "I'm thinking of not thinking."
> The monk asked, "How do you think of not thinking?"
> The master answered, "Nonthinking."
>
> (Bielefeldt, 1988, p. 188–189)

In contrast to the intensity of feelings and thoughts described in the following narrative, in popular culture there is a definite bias and an emphasis on the calm surface of meditation and an often wholesale disregard for the truth of our own thinking and perceptual processes and their products. However, during practice as tension builds up, as it often does, the Zen practitioner simply continues to sit. Guided by *mushotoku*, or no gaining mind, the practitioner permits whatever emerges into awareness without judgment, attachment, or aversion. Over time, these intense states will soften and have less impact. In this manner, difficult psychic states become workable and the practitioner forms a different relationship to internal processes and to others. The response to allowing and being with all these emerging, crystalizing, and dissolving mind moments, one tolerates the evolution of thinking processes as they transform into authentic thinking, which, as Kim notes, thinking that becomes "revaluated" (2007, p. 21) or "revalorized" (p. 121) in a manner that engenders "right action" (p. 121).

With these points in mind, as an introduction to this chapter and speaking from my own direct experience during *sesshin*, an extended and intense practice period, I offer the following narrative in terms of what can be described as oscillations ranging from passion to unbidden rage:

> I feel the bubbling over, watch the volcanic eruption, watch self, selves, others, form, melt crystallize, shatter in permutations of liquid psychic

> lava, emotional upsurge and outflow. Zazen increases the capacity for handling geometrically increasing intensities. ... Continued sitting in the wider oscillations of whatever rises and falls, as aspects of this one larger process, brings into the present situation an awareness of inner obstructions and dissolves anger, which, if suffered, transforms into passion evolving into awareness in the form of many different thoughts and feelings with variations in speed and intensity. Passion, longing for union with the divine, lover, universe, teachings, truth, life, death, moment, infinite moment, intimate contact with the depths of one's own being ... Passion of forms and images swirling, spewing multi-colored mind flowers, that blossom and melt away to the limits of what I can take and then back to breathing and sitting, the ringing bell. Up and slow walking once again.
>
> I sit with rage and find myself opening into passion or perhaps passion opening into what I imagine is "the me." Rage, passion's seal, and signpost, opening and/or closing—lock and key. Zen's gateless gate. "*Mu*," barrier and entrance all in one. Can one grow through rage, past rage's destructiveness until it burns itself into passion? From this zafu, if I embrace the horror and disturbance of felt rage, I can embrace the enlivening fires of passion. I swallow fire and dream rainbows. ... Rage, passion's burning bush. The deadliness of rage can feed the aliveness of passion. Raging passions, passionate rages. The serpent swallows its own tail and dissolves into infinity. Rage feels tense, tight, constricted in my body, nerves, muscles, bones, joints. The ache intensifies. Each heartbeat ripples through the body into the limbs, joints, to the ends of my fingers and toes. ... Yet, when the tail of rage's tiger is fully grasped, embraced, it becomes passion; passion, a multi-faceted gem that crystallizes into form and action. Permutations of lived passion: for peace, creature comforts, foods, Eros, connectedness, aliveness, flesh pleasures, music, passion for writing, painting, creating, and destroying, orgasmic passions ... All of it! ... passion that oscillate between work and play, love and hate mutually consumed and consuming. Play transforming to work, work becoming play. Love and hate passions that become split asunder, dissolve and merge.
>
> (Cooper, 2009, pp. 227–228)

In the ensuing discussion, it is important to keep in mind that the term "thoughts" serves as a shorthand for all mental productions, including thoughts, emotions, memories, wishes, fantasies, desires, and the processes that produce them. At the very least, thoughts, depending on how one relates to them, can easily become a problem or evolve into a solution.

The relationship between *zazen* (Zen meditation) and thinking has been problematic in Zen Buddhism since its inception within the Chan tradition in China. This problem has continued right through to the present day. This difficulty has typically been expressed in terms of the conflict between quietist and insight-oriented practices. On the one hand, a misunderstanding of Zen meditation creates the impossible expectation that thoughts must be eliminated.

However, the mind is supposed to think. That is its function. This misguided misperception of Zen meditation often engenders negative self-judgments when the misinformed practitioner fails at eliminating thoughts. A preoccupation with this project of thought-elimination can interfere with realizing basic truths about oneself, one's relationship to others, and in this manner, while well intentioned, such practices can become a misguided form of resistance.

Thoughts and Dōgen's Nondualism

From Dōgen's radical nondualistic and all-inclusive perspective, thoughts arise and must somehow be tolerated. Some thoughts punish, humiliate, persecute, and disturb one's sense of well-being. Some thoughts depress, discourage, and interfere with the ability to function. Other thoughts can take the form of fantasies and seduce the practitioner into states of imagined or felt ecstasy, dreams, or seemingly otherworldly visions of the sublime. Still other thoughts can engender states of "repose and ease," as Dōgen suggests in *Fukanzazengi*, "Universal Promotion of the Principles of Zazen," his first piece written upon his return from his studies with Tendō Nyojō in China in 1227 and revised in 1233. The Zen practitioner alternates through a continuum of infinite states between terror and delight. Dōgen poignantly describes these alternating thought processes associated with a nonexclusive ongoing awareness that operates free from attachment and aversion in *Zanmai-ō-zanmai*, "The Samādhi That Is the King of Samādhis" (1244):

> Just in the moment of sitting, investigate whether the universe is vertical, and whether it is horizontal. Just in the moment of sitting, what is the sitting itself? Is it a somersault? Is it a state of vigorous activity? Is it thinking? Is it beyond thinking? Is it doing something? Is it not doing anything? Is it sitting inside of sitting? Is it sitting inside of the body-mind? Is it sitting that is free of "the inside of sitting," "the inside of the body- mind," and so on? There should be investigation of thousands and tens of thousands of points like these. Sit in the full lotus posture with the body. Sit in the full lotus posture with the mind. Sit in the full lotus posture being free of body and mind.
> (Nishijima & Cross, 1997, p. 281)

But no matter where the thoughts go, no matter what emerges, as sitting in *zazen* continues, the body is still and contains whatever else one may be thinking. In this way, sitting engenders a pure receptiveness and readiness and a lived immediacy to the presently fully experienced moment.

Eigen's commentary on Bion's "faith in O" parallels the meditative experience. He writes:

> Bion describes how uncomfortable one may be in this open state. One must tolerate fragmentation, whirls of bits and pieces of meaning and

meaninglessness, chaotic blankness, dry periods, and psychic dust storms. Yes, Bion also suggests that such states can be trancelike and akin to hallucinosis.

(1985, pp. 219–220)

Shikantaza as the Practice Expression of Dōgen's Nondualism

Shikantaza or just sitting, the practice of *zazen* advocated by Dōgen, as noted, is foundational and functions as an expression of our original realization.[1] For instance, in the opening lines of *Bendowa*, "A Talk about Pursuing the Truth" (1231), he writes:

> For enjoyment of this samādhi, the practice of [za]zen, in the erect sitting posture, has been established as the authentic gate. This Dharma is abundantly present in each human being, but if we do not practice it, it does not manifest itself, and if we do not experience it, it cannot be realized.
> (Nishijima & Cross, 1994, p. 1)

In this regard, Dōgen describes the relationship between practice and realization as *shusho ichinyo* or the oneness of practice and realization. Despite his insistence on this point, thinking is often considered to be unreal and is typically minimized and therefore inconsequential or even viewed as an obstruction to religious unfolding. For example, commenting on the dialog between Yüeh Shan and the monk as it appears in *Shinji Shobogenzo*, Dōgen's collection of 300 koans, Daido John Loori asserts:

> Abide in neither thinking nor not-thinking. Thinking is linear and sequential—a separation from the reality that is the subject of thought, and thus is an abstraction rather than the reality itself.
> (2009, p. 176)

The advice to "Abide in neither thinking nor not-thinking," is well taken and points directly to the heart of *shikantaza*, just as Dōgen describes it from his radical nondualistic perspective. However, the instruction is qualified with a critique and devaluation of thinking and, although not explicitly stated or even intended, could generate the inference that thinking should somehow be eliminated because it is "unreal." It is important to keep in mind that from Dōgen's radical nondualism, which is reflected and expressed in *shikantaza* practice, abstraction is also suchness, an aspect of the currently manifesting reality. As unreal as thoughts are, they can exert powerful reality consequences, especially when mistaken for reality without question. The unconscious enactment of transference and countertransference dynamics that can manifest during the psychoanalytic encounter and that can engender a negative therapeutic reaction and derail the treatment dramatically exemplifies this point.

Regardless of alterations in our perceptual awareness, such as between the dualistic orientation of relative being and the unitive experience of absolute being, our lives are lived as one reality, described by Dōgen in the *Bussho* (Buddha nature) chapter of *Shobogenzo* (1241) as "Total Existence is the Buddha-nature" (Nishijima & Cross, 1996, p. 2).

Experientially, this is what Dōgen describes as *"Inmo"* or "suchness," as elaborated in Chapter Eight, "Dōgen's Expression of Suchness." It is when an individual takes either the relative or the absolute exclusively as the whole reality that problems ensue, especially when those thoughts are projected onto the world and its objects of perception, such as when false inferences become enacted. For example, considering the relation between form and emptiness, traditionally, Mahayana Buddhist teachings emphasize the negation of form as the key to realization. However, in a radical shift, Dōgen argues that realizing the true reality of being requires the simultaneous awareness of form and emptiness. Therefore, form is not negated. Form and emptiness both affirm and negate each other as two aspects of one reality.

This common albeit erroneous view of Zen Buddhist meditation is that meditation and thinking are antithetical and that thinking must be eliminated for the practitioner to be successful with meditation. For example, Izutsu, who views thinking as a major obstacle to realizational attainment, argues for "... a mistrust in thinking and an elimination of discursive thinking" (1982, pp. 147–60), typifies this common, albeit misguided view.

It is not clear whether Izutsu is simply advising the practitioner to cut through discursive thinking with *shōshiryo*, or "right thinking," as Kim suggests, or if he is arguing against all thinking in relation to contemplative practice. However, the slant of his argument implies a devaluation of thinking, and therefore Izutsu's comment serves as a typical example of a misguided critique of thinking. His view exemplifies a larger response to thinking in the history of Zen, as Abe observes: "In Zen, the positive and creative aspects of human thinking have been neglected and only its dualistic and discriminative aspects have been clearly realized as something to be overcome" (1985, p. 112). This negative attitude toward thinking flies in the face of the notion of *shōshiryo* or "right thinking," which, as part of the Buddhist Eightfold Path,[2] is foundational in operationalizing and clarifying through experience based on practice, the fundamental tenets of Zen Buddhism.

From the perspective described by what we may characterize as "antithinkers," thinking occupies the lowest rung on a ladder in a hierarchical progression of mind states. These factors have led Kim to assert, "... thinking has been almost incapacitated in the tradition" [as a result] they are still odd bedfellows today more than ever" (2007, p. 79).

Origins

Fujita traces back this negative view of thinking in relation to Chinese Chan Buddhism to an incorrect understanding of the 5th-century first ancestor of Zen in China, Bodhidharma's practice of wall gazing, in terms of the difference between *zazen* (sitting) and *shuzen* (learning meditation). Fujita writes: "Except for his own disciples (small in number), very few could understand the true meaning of what he was doing by facing the wall" (2011, p. 24).

Fujita describes *shuzen* as a form of "meditation to attain a special state of mind" referred to in Sanskrit as "*dhyāna*." In other words, *shuzen*, from this point of view, describes an instrumental or facilitative practice that is limited in scope by its focus on a specific goal. Drawing from its Indian roots, this goal can include the cessation of thought, the attainment of magical powers, or the induction of trance states. The practice thus becomes an instrument or a tool that is secondary to the projected goal, whatever that goal may be. The Chinese scholar-monk and historian, Tao-hsuan (596–667) who erroneously described Bodhidharma as a practitioner of *dhyāna*, fueled this confusion between Bodhidharma's practice of *zazen* and *shuzen*.

Nishijima summarizes this historical misunderstanding as follows:

> For a long time no one could understand the reason for that [sitting], and so they saw Bodhidharma as training in Zen meditation. Now, [the practice of] dhyāna is only one among many forms of conduct: how could it be all there was to the Saint? Yet because of this [practice], the people of that time who made chronicles subsequently listed him among those who were learning Zen meditation: they grouped him alongside people like withered trees and dead ash. Nevertheless, the Saint did not stop at [the practice of] dhyāna; and at the same time, of course, he did not go against [the practice of] dhyāna—just as the art of divination emerges from yin and yang without going against yin and yang.
>
> (Nishijima & Cross, 1996, p. 156)

Dōgen makes the distinction between *zazen* and *shuzen* very clear in *Fukanzazengi*. He makes a reference to *shuzen* by cogently and clearly asserting: "The zazen I speak of is not learning meditation. It is simply the Dharma gate of repose and bliss" (Waddell & Abe, 2002, p. 4). Heine stresses this point from a perspective that emphasizes Dōgen's radical nondualism. He writes:

> For Dōgen, any apparent distinction between the polarities of thought and thoughtlessness, means and end, or dynamism and quietude is overcome by the refutation of deficient views that fail to reflect the unremitting practice of zazen.
>
> (2020, p. 93)

For centuries, many Zen teachers have strived to expose and correct this erroneous instrumental and "quietist" view of *zazen*. For instance, the contemporary Zen master Sekkei Harada writes:

> I think there are many of you who think, "I must not think," so you suppress thought. This is the worst thing to do. You are suppressing the natural flow of the Dharma itself. Don't think of trying to suppress thought. By thinking, "Don't think, don't think," your essential nature is lost. Without any freedom or comfort, you only end up sitting and thinking of trying to get rid of suffering. This is the sickness of not knowing that the thought of getting rid of suffering is suffering.
>
> (2008, p. 33)

Dōgen has probably been one of the most outspoken critics of this "quietist" view with respect to his positioning of the terms used in the above opening *mondo* (encounter dialog) between Yüeh Shan and the nameless monk: *shiryo* (thinking), *fu-shiryo* (not thinking), and *hishiryo* (nonthinking, beyond thinking, without thinking, a-thinking, leaving thoughts alone, and beneath thinking) without prioritizing one over the other. For instance, in the *Hossho* (The Dharma nature) fascicle of his *Shobogenzo* (1243d), Dōgen writes: "The thinking and the not thinking are both the Dharma-nature" (Nishijima & Cross, 1997, p. 128).

Yet, in many quarters, whether explicitly or implicitly asserted, a devaluation of thinking still exists. Part of the problem stems from the fact that how we "understand" or rather how we translate practice can be determined by unconscious factors that support rationalizations that then, in turn, drive inappropriate ideas about practice. As a result, such erroneous views can cause serious relational problems such as misusing the teachings to rationalize egocentric agendas or to enact cultish, abusive, or exploitative behaviors. Practitioners can fall into the trap of turning these misguided ideas about practice against the self and against others. Such ideas often operate subliminally in the background of consciousness and guide the practitioner's experience of practice and resulting behaviors, often in extremely subtle ways.

Internally, misguided practices, driven by the false idea that we must eliminate thinking, can become coupled with wrong-minded evaluations, frequently, as mentioned above, in the form of harsh, negative self-judgment, for the failure to stop thinking during *zazen*. This misguided orientation dynamically splits mind. Part of the mind produces thoughts as it should and will, while another split-off part of the mind stands back in judgment, based on a failure of any attempts to eliminate thinking: "This thought good; that thought bad; thinking bad; no thoughts, good." This orientation, no matter how subtle, imposes unnecessary pressure on the practitioner and creates a practical problem because, to reiterate, the mind is supposed to think. That is the function of the mind. For example, psychoanalysis describes the unconscious operations of internalized persecutory early object images. When not identified and questioned, tremendous authority becomes attached to judgmental thoughts, forgetting that they are also just thoughts. Whether conscious or unconscious, the false quietist view that characterizes thinking as an obstacle to realization must be overcome—not by removing this false view, but by seeing through it. This false view that negates and attempts to annihilate thinking parallels a religious practice ideal of the mortification and negation of the flesh that devalues physical being as impure. Due to this posited contamination, physical being is erroneously implicated as functioning to obstruct higher spiritual realization or transcendence. The Buddha, who was deeply engaged in such practices for many years, eventually saw through the futility of this misguided dualistic conception and gave up such practices.

Further, this misguided approach can engender a vicious cycle that causes and perpetuates the suffering that Harada, Roshi alludes to in the above quote; in part, because the attention is on the actual thoughts themselves rather than on the activity that occurs with one's relationship to the thoughts, such as the tendency to eliminate them. This false view of realizational practice is embedded in the culture and can be deeply ingrained in the practitioner's unconscious. Even though cognitively one might "know better" intellectually, the view that thoughts should be eliminated can still operate to one degree or another unconsciously and influence how one responds to practice and how such misguided practice can function as an obstacle to the lived experience of what Dōgen describes in *Fukanzazengi* as "not meditation" but as *jijuyu zanmai* (self-fulfilling ease and joy). This approach to practice, that is, the attempt to eliminate thoughts or to focus exclusively on a specific object such as the breath, a body part, or a mantra, becomes a distraction from the actual practice of naturally just sitting and only sitting. The correct intention centers on simply sitting and allowing what will emerge naturally, unforced, and unfettered without attachment, aversion, or judgment. Just as eyes see, ears hear, nose smells, tongue tastes, the mind thinks. So, there is no need to defeat thinking. In fact, Zen teaches that a still mind is a dead mind. The notion of calm or stillness within the rising and falling of mental processes, not an elimination of mental processes, is the key. That is, as Dōgen emphasizes, it is one's actions and relationships that are important. In other words, it is the practitioner's attitude and relationship to thinking that is the issue. When the practitioner realizes this and can take the backward step, one's naturalness, if you will, evolves and the deeper sense of ease and joy, which has always been present, becomes more obvious.

Contrary to the bad rap that thinking continues to receive, thoughts and thinking processes certainly have positive uses. Making the distinctions and discriminations that derive through linear thinking, for example, contributes to healthy boundaries and to solving the many challenges and problems faced in daily life. Getting lost in the absolute can result in unhealthy and dangerous choices, including inappropriate boundary violations. We are all one, but we are also unique and separate. Many instances that occur in everyday life require that separations remain intact; that differences are respected and honored; and that healthy distances remain in place, while at the same time, realizing the fundamental interconnectedness of all beings. For example, I often tell my New York City students that it is essential to distinguish between green and red lights when we engage the very busy crossing at 34th St and Lexington Avenue. That despite our absolute oneness, we don't want to "merge" with a speeding taxi when crossing the street!

Notes

1 For details and guided practice session, see Chapter Fourteen, *Shikantaza*: "Basic Fact of Sitting" Practice Session.
2 Eightfold Path: Right Understanding, Right Thinking, Right Speech, Right Action, Right Livelihood, Right Effort, Right Mindfulness and Right Concentration.

References

Abe, M. (1985). *Zen and Western Thought*. Honolulu: University of Hawaii Press.
Bielefeldt, C. (1988). *Dogen's Manuals of Zen Meditation*. Berkeley: University of California Press.
Cooper, P. (2009). Oscillations reload. In: D. Mathers. M. Miller & O. Ando (Eds.), *Self and No-self: Continuing the Dialogue Between Buddhism and Psychotherapy* (pp. 217–230). London: Routledge.
Dōgen, E. (1227). *Fukanzazengi*. In: M. Abe & N. Waddell (Eds.), *The Heart of Dōgen's Shobogenzo* (pp. 1–6). Albany: S.U.N.Y. Press, 2002.
Dōgen, E. (1231). *Bendowa*. In: G. Nishijima & C. Cross (Trans & Eds.), *Master Dogen's Shobogenzo, Book 1* (pp. 1–23). London: Windbell Publications, 1994.
Dōgen, E. (1241). *Bussho*. In: G. Nishijima & C. Cross (Trans. & Eds), *Master Dogen's Shobogenzo, Book 2* (pp. 1–32). London: Windbell Publications, 1996.
Dōgen, E. (1243d). *Hossho*. In: Nishijima & C. Cross (Trans. & Eds.), *Master Dogen's Shobogenzo, Book 3* (pp. 125–129). London: Windbell Publications, 1997.
Dōgen, E. (1244). *Zanmai O Zanmai*. In: G. Nishijima & C. Cross (Trans. & Eds.), *Master Dogen's Shobogenzo, Book 2* (pp. 281–284). London: Windbell Publications, 1997.
Eigen, M. (1985). Toward Bion's starting point: Between catastrophe and faith. *International Journal of Psychoanalysis*, 66:321–330.
Fujita, I. (2011). My Footnotes on zazen: zazen is not shuzen (1). *Dharma Eye*, 28:24–27.
Harada, S. (2008). *The Essence of Zen: The Teachings of Sekkei Harada*. Boston, MA: Wisdom Publications.
Heine, S. (2020). *Readings of Dōgen's Treasury of the True Dharma Eye*. New York: Columbia University Press.
Izutsu, T. (1982). *Toward a Philosophy of Zen Buddhism*. Boulder, CO: Prajna Press.
Kim, H. (2007). *Dōgen on Meditation and Thinking: A Reflection on His View of Zen*. Albany: State University of New York Press.
Loori, J. (2009). *The True Dharma Eye: Zen Master Dōgen's Three Hundred Kōans*. Boulder: Shambhala.
Nishijima, G. & Cross, C. (1994). *Master Dogen's Shobogenzo, Book 1*. London: Windbell Publications.
Nishijima, G. & Cross, C. (1996). *Master Dogen's Shobogenzo, Book 2*. London: Windbell Publications.
Waddell & Abe. (2002). *The Heart of Dōgen's Shobogenzo*. Albany: State University of New York Press.

Chapter 13

Ada
A Clinical Study

This chapter is intended as a response to the often-asked question, "How does Zen practice influence my approach to psychoanalysis?" While there are many ways of responding to this question, the focus in this discussion centers on *Inmo*, or suchness, described from Dōgen's perspective in Chapter Seven, "Dōgen's Expression of Suchness." Consider this encounter dialog between Yunyan Tansheng (780–841) and his student Dongshan Liangjie (807–869) who founded the *Caodong* school, which was transmitted to Japan by Dōgen and evolved into the Sōtō Zen school.

Dongshan was preparing to leave Yunyan and planning to visit other renowned teachers as the story goes:

> Just when Dongshan was about to depart, he said, "If in the future someone happens to ask whether I can describe the master's truth or not, how should I answer them?"
> After a long pause, Yunyan said, "Just this is it."
> Dongshan sighed.
>
> (Ferguson, 2000, p. 183)

Commenting on this encounter, Leighton notes that "Dongshan would realize the reality of teaching as the mutual recognition of suchness and the complex relationship that intimately expresses the full dynamic of the practice of suchness" (2015, p. 33).

This highly instructive encounter dialog points to and expresses the reality of suchness or reality as it is. In the phrase "Just this is it," "this" functions as a simple yet cogent expression of their shared beyond words presence. That is, shared presence occurs in the dependently co-arising relational context unique to Dongshan and Yunyan. There is an immediacy and a simplicity in this lived and shared presence that transcends linear, logical thinking that is unique to the two individuals who participate in the psychoanalytic encounter.

Caution

The following brief clinical vignette emphasizes and highlights the Zen influence of lived presence, which is captured in the above conversation and embodied in Yunyan's terse yet cogent expression "Just this is it!" However, the reader is cautioned that this example exaggerates the Zen influence to bring it into the foreground. It is important to understand that I do not disregard sound psychoanalytic principles and practices when relevant. I find interpretations, for example, useful and necessary when the timing and context are appropriate. This is true within the long-term context of my work with Ada, from which the following material is drawn from. On the occasions when I would make interpretations, Ada would respond, for the most part, attentively and with whole-hearted sincerity. She is very curious, conscientious, and eager to understand how her inner life influences her relationships and her way of being in the world. However, despite the relevance or accuracy of the interpretations and the genuine nature of Ada's responses, they seemed to shift the shared feeling and energy of the moment away and to distract us from the simple act and the benefit of shared connectedness and a sense of lived presence. In this regard, despite the accuracy of interpretations, considering the early family relational dynamics, they can also function as transference/countertransference enactments. Additionally, it is important to keep in mind that there is so much more to the psychoanalytic encounter than interpretations. The Australian psychoanalyst Judith Pickering, for example, notes:

> This relationship is imbued with certain 'psychotherapeutic virtues'. Among these are free-floating attention, pure presence, reverie, contemplation, attunement, resonance, equanimity, calm, reflective capacity, compassion, loving-kindness, patience, understanding, open-mindedness, generosity and gentleness of spirit, discernment, intuition, courage, and truthfulness.
>
> (2019, p. 4)

Many of these attributes will be evident in the following vignette. However, keep in mind that this material simply highlights one moment in a long-term treatment that exemplifies my point and demonstrates one way that "Just this is it," and Dōgen's elaboration of *"Inmo"* or suchness, coupled with Zen study and practice, influences my clinical work.

It is important to keep in mind that, as noted above, both Zen and psychoanalysis share identities, similarities, and differences, which can be highly fluid depending on how perceptual capacities are operating, for example, in terms of what Matte-Blanco describes as symmetrical and asymmetrical aspects of conscious and unconscious and how they interact, or in terms of this discussion, between unitive and differentiated experiences.[1]

Further, speaking from a subjective and experiential perspective and the ineffable, unknowable O of the analytic encounter, Bion observes:

> No one can ever know what happens in the analytic session, the thing-in-itself, O; we can only speak of what the analyst or patient feels happens, his emotional experience, that which I denote by T.[2] We know what the participants say happens, or the emotional state engendered by the verbalization of the analyst or patient in the listener.
>
> (1965, p. 33)

With Bion's cautionary remarks in mind, it will be helpful to keep in mind the highly subjective nature of human experience. From this perspective, the following report describes only what I think happened or what I would like to think happened and what I would like the reader to think happened. However, what is important from the realizational perspective is to be attentive to what gets evoked in you as reader ("listener") and what influence, if any, this material exerts in terms of your own orientation to the psychoanalytic encounter.

Ada

Ada expressed concerns regarding her feeling sensitive and vulnerable to what she feared and described as "crossing boundaries." She expressed it in the question: "How can I make any impositions on you to ask for or expect any favors from you?" I responded by asking: "In terms of what?" After a period of anxious silence, she then hesitatingly explained that she needed to reschedule our sessions to accommodate changes in a new work schedule. The required change was related to a promotion that she had successfully competed for and had just been awarded. Her increased responsibilities as a project manager demanded increased hours and a possibly unpredictable work schedule.

We had covered various versions of this situation in her personal and family life many times and we both knew the transference origins of her sensitivity, vulnerability, and hesitation. We both knew why this felt to Ada like an imposition and evoked a fear of crossing boundaries. This time, we simply continued to silently sit together with her concerns, with her feelings, with the situation, with her internal fears, and with her real needs. She soon began to describe a feeling of calmness and peace. The session ended and she left without further dialog between us except for the usual "see you tomorrow."

The following day, Ada arrived 20 minutes early (she usually arrives right on time, if not a few minutes late). I asked her about it by simply noting, "You arrived early today." She said that she had wanted to recapture the feeling of well-being that sitting with me at the end of the previous day's session engendered for her. She began the session by explaining her understanding of the transference dynamics. In her experience, any shift on my part—either toward or away—such as through making an interpretation, would have destroyed the intimacy and peacefulness of the silence, and, even though she knew better, would have felt like an abandonment to her. Whether the interpretation was accurate or not, I would have been experienced by her as abandoning the experiential space of the shared lived moment. I would have disrupted the deep connection that she was feeling in the moment through the shared silence.

In this situation, I believe that an interpretation would have functioned as a counter-resistance to the evolution of the Truth, the O of the session, and of the intimacy evoked by the unitive nature of the experiential moment.

We pursued this shared understanding further in the following session. Ada's self-hatred had shifted into the foreground of her experience. She confused a legitimate desire to be successful in life and her appropriate assertiveness with greed and aggression. These feelings had spilled over into the session. Her wish for making a legitimate and needed request felt like a violation of our boundaries. She also felt that I would view her as greedy and aggressive for competing for the promotion and higher salary. She was afraid that I would view her negatively and that I would act out my negativity by withdrawal of attention and harsh criticism. She experienced her promotion and her increase in salary as manifestations of her greed and aggression and imagined that I would be judgmental of her achievement. We both understood the early object relations that perpetuated her fears as they had been spoken about many times before during our work together through dialog, notations, and transference interpretations based on harsh negative self-perceptions that she projected into me.

These self-perceptions and imagined expectations of my reactions, we discovered, despite their harshness, felt "safer" than the deeper, more vulnerable feelings that were emerging through my undivided attention and silent presence no matter what. Ada imagined that she would be acting aggressively and that she would be perceived as aggressive by me if she asserted these needs. As noted, she also considered her wish to express her needs as a violation of our boundaries. She was welling over with feelings and feared that she would "flood the room and wash me away." Not unlike her early objects, I simply could not and would not handle them. She wondered if I would be strong enough, compassionate enough, and present enough to willingly sit with and hold her feelings, which she felt as an acknowledgement of her needs, hunger, and longings. In short, would I love her unconditionally no matter what? My capacity for acceptance, to love unconditionally meant sitting still, staying right where I was—in the present moment, attending the moment, embracing the moment, in full acceptance of the suchness of being-as-it-is. Together could we, as the old Zen teaching story asserts, "Taste the strawberries!"[5] At this point, she said that she felt anxious but that it was a "good kind of anxiety," that there was something fundamentally anxious about feeling fully alive, mutually present, and loved. Further, the love felt in this moment was a deeply shared transformation that began for me as an analyst as a countertransference reaction of my own. Ada was a very attractive young woman who evoked my erotic feelings and associated fantasies, which over time, as I first became aware of my fantasies and associated desires, allowed them to unfold and began to treat these internal states as objects of analysis, as Ogden describes (1997). In other words, relating to these internal experiences from a neutral position, free from grasping or rejecting, they opened both the psychic and relational space into a deeper feeling of mutuality beyond these earlier erotic and libidinal desires through our work together. We were both experiencing transformations. Again, as I noted above, we both understood the early transference dynamics. I understood my own countertransference reactions. There was no need for discussion or interpretation, simply just sitting in the reality of the shared moment. This shared experience is the living unsayable, ineffable O or emotional truth of the session. My decision to remain silent derived intuitively and spontaneously in the lived moment. It is only in the process of communicating this experience through language that requires logical sequential thought to be comprehensible.

From a Bionic perspective, we might say that Ada communicated the importance and significance of true and genuine presence in the not-knowing of the moment and sitting with and patiently waiting for the evolution of the uniqueness of Ada's O or emotional Truth without "irritable grasping after facts" (Bion, 1970, p. 125) or making interpretations. As Abe notes, this moment is "not *something* unnameable, but *the unnameable*" (1992, p. 46). In contrast to Bion, Dōgen views the truth as always present. Waiting for evolution is not necessary. In this regard, I could respond only to Ada, being-as-she-is, in the present moment as Ogden describes it as "... without trying to ferret out what the story was 'really about'; the story was not about anything; the story was the story; O is O" (2004, p. 297). Just this is it! In conclusion, we could say that Ada's experience, I hope, conveys the difference between talking *about* an experience, such as through interpretation and simply being the experience in the evolving now of the suchness of the session.

Notes

1 For a detailed explication of Matte-Blanco's notions in relation to the Zen unconscious, see P. Cooper 2000 and 2010, pp. 123–147.
2 Emotional Truth.
3 P. Cooper 2014.

References

Abe, M. (1992). Dōgen on Buddha Nature. In: S. Heine (Ed.), *A Study of Dōgen: His Philosophy and Religion* (pp. 35–76). Albany: State University of New York Press.
Bion, W. (1965). *Transformations*. London: Karnac.
Bion, W. (1970). *Attention and Interpretation*. London: Karnac.
Cooper, P. (2000). Unconscious process: Zen and psychoanalytic versions. *Journal of Religion and Health*, 39(1):57–69.
Cooper, P. (2010). *The Zen Impulse and the Psychoanalytic Encounter*. London: Routledge.
Cooper, P. (2014). Taste the strawberries. *American Journal of Psychoanalysis*, 74:147–161.

Ferguson, A. (2000). *Zen's Chinese Heritage: The Masters and their Teachings*. Boston, MA: Wisdom Publications.
Leighton, D. (2015). *Just This Is It: Dongshan and the Practice of Suchness*. Boston, MA: Shambhala.
Ogden, T. (1997). Reverie and interpretation: Henry James (1884). *Psychoanalytic Quarterly*, 66:567–595.
Ogden, T. (2004). An introduction to the reading of Bion. *International Journal of Psycho-Analysis*, 85:285–300.
Pickering, J. (2019). *The Search for Meaning in Psychotherapy: Spiritual Practice, The Apophatic Way and Bion*. New York & London: Routledge.

Chapter 14

Shikantaza
"Basic Fact of Sitting" Practice Session[1]

This chapter, which serves as an experiential conclusion to this offering, centers on a variation on the meditation practiced earlier in Chapter Three, "*Mokusho*: Silent Illumination." I have mentioned *shikantaza* or just sitting frequently in previous chapters in terms of the significance of experience as the nexus of both Zen and psychoanalysis from the realizational perspective. Both direct and indirect discussions and references to *shikantaza* are sprinkled throughout Dōgen's writings. For example, in the *Bendowa* (1231) chapter of his *Shobogenzo*, he writes: "This Dharma is abundantly present in each human being, but if we do not practice it, it does not manifest itself, and if we do not experience it, it cannot be realized" (Nishijima & Cross, 1994, pp. 1–23). In the *Hensan* chapter of his *Shobogenzo*, he refers to practice as "thorough investigation." He provides explicit instructions for *shikantaza* in *Fukanzazengi*, "Universal Promotion of the Principles of Zazen" (1227). He offers an abbreviated version in *Zazengi*, "The Principles of Zazen" (1243c), chapter of his *Shobogenzo*. He elaborates on the origins, rationale, and underlying principles of the practice in *Bendowa* (1231) and in *Zazenshin* (1243b).[2]

The two opening sentences to *Zanmai O Zanmai* "The Samadhi the is the King of Samadhis," (1244) Dōgen conveys a strong sense of enthusiasm and passion for *shikantaza* practice. He writes:

> To transcend the whole universe at once, to live a great and valuable life in the house of the Buddhist patriarchs, is to sit in the full lotus posture. To tread over the heads of non-Buddhists and demons; to become, in the inner sanctum of the Buddhist patriarchs, a person in the concrete state, is to sit in the full lotus posture.
> (Nishijima & Cross, 1997, p. 281)

Definition

As mentioned previously, and as will be mentioned again, since it is important, *shikantaza* means "just sitting" or only sitting. Kim describes *shikantaza* as follows:

It is that seated meditation which is objectless, imageless, themeless, with no internal or external devices or supports, and is nonconcentrative, decentered, and open-ended. Yet it is a heightened, sustained, and total awareness of the self and the world. It seeks no attainment whatsoever, be it enlightenment, an extraordinary religious experience, supernormal powers, or Buddhahood.... It requires single-minded earnestness resolve and urgency on the part of the meditator.

(2007, p. 24)

Zazen is a general term for Zen meditation practice. There are many different methods, such as *zuisokukan* or following the breath, *susokukan*, or breath counting, *kanna zen*, or koan concentration and *shikantaza*, or just sitting, the subject of this chapter. *Shikantaza* is a specific form of *zazen* typically associated, but not exclusively, with the Sōtō Zen tradition. *Shikantaza* is the Japanese Sōtō Zen practice that derives from the Chinese Chan practice of *mokusho* (Chinese: *mozhao*), silent illumination or serene reflection, which was discussed in Chapter Three. The Chinese Chan teacher Sheng Yen describes *shikantaza* as synonymous with *mokusho*. He writes:

In the Japanese Sōtō Zen School of Dōgen, this method of meditation is called *shikantaza* or, literally, "Just sit, nothing more." In the practice of *shikantaza*, one concerns oneself with sitting, and sitting only. When a distracting thought arises one says to oneself, "All I am doing is sitting; there is nothing else to do, nothing to accomplish. Just sit."

(2001, p. 150)

As with *mokusho*, the underlying theme is to keep the practice simple. The way to keeping it simple is through *shikantaza* or "just sitting." The contemporary Zen Buddhist teacher and Dōgen scholar Shohaku Okumura notes: "This is really simple practice; we do nothing but sit in the zazen posture breathing easily, keeping the eyes open, staying awake, and letting go. That's all we do in zazen; we do nothing else" (oral teaching May 8, 2022).

Simplicity is implied in the term *shikantaza*, which can be broken down as follows: *Shikan* means to sit; *Ta* means to hit the target, which in this practice is the reality of the present moment; and *Za* means *zazen* or meditation. So, *shikantaza* means just sitting in meditation and being present to the moment and nothing else. As an aside, this is Bion's recommendation for sitting with the patient. That is, as he says, without memory, desire, or understanding, and, following the British poet John Keats (1795–1821), by tolerating "not knowing" and sitting "without irritable reaching after facts" (Bion, 1970, p. 125).

In this manner, both the Zen practitioner and the psychoanalyst face reality directly. This includes facing thoughts, feelings, sensations, perceptions, discomfort, boredom, and frustrations, as well as the feeling of joy and sense of ease. All these experiences can emerge as part of the present reality. When the analyst sits with a patient, the analyst is sitting directly in reality and the shared reality that emerges during the psychoanalytic encounter. Nishijima notes:

> To arrive at the truth does not mean to get something—it just means to realize reality itself, and to live fully in this present moment.
>
> (2003, p. 207)

And:

> When we sit in Zazen we face reality directly. We face thoughts, emotions, and discomfort (both physical and mental), We also see that reality is something more than just thoughts or just the body.
>
> (2003, p. 13)

Bion observes that facing reality through "Faith in 'O'" can be "catastrophic." In both *zazen* and psychoanalysis, the practitioner confronts it directly. It requires being lived through and experienced.

I will begin with some discussion about *shikantaza* practice and then I will proceed directly into a period of silent practice. The silent period will be marked by the ringing of the bell three times and will end with a single bell. In the previous meditation session, the focus was on *mokusho*. As I pointed out in that session, in Zen practice, regardless of the method, it is very important to harmonize body, breath, and mind. Dōgen quotes Buddha Shakyamuni, who says, "We should sit like coiled dragons," which suggests a sitting posture in which there is stability and power without undue rigidity or exertion.

In *Zanmai O Zanmai* (1244), Dōgen writes:

> For this reason, the Buddha teaches his disciples to sit in the full lotus posture, sitting with the mind upright. Why? [Because] if the body is upright, the mind is easily set right. When the body sits upright, the mind is not weary, the mind is regulated, the intention is right, and the attention is bound to what is immediately present. If the mind races or becomes distracted and if the body leans or becomes agitated, [sitting upright] regulates them and causes them to recover.
>
> (Nishijima & Cross, 1997, p. 282)

That is, practice starts with a still and relaxed body in correct posture. Focus then centers on a calm mind and a natural breath rhythm. When the body becomes relaxed, truly relaxed, the mind becomes calm and clear. Keep in mind that calmness of mind is not measured by the frequency and content of thoughts, but by one's relationship to them. When the mind becomes calm and clear, the body relaxes. It's really that simple. This is so because from the nondualistic perspective of Zen Buddhism, body and mind are one. The body is the more obvious and the material aspect of mind and the mind and the mental processes are the subtle and often unconscious aspects of the body. Think of this relationship as a continuum. *Shikantaza* is a whole body/mind practice—"Whole Being." This practice begins with what is most obvious and accessible, by getting situated properly. So first check the posture. The spine is erect but not stiff, the shoulders and arms are in a comfortable and relaxed position. If using a chair, sit toward the front of the chair. Place the feet flat on the floor with the heels aligned with the front of the knees. Place the left hand in the right hand with the left palm facing up with the thumb tips slightly touching. During practice, take notice of excess pressure on the thumb tips. This means you are working too hard and pressuring yourself, so gently back off. If, on the other hand, the thumbs are drifting apart, this means you are getting drowsy or you are lost in thought, so again, simply adjust the posture and the thumbs and be in the moment. You want to be relaxed, but not lax or lazy. You want to be focused and centered, but not rigid or uptight. Entry into practice requires intention and decisiveness. The intention is to "Raise *Bodhicitta*." *Bodhicitta* means "awake mind." In practice, it means sitting with the rise and fall of all experience without attachment or aversion; without grasping or pushing away; without valuing or devaluing any experience. This is Dōgen's practice of *shikantaza*, which, to repeat, means just sitting. We just sit no matter what! These old sayings capture this sense of decisiveness: "Practice like your head is on fire!" "Practice as if you swallowed a red-hot iron ball and you are trying to spit it out!" If your head were on fire, you would not think about it would you? You would immediately make every effort to put the fire out. This is immediate or without mediation. In other words, there is no deliberation or conceptual thought between the awareness of the experience and your response to the experience, including your experience of rising and falling conceptual thoughts. Another of Dōgen's quotes is to "Practice until you break the cushion!" Sitting with the rising and falling of all experience without attachment or aversion. This isn't an "anything goes" attitude. Decisiveness in practice doesn't mean getting stressed out about it either. Simply stay present and focused and allow the practice to unfold.

In addition to the intention to raise *Bodhicitta*, it is important to practice with *mushotoku*, which means "no gaining mind." In other words, let go of any goals or expectations. Just allow the ongoing flow of the lived present to evolve on its own, free from any expectations. Again, in parallel to Wilfred Bion, he speaks of sitting with the patient in a state of "negative capability" (1970, p. 125), another term that he borrows from John Keats that means to be free of expectations and simply allow the evolution of the session to unfold.

The "steps" that will be practiced in a moment provide a structure, but they are simply guidelines, not rules. Over time, direct experience will demonstrate that they can shift, reorder themselves, intermingle, rise, and fall like any other experience and flow in a seamless manner, melting together into one continuous and natural flow.

The practice will begin with a body scan to develop a feeling of relaxation and then expand the attention to an awareness of the whole body; an awareness of just sitting, just noticing, and feeling the full presence of body and mind just sitting. As mentioned above, the practice will begin with three soundings of the bell. Then some instructions will be provided, which will lead into a few minutes of silent practice. One bell will sound to end the practice period.

Three Rings

Now tuck the chin in toward the throat a bit and cast the eyes downward at about a 45-degree angle to the floor. Use a soft gaze. Begin with the eyes gently closed, but during the silent period, feel free to open the eyes. If the eyes are open, simply notice that they are open, and if the eyes are closed, just notice that they are closed. Now please bring the attention to the breath. At the end of the next exhalation, take in a full deep breath to full capacity, but without straining. Now exhale slowly until the breath is completely exhausted and allow the next inhalation to come by itself, as if the breath is breathing the body. Repeat this process a few times, deepening a sense of ease with each exhalation and passively allowing the breath to return. Now follow the breath to the crown of the head and feel the awareness spreading out across the scalp, just noticing what's going on, feel the awareness spreading along with the breath flowing into the forehead, and the back of the neck, along the sides of the head into the temples, into the eyelids, nose, nostrils, cheeks, jaw, and chin. Feel the shoulders relaxing and follow this relaxed feeling in the upper arms, elbows, forearms, wrists, palms, and fingers. You might notice an energy, a warmth, or a tingling sensation in the palms of your hands. Follow the breath and this energy, if you feel it, back up the arms and into and along the shoulders, into the throat, the upper chest, ribcage, and upper back just breathing gently, noticing, and relaxing, not trying to change anything, but just noticing. Follow the awareness down the spine and into all of the back muscles, just noticing, around the waste into the abdomen, buttocks, groin, thighs, knees, shins, calves, ankles, feet, and toes.

Now that you have completed the body scan, begin to feel a sense of the whole body just sitting. You may begin to notice a lightness in the body, a feeling of peaceful calm awareness. You may begin to notice that your field of awareness naturally expands and includes the space around you and into the wider environment. As awareness magnifies and spreads out, you might notice little details such as sounds as they rise from and fall back into the larger matrix of silence. However, you don't get caught by them, you just notice. You may feel a sense of connectedness and oneness. The whole environment becomes you sitting here and now, the mountains and rivers are sitting together with you. The sky is sitting with you. The streets outside are sitting with you. Everything is in its natural state, just being as it is. There may be lots going on; the sound of birds, winds, church bells, voices on the street, cars, all held and contained within the larger matrix of the deep silence that we are all part of. You simply notice these details, but they don't catch you. You clearly notice but your mind does not follow. This natural sense of clarity is illumination. Not being pulled, not allowing your mind to trail off is silence. Together, this process is *shikantaza*, just sitting. You may also find yourself drifting off on thought trains. This is natural. When you notice this drifting off, without judgment, gently bring yourself back to your awareness of the present environment and continue just sitting and just noticing. Just as you shifted from the awareness of individual body parts to a sense of the whole body just sitting, begin to experience this larger environment as the Whole Body on this wider cosmic scale. Whole Being is Buddha Nature. You *are* the environment just sitting and the environment is you just sitting.

THREE MINUTES

Single Bell

Thank you for your presence and for your sincere practice, and please remember to keep practicing. It is extremely important not only for you, but also for the benefit of all beings and for the planet.

Notes

1 *Shikantaza*, "Basic Fact of Sitting," guided audio practice instruction link: https://soundcloud.com/paul-cooper-290569931/basic-fact-of-sitting-12-20-2020mp3
2 See C. Bielefeldt (1998). *Dōgen's Manuals of Zen Meditation* for a thorough examination of this topic.

References

Bielefeldt, C. (1988). *Dogen's Manuals of Zen Meditation*. Berkeley: University of California Press.
Bion, W. (1970). *Attention and Interpretation*. London: Karnac.
Dōgen, E. (1227). *Fukanzazengi*. In: M. Abe & N. Waddell (Eds.), *The Heart of Dōgen's Shobogenzo* (pp. 1–6). Albany: S.U.N.Y. Press, 2002.
Dōgen, E. (1231). *Bendowa*. In: G. Nishijima & C. Cross (Trans. & Eds.), In: G. Nishijima & C. Cross (Trans. & Eds.), *Master Dogen's Shobogenzo, Book 1* (pp. 1–23). London: Windbell Publications, 1994.
Dōgen, E. (1243b). *Zazenshin*. In: G. Nishijima & C. Cross (Trans. & Eds.), *Master Dogen's Shobogenzo, Book 2* (pp. 91–106). London: Windbell Publications, 1996.
Dōgen, E. (1243c). *Zazengi*. In: M. Abe & N. Waddell (Trans. & Eds.), *The Heart of Dōgen's Shobogenzo* (pp. 109–110). Albany: S.U.N.Y. Press, 2002.
Dōgen, E. (1244). *Zanmai O Zanmai*. In: G. Nishijima & C. Cross (Trans. & Eds.), *Master Dogen's Shobogenzo, Book 2* (pp. 281–284). London: Windbell Publications, 1997.
Kim, H. (2007). *Dōgen on Meditation and Thinking: A Reflection on His View of Zen*. Albany: State University of New York Press.
Nishijima, G. (2003). *Master Dogen's Shinji Shobogenzo: 301 Koan Stories*. Essex: Windbell Publications.
Yen, S. (2001). *Hoofprints of the Ox*. Oxford. Oxford University Press.

Index

Abe, Masao 121, 149, 158
absolute/ultimate reality 17, 18, 21, 62, 97, 102, 104, 105, 107, 116, 129, 137, 138–139, 140, 149; *see also* "O" (Bion)
absolutism 92
accommodation/assimilation 7, 34, 35, 42, 89, 115; Buddhist transferability 124–126; interaction between psychoanalysis and Zen Buddhism 117–119, 124–125; *karma* 126–127; narrative derivatives 116, 117; psychoanalytic encounter 116–117; religious expression 120–122; resistance to 42–44, 120, 126–127; Zen infusion into psychoanalysis 123–124
actional/relational orientation 57, 98, 120, 121–122, 125, 138
Adams, W. 69, 73–74
Alexander, Franz 78, 123
Alfano, C. 69, 74–76
American Zen 118
analytic self 118
anatta see no-self
Anderson, Reb 36–37
assimilation *see* accommodation/assimilation
at-one-ment 93, 105, 110, 137–138, 140
attachment 17, 24, 25, 48, 60, 72–73, 77, 91, 100, 118, 122, 124, 147, 163
attention 24, 26, 71–72, 73
Attention and Interpretation (Bion) 15, 19, 44, 81, 105, 106, 125, 133
authentic practice 9, 18, 23, 24, 56, 130; *see also shikantaza*
authoritarianism 45

aversion 25, 48, 60, 77, 91, 92, 100, 122, 124, 147, 163
avidya see ignorance (*avidya*)

backward step, taking 11–12, 25, 82, 99, 137, 152
Bankei 52
Beat Zen 118
Bendowa (Dōgen) 7, 9, 139, 148, 160
Bhavachakra (Wheel of Life and Death) 16, 38, 92, 106
Bielefeldt, C. 64
Bion, Wilfred 5, 6, 10, 14, 16–19, 43–44, 69, 70, 81–82, 129–130, 131–132, 140–141, 161, 163; at-one-ment 93, 105, 110, 137–138, 140; on experience 15, 125–126, 129–130, 132–133, 139; "F" 108; ideas, resistance to 120–121; invariance 5, 7, 16; "K" 15, 16, 76, 78, 93, 102, 105, 106, 107, 109–112, 116, 133, 137, 140; on language 6, 15, 16, 47, 58, 81, 103, 133; medical view 18; on mystical dimensions of psychoanalysis 77; negative capability 72–73, 74, 137; on not knowing 74, 136, 141; "O" 76, 77–78, 79, 94, 96, 99, 101, 102–103, 104–109, 115, 116, 133, 136, 137, 139, 140, 147–148, 155, 157, 158, 162; on openness 17, 71, 134, 135, 137; on present moment 82, 100–101, 105–106; on psychoanalysis 119–120, 124, 125–126; on psychoanalytic experience 15–16; on relinquishment of desires/memories/understanding 17, 18, 28, 70, 71, 74, 82, 99–100,

105, 106, 110, 111, 131, 132, 161;
on resistance to becoming of "O"
106–107, 109; transformations 16,
132, 133, 136, 137, 157, 158; on
unconscious communications 138;
and Watts 43, 80–81; on wholeness
101, 129
Blake, William 76
Bleandonu, Gerard 19, 44
Bobrow, Joseph 69–70, 71–72,
76–77, 123
Bodhicitta 24, 98, 99, 163
Bodhidharma 9, 21, 26, 65, 66, 150
body 27, 37, 99, 164; and mind 162;
and ritual 37; sitting posture 24, 27,
131, 147, 160, 162, 163
Book of Serenity, The 110
Buddha 9, 37, 162
Byrne, Christopher 22, 52

calmness 152, 156, 162
Caodong school 22, 53–54, 154
Chan Buddhism 4, 22, 23, 54, 57, 58,
64, 146, 150, 161
circular logic 98
Cobb, J. 121
Cogitations (Bion) 105
cognition 117, 137–138, 139
Cooper, P. 70
counterculture movement 44, 115
countertransference 78, 94, 124–125,
126, 134, 149, 155, 157–158
Cross, C. 90

Dahui Zonggao 52, 54, 58, 63
Daiman 90
delusion 53–54, 60, 92, 137
DeMartino, Robert 4
dependent co-arising (*pratītyasamutpāda*)
9, 10, 17, 24, 35, 41, 74, 75, 78, 89,
92–95, 125, 154
dhyana 150
Dictionary of the Work of W.R. Bion, The
(Lopez-Corvo) 79
discrimination 60, 62, 65, 75
Dōgen 3, 4, 6, 7, 10, 14, 18, 21, 35,
51–52, 61–63, 82, 94, 107, 110,
111, 116, 129, 130, 131, 141,
158, 160, 163; action/relational
orientation of 98, 120, 121–122,
125, 138, 152; authentic practice 9,
18, 56, 130; on body 37; and Dahui
Zonggao 58; on delusion 137; on
distinction between *zazen* and *shuzen*
150; on emptiness 78, 90–91; on
existence 140; *hensan* (thorough
investigation/exploration) 34, 37–38,
131, 135, 160; on investigation of
mind moments 25; *jijuyu zanmai*
(self-fulfilling ease and joy) 152; and
kōan 56, 59, 60, 61–63; on language
47, 57, 62, 122–123; nondualism
of 6, 44, 54, 56, 61–62, 63, 65, 66,
70, 78, 96, 98–99, 111, 139, 140,
147–149, 150; on no-self 90; on
one mind 25–26; on oneness and
discrimination 75; oneness of practice
and realization 6, 44, 54, 56, 148; on
openness 134, 135; and orthodoxy 36;
on present moment 82, 98, 131; on
quietist practices 64; on realization
18, 26; on sitting posture 131, 147,
162; on suchness 97–100, 135, 140,
149, 155; Suzuki's criticism of 52,
53, 54, 56, 64–65, 66; on thinking
57, 151; on thorough exploration
37–38, 135; *Uji* 17; on *zazen* 139,
148; *see also shikantaza*
Dongshan Liangjie 154
dualism 6, 43, 44, 60, 61, 93, 139,
140, 152; of Fromm 47, 48; "K"
and "O" 109, 111, 140; noumena
and phenomena 46; secular-religious
dichotomy 9; sense and non-sense
139; of Suzuki 56
dukkha 72

Eaton, J. 70
Eckhart, Meister 44, 77
ego 23, 99
Eigen, Michael 5, 82, 108, 147–148
Eightfold Noble Path 7, 149
Eisai 52
Elements of Psychoanalysis (Bion) 104
emotional elbow room 125
emotional experience 71, 77, 102, 103,
109, 133, 136, 138, 156
emotional truth 15, 47, 106, 108, 130,
132, 137, 157, 158; *see also* "O" (Bion)
emptiness (*śūnyatā*) 7, 9, 17, 24, 74,
75, 89–91, 93, 121, 140, 149; being
and nonbeing 89; embodied 78; and
ignorance 92; nihilist orientation
of 90; and "O" 76, 77–78, 94, 108;

and totalistic countertransference 125; *see also* dependent co-arising (*pratītyasamutpāda*)
enlightenment 9, 121; *Bodhicitta* 24, 98, 99, 163; Caodong view of 53–54; experiences 46; practice as expression of 54, 58; Suzuki on 56; as a unique and discrete event 53; *see also* realization
Epstein, M. 70
Escape from Freedom (Fromm) 44
Evans-Wentz, W. 132
evenly suspended attention 73
evolutions (Bion) 10, 73
experience 14–15, 19, 37–38, 125–126, 129–130, 139, 156, 160; Bion on 15, 125–126, 129–130, 132–133, 139; and dependent co-arising 93, 94; emotional 71, 77, 102, 103, 109, 133, 136, 138, 156; and emptiness 90, 92, 94; expression of 16; Fromm on 45–46; and *hensan* 135; individual, uniqueness of 16, 71, 103, 107, 133, 136, 141; and language 16, 46, 57–58; middle way 72, 82; personal, "O" as 107–108; primacy of 45–46, 132–134; psychoanalytic 15–16, 95; realizational perspective 16–18; sensuous 6, 15, 47, 77, 100, 101, 103, 109, 110, 111, 119, 126, 133; shift from objective orientation to subjective orientation 119–120; subjective nature of 70, 82, 156; Suzuki on 34, 41; and thinking/ thought 57–58; transcendent attunement 74–76; *see also* "O" (Bion)
expressive practice 53–54, 56, 66

"F" (Bion) 108
facilitative practice 44, 54, 55–59, 60, 150
Fader, L. 39
Faure, Bernard 40, 54, 66, 124
Ferro, Antonino 116, 117, 131, 134, 138
Finn, Mark 3, 80
forced memories 10, 73
form 76, 78, 90, 93, 140, 149
Four Noble Truths 7
freedom 7, 45; and orthodoxy 36; spiritual 35, 41, 42; Suzuki on 42–43; Watts on 41, 42

Freud, Sigmund 14, 45–46, 73, 74, 92, 120, 123
Fromm, Erich 4, 40, 44–47, 48, 119, 124
Fujita, I. 150
Fukanzazengi (Dōgen) 18, 66, 97, 98, 99, 137, 147, 150, 152, 160

Genjokoan 10, 63
grasping 25, 26, 48, 77, 96, 99, 158
Grotstein, J. 71, 115
gujin (total exertion/total penetration) 135

Hábito, Rubin 120
Hakuin 65
Harada, Sekkei 151, 152
Harrington, A. 33, 40–41
Harrison, J. 69
Healing Breath: Zen for Christians and Buddhists in a Wounded World (Hábito) 120
Heart Sutra 78, 90, 93
Heine, Steven 3, 5, 37, 40, 56, 58, 65, 121, 122–123, 150
hensan (thorough investigation/ exploration) 34, 37–38, 131, 135, 160
Herrigel, Eugen 79
Hershock, Peter 7, 58, 119, 122
Homeless Kodo *see* Sawaki, Kodo
Hongzhi Zhengjue 22, 52, 53
Hopkins, Jeffrey 91
Horney, Karen 38–39, 124, 135–136
Hossho (Dōgen) 26
Huike 26
Huineng (Daikan) 5, 24, 96
Huxley, Aldous 38

ignorance (*avidya*) 25, 91–92, 93, 106–107, 122
Ikka Myoju (Dōgen) 59–60
Immo (suchness) 17, 61, 65, 96–101, 135, 140, 148, 149, 154, 155, 157, 158
impermanence 24, 98, 106
incommunicado core 77
inherent existence 9, 24, 89, 90, 91, 92, 93, 106, 126, 140
intention 71–72; and *Immo* 97, 98; and *kōan* 63; and *mokusho* 24–26; and "O" 108–109; and *shikantaza* 163
intertextual analysis 56
intuition 10, 11, 81, 105, 130, 139; experience 15, 16, 133, 135, 140; of

"O" 78, 110, 111, 137; *prajna* 73, 75, 78, 132; and realization 76, 100, 137–138; and sensory experience 77; and suchness 100; wisdom 28
invariance 5, 7, 16
Ives, C. 121
Iwamura, J. 33
Izutsu, T. 149

jijuyu zanmai (self-fulfilling ease and joy) 152
Joshu 110
Jung, C. 39–40

"K" (Bion) 76, 102, 105, 109–112, 133, 137, 140; configuration 109; definition of 106; and language 15, 16, 93, 109–112, 133; and "O" 78, 107, 109–111, 116
kanna-zen 54, 57, 58, 62, 66, 161
Kant, I. 103, 104, 106, 111, 139
Kapleau, Phillip 43, 44
karma 16, 126–127, 133
Kasulis, Thomas 75
Katagiri, Dainin 43
Keats, John 44, 72–73, 137, 161, 163
Kelman, H. 124
Kennedy, Robert 120
Kenzo, Awa 79
Kerouac, Jack 38
Kim, H. 75, 121, 122, 125, 138, 145, 149, 160–161
kōan 53, 54, 56–57, 58, 59–63, 110
Koestler, A. 39
Kyoto school 124

language 16, 56, 61, 63, 158; Bion on 6, 15, 16, 47, 58, 81, 103, 133; devaluation of 44, 46, 47–48, 57; Dōgen on 47, 57, 62, 122–123; and "K" 15, 16, 93, 109–112, 133; and "O" 78, 105; in psychoanalytic encounter 117; and psychoanalytic experience 15, 47; *see also* thinking/thoughts
Leighton, D. 154
Linji school 52, 53, 54
Living Zen, Loving God (Hábito) 120
Loori, John 148
Lopez-Corvo, R. 44, 70, 79–80
Lotus Sutra 97
Luria, Isaac 44

Maezumi, Taizan 17, 43
Mahayana Buddhism 4, 7, 9, 89, 92, 127, 140, 149
Matte-Blanco, Ignacio 126, 155
McDaniel, R. 43
Memoir of the Future (Bion) 15
memory(ies): Bion on 10, 82, 100; forced 10, 73; relinquishment of 17, 18, 28, 70, 71, 74, 82, 99–100, 105, 106, 110, 111, 131, 132, 161; *vs.* remembering 10; spontaneously arising (evolutions) 10, 72, 73
Mendoza, S. 69–70, 77–78
Merton, Thomas 34
middle way 48, 72, 77, 82, 92, 93, 99
Milton, John 16–17, 44, 136
mindfulness meditation 18, 70, 72, 73
mind-to-mind transmission 122–123
mokusho (silent illumination) 18, 21, 52, 63, 64, 161; critique of 53; intention of 24–26; origins of 21–23; practice 26–28; quietist view of 21, 22; simplicity of 22, 23–24; sitting 24–25, 26; True Dharma Eye 25; *see also shikantaza*
moment-to-moment being 17, 54
Moncayo, Raul 3–4, 80
Mozhao Ming (Hongzhi Zhengjue) 22
mu (being without) 90–91
mushotoku (no gaining mind) 125, 131, 138, 140, 141, 145, 163
mystical dimensions of psychoanalysis 77

Nagao, Gadjin 78, 89, 93
Nagarjuna 7, 93
Nangaku 5, 6, 136
narrative derivatives 116, 117
negative capability 72–73, 74, 137, 163
Nichol, D. 70
nihilism 11, 35, 46, 60, 61, 90, 92
Nirodha 72, 77
Nishijima, Gudo 6, 56, 62, 90, 150, 162
no fixed point 7, 10–12, 115
nonattachment 25, 70, 72–73, 77
nondualism 95, 111; body and mind 162; of Dōgen 6, 44, 54, 56, 61–62, 63, 65, 66, 70, 75, 78, 96, 98–99, 139, 140, 147–149, 150; embodied emptiness 78; practice and realization 6, 44, 54, 56, 64, 66; realizational perspective 17–18; and suchness

98–99; thoughts 65, 147–148; and transcendent attunement 75
no-self 11, 24, 89, 90
"Notes on Memory and Desire" (Bion) 18, 19, 71, 100, 102, 106, 125, 131
not knowing 74, 92, 102, 106, 134–137, 139, 141, 158, 161; *see also* ignorance (*avidya*)
noumena 46, 111, 139, 140

"O" (Bion) 15, 16, 70, 76, 79, 102–103, 104–105, 115, 133, 139, 140, 156, 157, 158, 162; definition of 105–106; and emptiness 77–78, 94; and ignorance (*avidya*) 106–107; intention 108–109; intuition of 78, 110, 111, 137; and "K" 78, 107, 109–111, 116; and meditation 147–148; as personal experience 107–108; and suchness 96, 99, 101; transformations in 136; and Zen notion of origin 70
Oedipal conflict 123
Ogden, Thomas 94, 105, 117, 131, 158
Okumura, Shohaku 62, 161
one mind 25–26
oneness 138–139, 164; and distinction 75, 76; and *mokusho* 21; of practice and realization 6, 44, 54, 56, 148
openness 70, 71; to not knowing 74, 134–137, 139; in psychoanalytic encounter 28, 38; revelatory 69, 73–74

Paradise Lost (Milton) 16–17
Pelled, E. 70
phenomena 46, 111, 140; and dependent co-arising 93, 94; and emptiness 9, 89, 91, 92
Pickering, Judith 155
Plato 44
practice(s) 7, 19, 37, 125–126, 129–130, 133, 139, 160; authentic 9, 18, 23, 24, 56, 130; and doctrine 53; expressive 53–54, 56, 66; facilitative 44, 54, 55–59, 60, 150; misguided ideas about 151, 152; quietist 21, 22, 52, 53, 63, 64, 65, 66, 146, 151, 152; reading 9–10; and realization 5–6, 44, 54, 56, 64, 65, 148; and theory 71, 118; wall gazing 21, 65, 150; *see also kōan; mokusho; shikantaza; zazen*

prajna 23, 73, 75, 78, 132; *see also* intuition
pratītyasamutpāda see dependent co-arising (*pratītyasamutpāda*)
preconceptions 16, 82, 90, 133, 140–141; and assimilation/accommodation 35, 118, 123, 124; and negative capability 73; and no fixed point 10, 11; and "O" 105, 107, 137; in psychoanalytic encounter 116, 117, 134; and spiritual freedom 35
pre-reflective experience 75
present moment 6, 11, 54, 82, 130, 131, 157, 158, 162; and expressive practice 54; and *mokusho* 24, 25, 27; and "O" 105–106; and suchness 96, 98, 100–101
projective identification 116–117
psychoanalysis 9, 14, 94–95; experiential orientation to 15–16, 45–46, 104; influence of Suzuki on 38–41; insight 46; knowing about 16; and medical as a model 119–120; mystical dimensions of 77; and resistance 120–121; shift from objective orientation to subjective orientation 119, 120; uniqueness of 119; violation of boundaries (clinical study) 156–158; and Zen Buddhism 3–4, 6, 11, 12, 44, 79–80, 81, 117–119, 123–127, 130, 131–132, 138–140, 155; Zen infusion into 123–124
psychoanalytic cure 106, 125
psychoanalytic listening 70, 71, 72, 73, 77, 94, 95

Racker, Heinrich 124
reading practice 9–10
reality 73–74, 89, 102, 133, 161–162; absolute/ultimate 17, 18, 21, 62, 97, 102, 104, 105, 107, 116, 129, 137, 138–139, 140, 149; and curtain of illusion 104; and dependent co-arising 93; and emptiness 90, 149; and language 6, 47, 48, 62; and middle way 93; and no fixed point 10; and no-self 11; and perceptual shifts 139; of psychoanalytic experience 103–104; relative 18, 21, 62, 109, 116, 138, 139, 140, 149; and sensuous experience 77; and

suchness 96, 97, 154; and thinking/
  thoughts 62, 63, 148; *see also* "O"
  (Bion); present moment
realization 6, 8, 12, 16–18, 19, 26, 53,
  82, 111, 122, 130–132, 140; and
  cognition 137–138; of emptiness 78,
  91; Fromm 45; and ignorance 91, 92;
  and intuition 76, 100, 137–138; and
  kōan 56–57; and language 56, 57,
  122–123; medical view 18; openness
  to not knowing 134–137, 139; and
  practice 5–6, 44, 54, 56, 64, 65, 148;
  and present moment 98; primacy of
  experience 132–134; religious vertex
  18; and self-experience 26; shift from
  static mind states to action/relational
  functioning 138; and thinking 56,
  57, 149, 152; Watts on 43
Reiner, A. 102
relative reality 18, 21, 62, 109, 116,
  138, 139, 140, 149
religious expression 120–122
religious vertex 18, 108
relinquishment of desires/memories/
  understanding (Bion) 17, 18, 28, 70,
  71, 74, 82, 99–100, 105, 106, 110,
  111, 131, 132, 161
remembering, *vs.* memory 10
resistance: to assimilation/
  accommodation 42–44, 120, 126–
  127; to authentic practice 23, 24; to
  becoming of "O" 106–107, 109
revelatory openness 69, 73–74
reverie 73, 75, 76, 81, 94, 95, 116
Rhode, E. 106, 108, 134–135
Rinzai school 34, 35, 51, 52, 53, 54,
  55, 107
rituals 36–37
Roberts, Shinshu 17
Rubin, J. 70, 71

Salvatti, A. 90, 102
samādhi 23, 131, 139, 148
samsara 63
samskaras 16, 126, 133
Sasaki, Ruth Fuller 43
satori 55, 56, 57, 60, 64, 107, 131
Sawaki, Kodo 26, 44
Schlütter, M. 53
secular Buddhism 6, 120
secular mindfulness 6–7, 127
secular-religious dichotomy 9
selected fact 99, 103

self-sense/I-sense 11
sense of ease 28, 152, 161, 164
sensuous experience 111, 119, 126;
  and desires 101; and language 6,
  15, 47, 103, 110, 133; and mystical
  dimensions of psychoanalysis 77; and
  "O" 109, 110
sesshin 145
shamata/shamatha (calm abiding) 22, 52
Shepherd, R. D. 55
Shibi Xuansha 59–62
shikantaza 6, 12, 18–19, 21, 96, 123,
  131, 138, 160–165; criticisms of 52,
  53, 63; definition of 160–161; and
  kanna-zen 54, 58, 66; and *kāon* 59;
  practice 38, 54, 64–65, 162–165;
  quietist view of 52, 53, 63, 66; and
  realization 53, 65; simplicity of 161;
  and suchness 65, 99–100; Suzuki
  on 52, 56, 63, 64–65; and thinking
  148–149
shinjin datsuraku (dropping off body and
  mind) 99, 137
Shinji Shobogenzo (Dōgen) 58, 62, 148
Shobogenzo (Dōgen) 6, 90, 97, 131, 149,
  150, 160
Shoji (Dōgen) 37
shoshiryo (right thinking) 149
shusho ichinyo (practice realization
  oneness) 6, 44, 54, 56, 148
shuzen (learning meditation) 65–66,
  99, 150
silence 44, 46, 156–157, 158, 162
silent illumination *see mokusho* (silent
  illumination)
sincerity, and wholeheartedness 38–39,
  135–136
sitting posture 24, 27, 131, 147, 160,
  162, 163
Six Realms 38
Smith, Huston 55
Soku-Shin-Ze-Butsu (Dōgen) 25
Sōtō Zen Buddhism 3, 18, 19, 22, 35,
  44, 48, 51–52, 53, 58, 66, 125, 161
Spirit of Zen, The (Watts) 43
spiritual freedom 35, 41, 42
spontaneously arising memories
  (evolutions) 10, 72, 73
stillness 23, 27, 28, 37, 65, 152, 157, 162
suchness 17, 61, 65, 96–101, 135, 140,
  148, 149, 154, 155, 157, 158
suffering 7, 93, 151, 152; and
  attachment 72; and ignorance 91; and

impermanence 24; and relative view 18; source of 106
śūnyatā see emptiness (*śūnyatā*)
susokukan 161
Suzuki, D. T. 4, 8, 33–35, 36, 37, 44, 51, 66, 81, 123, 124, 135; criticism of 39, 56, 58, 63–66; and Fromm 44–45, 46, 47; hybrid Zen 33, 34; influence on psychoanalysis 38–41; on practice 55, 58; Rinzai Zen orientation 34, 35, 51; on *shikantaza* 52, 63, 64–65; on *shusho ichinyo* 54; view of *kōan* 56–57; and Watts 41, 42–43; writings, limitations of 66; writings, representation of Dōgen/Sōtō Zen in 51–52
Suzuki, Shunryu 43, 55, 82
Symington, Joan 70, 72, 73, 77, 92, 120, 129, 131
Symington, Neville 70, 72, 73, 77, 92, 120, 129, 131

Ta-hui *see* Dahui Zonggao
Tao-hsuan 150
teacher-student relationship 122
Tendo Nyojo 52, 58, 147
Theravada Buddhism 6–7, 18, 70, 73
thing-in-itself 103, 104, 106, 111, 132, 139
thinking/thoughts 24–25, 60, 61, 62, 63, 122, 145, 146; devaluation of 46, 47–48, 57, 65, 149–150, 151; discursive 61, 73, 76, 105, 110, 149; Dōgen on 57; elimination 146–147, 149, 151, 152; judgmental thoughts 151–152; and nondualism of Dōgen 65, 147–148; and "O" 78; positive uses of 152; revaluated 23, 122, 145; *shikantaza* 148–149; *shoshiryo* (right thinking) 149; and *zazen* 146–147; *see also* language
Three Marks of Existence 24, 106
Three Pillars of Zen (Kapleau) 43, 44
Three Poisonous Minds 25, 26, 60, 122
totalistic countertransference 78, 124–125, 126
transcendent attunement 74–76
transference 94, 107, 117, 133, 149, 155, 156
transformations 16, 132, 133, 136, 137, 157, 158
Transformations (Bion) 16, 104, 106, 132

traversing the caesura 69, 74
True Dharma Eye 25

Uji 17
unconscious 70, 71, 126; communications 76, 116–117, 122, 138; and ignorance 92; preconceptions 16, 82, 117, 123
universal mysticism 8

van der Braak, Andre 8, 34, 35
Vermote, Rudi 102, 136, 138
vipassana/vipashyana (insight) 6–7, 22, 52, 73

wall gazing 21, 65, 150
wato 58, 63
Watts, Alan 8, 41–44, 66, 70, 80–81
Way of Zen, The (Watts) 41, 42, 66, 70, 80–81
wholeheartedness of spirit 38–39, 135–136
wholeness 101, 129
Wienpahl, Paul 46–47
Winnicott, D. 77, 94
wisdom 122, 132; and emptiness 78; intuitive 28, 78; and silence 22, 54
Wright, Dale 9, 36, 46

Yamada Koun 120
Yamada, S. 79
Yasutani, Hakuun 44
Yen, Sheng 22, 24, 54, 57, 161
Yongjia Xuanjue 23, 54
Yüeh Shan 145, 148, 151
Yunyan Tansheng 96, 154, 155

Zanmai O Zanmai (Dōgen) 131, 147, 160, 162
zazen 6, 8, 9, 26, 37, 38, 58, 59, 60, 129, 139, 161, 162; Dōgen on 66, 97, 99, 150; intention 43; and negative self-judgments 151; practice 27; quietist view of 65, 151, 152; Rinzai notion of 64; Sawaki on 26, 44; *vs. shuzen* 150; Sōtō notion of 64; and thinking 146–147, 149; Watts on 43; *see also shikantaza*
Zen and Psychotherapy: Partners in Liberation (Bobrow) 123
Zen and the Art of Archery (Herrigel) 79
Zen Buddhism 3, 7–8, 9, 14, 33, 51, 115; and authentic practice 9;

criticism of 39; durable heritage of 5; impact on West 34; Japanese 8; Lopez-Corvo's references to 79–80; misunderstandings in West 41, 46–47; modernist 7, 33, 34, 38; orthodoxy 36; and psychoanalysis 3–4, 6, 11, 12, 44, 79–80, 81, 117–119, 123–127, 130, 131–132, 138–140, 155; reimagining of 34; rift between objective and subjective approaches 119; Rinzai 34, 35, 51, 52, 53, 54, 55, 107; rituals in 36–37; Sōtō 3, 18, 19, 22, 35, 44, 48, 51–52, 53, 58, 66, 125, 161; as a structured religious system 8; as a subdiscipline of psychoanalysis 124; Suzuki 33–34, 35, 36, 37, 38–41, 42–43, 44–45; traditional 7, 9, 34, 38; as a way of life 8; and western individualism 35–36

Zen Dust (Sasaki) 43

Zen Gifts to Christians (Kennedy) 120

Zen kōan as a Means of Attaining Enlightenment, The (Suzuki) 55

Zen Mind, Beginner's Mind (Suzuki) 43, 55

Zen Spirit, Christian Spirit (Kennedy) 120

Zhang, Y. 70, 80–81

zuisokukan 161

For Product Safety Concerns and Information please contact our EU representative GPSR@taylorandfrancis.com
Taylor & Francis Verlag GmbH, Kaufingerstraße 24, 80331 München, Germany

www.ingramcontent.com/pod-product-compliance
Lightning Source LLC
Chambersburg PA
CBHW050537300426
44113CB00012B/2144